Women, Writing and Religion in England and Beyond, 650–1100

Studies in Early Medieval History

Series editor: Ian Wood
Concise books on current areas of debate in late antiquity/early medieval studies, covering history, archaeology, cultural and social studies, and the interfaces between them.

Women, Writing and Religion in England and Beyond, 650–1100

Diane Watt

BLOOMSBURY ACADEMIC
LONDON • NEW YORK • OXFORD • NEW DELHI • SYDNEY

BLOOMSBURY ACADEMIC
Bloomsbury Publishing Plc
50 Bedford Square, London, WC1B 3DP, UK
1385 Broadway, New York, NY 10018, USA
29 Earlsfort Terrace, Dublin 2, Ireland

BLOOMSBURY, BLOOMSBURY ACADEMIC and the Diana logo are trademarks of
Bloomsbury Publishing Plc

First published in Great Britain 2020
This paperback edition published in 2021

Cover design: Terry Woodley
Cover image © MS Clm 1086, folio 71v. Includes the cipher with Hygeburg's name.
Bayerische Staatsbibliothek München, Clm 1086, Folio 71v.

A catalogue record for this book is available from the British Library.

A catalog record for this book is available from the Library of Congress.

ISBN: HB: 978-1-4742-7062-5
       PB: 978-1-3502-3972-2
     ePDF: 978-1-4742-7065-6
    eBook: 978-1-4742-7064-9

Series: Studies in Early Medieval History

Typeset by RefineCatch Limited, Bungay, Suffolk

To find out more about our authors and books, visit www.bloomsbury.com
and sign up for our newsletters.

In memory of William Watt (1962–2019)

Contents

Illustrations

Acknowledgements

I first began work on this book more than ten years ago and in that time I have accrued many debts to individuals and organizations, including academics, archivists, universities, libraries and funding bodies. This project began when I was based at Aberystwyth University, and I am grateful to my colleagues there who made it such an enjoyable place to live and work. Indeed I spoke about this project at my inaugural lecture which was held at the National Library of Wales and attended by so many of my friends and fellow scholars, including members of the Institute of Medieval and Early Modern Studies, a partnership between Aberystwyth and Bangor Universities that provided a collegiate environment in which this research could develop and flourish in its early stages. The book itself was written after I moved to the University of Surrey, and so I would like to thank my fellow medievalists here, past and present, especially Venetia Bridges, Shazia Jagot and Amy Morgan. Special mention should also be made of the encouragement offered by three other colleagues, Sabine Braun, Grev Corbett and Adeline Johns-Putra, and by the research support team, especially Marcela Acuna-Rivera, Sue Starbuck and Tamsin Woodward-Smith.

I have benefited from a variety of departmental, school and faculty funding provided by both Aberystwyth University and the University of Surrey, including a Sir David Hughes Parry Award in 2011 that enabled me to undertake some preliminary manuscript research at Cardiff Central Library. Further generous financial support came in the form of a Leverhulme International Networks grant (IN-2014-038) that ran from 2015 to 2017 and a Leverhulme Major Research Fellowship (MRF-2016-014) that ran from 2017 to 2019 and funded a number of archival trips and also provided me with invaluable time to complete this book. I am especially grateful to the partners of the international research network 'Women's Literary Culture and the Medieval Canon' for providing a stimulating environment to discuss some of my ideas: Amy Appleford, Liz Herbert McAvoy, Laura Saetveit Miles, Sue Niebrzydowski, Denis Renevey, Corinne Saunders, Nancy Bradley Warren and the project facilitator, Lynette Kerridge (who also read through an early draft of the book). Other scholars who in different ways have contributed to this project, whether by reading draft chapters, by sharing their own research or in other ways, include Virginia

Blanton, Katie Bugyis, Catherine Clarke, Aidan Conti, Mary Dockray-Millar, Michael Drout, Ruth Evans, Robert Ireland, Eileen Joy, Stephen Knight, Kathryn Maude, Patrick Sims-Williams and Jocelyn Wogan-Browne. Special mention should be made of Antony Smith from the Department of Geography and Earth Sciences at Aberystwyth University who kindly helped me produce the location map for this book.

Much of the research for this book was conducted at the Hugh Owen Library at Aberystwyth University, the British Library in London, the National Library of Wales in Aberystwyth and Surrey University Library, and I was also granted valuable access to Birkbeck University Library and the Maughan Library at King's College London. In addition, I was able to examine important early manuscripts and consult other relevant material in a number of other major collections: the Badische Landesbibliothek in Karlsruhe, the Bayerische Staatsbibliothek in Munich, the Bodleian Library, University of Oxford, Cambridge University Library, Cardiff Central Library, Lambeth Palace Library in London, the Österreichische Nationalbibliothek in Vienna, the Stiftsbibliothek in St Gallen, and Trinity College Library in Dublin. Cornelia Hopf of the Forschungsbibliothek in Gotha kindly answered my questions about Codex Memb. I.81.

I am grateful for the many opportunities I have had to present my work on the project at research seminars, colloquia and conferences and extend my thanks to the scholars who very generously invited me to speak and acted as my hosts. Special mention should be made of the talks and lectures delivered at the Universities of Birmingham (Victoria Flood and Oliver Herford), Cambridge (Helen Cooper and Barry Windeatt), Leeds (Axel Müller), Oxford (Vincent Gillespie), Pennsylvania (Courtney Rydel and David Wallace), and those at Birkbeck, University of London (Heike Bauer), the Central European University, Budapest (Gerhard Jaritz), and Keio University, Tokyo (Takami Matsuda and Naoë Kukita Yoshikawa). I also had the pleasure of speaking about research that fed into this book at a Gender and Medieval Studies conference held at King's College London (invited by Clare Lees, Robert Mills, and Sarah Salih), the conference on 'Barking Abbey and its Texts' held at City University New York (invited by Jennifer Brown and Donna Alfano Bussell), the Northeast Modern Language Association Annual Convention in Montreal (in a session organized by Susannah Chewning), the London Old and Middle English Research Seminar at the Institute of English Studies (invited by Catherine Nall and Katie Normington), the International Anchoritic Society annual conference held at Gregynog, University of Wales (invited by Liz Herbert McAvoy and Michelle

Sauer), the Women's Literary Culture and the Medieval Canon international network event held at Boston University (hosted locally by Amy Appleford), the annual International Medieval Congress at the University of Leeds in 2016 and 2018 (in sessions organized by Kathryn Maude and Catherine Clarke, respectively) and, in a joint presentation with Mary Dockray-Miller, at the conference on 'The Medieval Canon in the Digital Age' held at the University of Ghent (invited by Jeroen De Gussem, Jeroen Deploige, Wim Verbaal, and Mike Kestemont). This book was completed at a time of fierce debates about misogyny and trans* scholarship within medieval studies and the misappropriation of the Middle Ages by white supremacists and other political factions. I am particularly grateful to scholars such as Gabrielle M. W. Bychowski, Jonathan Hsy and Dorothy Kim for helping me to begin to understand some of the issues at stake, and I hope that this book has benefited, albeit indirectly, from what I have learnt.

Chapter 1 of this book first appeared as 'Lost Books: Abbess Hildelith and the Literary Culture of Barking Abbey', *Philological Quarterly* 91 (2012), 1–22, although it has subsequently been revised. The first four sections of Chapter 2 were first published as 'The Earliest Women's Writing? Anglo-Saxon Literary Cultures and Communities', *Women's Writing*, 20 (2013), 537–54 (https://www.tandfonline.com), and they too appear here in revised form. In Chapter 3 I rework and substantially expand upon material that first appeared in 'A Fragmentary Archive: Migratory Feelings in Early Anglo-Saxon Women's Letters', *The Journal of Homosexuality*, 64 (2017), 415–29 (https://www.tandfonline.com). I would like to thank Taylor & Francis and *Philological Quarterly* for permission to reproduce this material in the present book. This book has benefited greatly from the feedback of anonymous readers and the series editor, Ian Wood, and the assistance and support offered by Alice Wright, Lily Mac Mahon and the team at Bloomsbury Academic, and by Douglas Matthews.

As always, I am enormously grateful to Heike Bauer for her encouragement and patient support throughout. Lily, Molly, Elsa, Bobby, and also Rufus and Floyd, both very much missed, provided much needed companionship during, and distraction from, the writing of the book.

Note on the Texts and Translations

Most of the original works discussed in this book are written in Latin. Some are in Old English. The aim is to make them accessible to a wide audience. Published translations have been used where available (sometimes in slightly emended form), unless otherwise specified, and editions of the original texts are mentioned in the notes and bibliography. However, where I quote at length or where I wish to pay close attention to specific words and phrases, I provide both the original text and the translation.

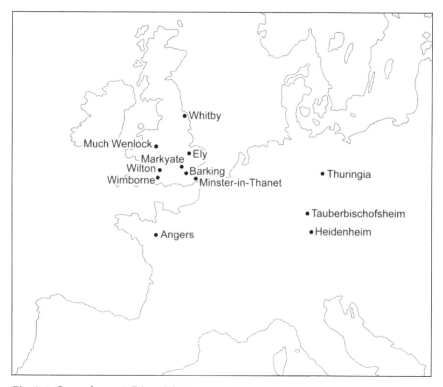

Fig. 0.1 General map © Diane Watt.

Introduction

Were there any women writers in the early Middle Ages? This question has often been posed to me while I have been working on this book. The answer should be straightforward. *Women, Writing and Religion in England and Beyond, 650–1100* explains why it is not. It explores the conditions that enabled a rich and varied literary culture to thrive in women's religious communities in the early Middle Ages and the reasons why that remarkable culture is almost invisible today. As I will outline in the next section of this introduction, histories of English Literature, including women's literary histories, have tended to exclude completely or to marginalize the contributions of early medieval women, focusing instead on a small group of women from the twelfth to the fifteenth century, notably the courtly writer, Marie de France (*fl.*1180), and the visionaries Julian of Norwich (1342/3–after 1416) and Margery Kempe (*c.* 1373–after 1439). This book, with its focus on the interconnected literary and religious cultures of English women in the centuries before 1100, demonstrates that the late medieval women writers and visionaries, who are often viewed as exceptional, are in fact part of a much longer tradition. It identifies early authors whose position as foremothers in the canon of English women's writers has been overlooked for too long. Two of the most notable examples are Leoba (*d.* 782), an early medieval English missionary and abbess of Tauberbischofsheim, in what is now Germany, and Hugeburc (*fl.* 760–80), an English nun who joined the Benedictine monastery of Heidenheim. Leoba was a correspondent of Boniface, and her one surviving letter also contains the first extant example of poetry known to have been authored by an English woman.[1] Hugeburc, who wrote lives of the brothers St Willibald and St Wynnebald, lays claim to the title of first named English woman writer of a full-length literary narrative. Both Leoba and Hugeburc have been neglected in English literary histories because, as women who joined monastic houses in Francia, they are, as Aidan Conti observes in relation to Hugeburc, 'more suited to those who work within a Carolingian rather than Anglo-Saxon timeframe'.[2] But these two women are also part of an English literary tradition. By analysing these, and other early examples of women's writing, and by locating them within a wide-ranging exploration of early medieval religious women's engagement with literary culture, this book offers a new perspective on early English literary production more broadly, one that places religious women at its very centre.

Given the sparse body of extant texts composed before 1100 that are generally recognized as being women authored, the approach I adopt in this study is in part *speculative*. I am concerned with piecing together the evidence of what remains and what has been lost to provide a fuller understanding of the extent to which early religious women were involved in the production, consumption, circulation and preservation of poems, prayers, letters, devotional works, histories and hagiographies. This speculation includes, but is not limited to, assessing whether or not a case for female authorship of certain key surviving anonymous works can be made. At the same time, it is important to speculate about why so few women-authored texts are seen to have survived. Jennifer Summit, in her study *Lost Property* (2000) has argued persuasively that early women writers are *constructed* from the beginning as lost, even when they are present in the written record.[3] However, it is also the case that early women's writing *was* lost, suppressed and deliberately destroyed. Christine Fell makes the argument that the reason the collection now known to us as the Boniface correspondence, in which the Leoba letter is preserved, has survived to the present day is simply that it was located in Continental Europe 'whereas most equivalent material in England either failed to survive the Viking raids, the Norman Conquest, or the Dissolution of the Monasteries and related hazards'.[4] The libraries attached to the great early medieval English women's religious houses have been obliterated or dispersed, and many texts written by women have become detached from the contextual information that would make their authorship apparent. Tellingly, however, Fell notes that such 'equivalent material in England' may also not have been considered 'worthy of preservation in the first instance'.[5] Works by women may well have been dismissed as lacking value, being old-fashioned (and thus dispensable or replaceable) and lacking authority. To put this simply, women were often dismissed as being unworthy authors, and their roles in the production of literary works were overlooked, ignored and forgotten.

Throughout the Middle Ages, the idea of the author (*auctor* in Latin) was associated with ideas of *authority* or *auctoritas*.[6] Medieval texts most often circulated anonymously, or were ascribed or re-ascribed (regardless of who actually wrote them) to renowned figures from the past, who were almost invariably male. No matter how powerful they were in religious or political terms, medieval women were perceived by others – and perceived themselves – as lacking the authority to be described as authors. In many ways the situation has not changed today, with anonymous early medieval literary works in particular (such as *Beowulf*) generally seen to be the product of an individual male imagination. Figures whose names are known, men like the poet Caedmon, or Archbishop Wulfstan, take on an almost iconic status that is simply not granted to their female counterparts, the Abbesses Leoba and Hild (Caedmon's patron). Yet in the early Middle Ages, and indeed in the later Middle Ages too, literary production was closely linked to orality. As evidenced so clearly by Hugeburc's account of Willibald's travels, which is based on his own testimony, it was highly collaborative, dependent on the contributions of religious communities as archivists and preservers of memory and on patrons, scribes, compilers, commentators and translators, as well as on writers in the more conventional sense. With the criteria of originality that lies at the heart of modern understandings of what it means to author a work being so completely irrelevant to medieval conceptions, those responsible for the production of texts often drew freely on other sources, oral or written, without acknowledging any debts. At the same time, literary reception was communal, with books read aloud publicly or within closed groups, and exchanged, shared and copied amongst networks of readers. One of the aims of this book is to highlight the complexity of literary culture in the early Middle Ages in order to make sense of women's roles within it. For this reason considerable attention is paid not only to works written by women, or potentially written by them, but also to works produced for women, either as patrons or as readers, and to works that seem indebted to women's accounts, oral as well as written, including hagiographical literature. My focus in this study is primarily on works composed by or for women rather than on women scribes but it could easily be extended to include them, and indeed my thinking is deeply indebted to the pioneering work on women's involvement in manuscript production and reception in volumes such as *The Golden Age of Anglo-Saxon Art*, edited by Janet Backhouse, D. H. Turner and Leslie Webber (1984) and the publications of both Michelle P. Brown and Rosamond McKitterick, as well as more recent scholarship in the field.[7] Similarly, important work by scholars such as Mechthild Gretsch and Joyce Hill on an Old English version of the *Rule of St Benedict* produced for women religious enables us to understand better how works might be written or adapted to suit the needs of a female audience.[8] Only a nuanced understanding of the production and reception of texts as communal rather than individual will succeed in rendering visible the contribution of women.

A central argument of this book is that monastic writers (historians, hagiographers, and writers of works of instruction and/or encouragement), some of whom were writing specifically for female patrons, overwrote female authorities and women's texts in the sense that they rewrote women's narratives, replacing their oral or written accounts, the 'underwriting', with new versions.[9] Such overwriting was often intended to improve, modernize and preserve the earlier material rather than destroy or censor it, and the underwriting may well have continued to circulate and be read for some considerable time after. The very fact that throughout the Middle Ages multiple versions of saints' lives survive suggests that the process of overwriting was an inherent aspect of a genre that required continual revision, updating and translation. I also use the concept of overwriting in a more metaphorical sense to describe the complex relationship between male authors and their female subjects and to capture the ways in which texts can attempt to control and circumscribe female autonomy. This book explores all of these different forms of overwriting.

The first two chapters of this book consider women's engagement with literary culture in the seventh and early eighth century in the double monasteries at Whitby, Ely and Barking in Bede's *Ecclesiastical History* and a range of other texts. These chapters argue that Bede systematically overwrote women as authorities while he appropriated their work, but at the same time he preserved the names and reputations of the more powerful abbesses and nuns. The correspondence of St Boniface offers further evidence of a dense literary network and intense engagement with literary culture on the part of cloistered women in England who corresponded with Boniface and his circle and of those who served as missionaries on the continent. The next two chapters consequently focus on surviving works authored by women – works which escaped being overwritten. They consider the eighth-century letters by English nuns who wrote to Boniface and his supporters, and the eighth- and ninth-century letters and saints' lives produced by, for and about the missionary women who travelled to Germany. Of these texts, only Rudolf of Fulda's *Life of Leoba* (written *c.* 836) might, in its appropriation of female sources, be described as having been overwritten in the way that the written and oral accounts of the Whitby, Ely and Barking nuns were. However, the lives of Willibald and Wynnebald *were* thought to be anonymous until the twentieth century when Hugeburc's name was found to be encrypted within them, so even the authorship of these texts was, in a different sense, overwritten, albeit by the author herself.[10] The final two chapters run in parallel to the first two, considering the extent to which some of the extensive work produced in the late eleventh century by, for and about women by Goscelin of

St Bertin also overwrites women as authors and authorities, focusing in this case on the writings associated with Wilton Abbey.

Having already indicated that there is indeed a wealth of evidence of early medieval women's engagement with literary culture, once we begin to look for it, I consider why it has not hitherto received more critical attention. Why have literary critics, and feminist literary critics in particular, so consistently overlooked this material, or, more to the point, why have they failed to see what this material tells us about women's roles in early literary production? Is it simply that the material is too challenging? Or are a number of complex factors at work that have worked to suppress the evidence of women's literary agency?

Delving deeper: Recovering 'the Dark Ages of the female imagination'

This book argues that an understanding of early women's engagement with literary culture is crucial to understanding women's literary history and, more specifically, what is distinctive about early literary culture and what remains the same in later periods. It is perhaps surprising that this case still needs to be made. Joan M. Ferrante, in her groundbreaking book *To The Glory of Her Sex: Women's Roles in the Composition of Medieval Texts* (1997), observed that 'history in any form from the Middle Ages to the present which does not include the role of women is not true history'.[11] Yet monumental studies of literary history, even those published in the relatively recent past, continue to give short shrift to women, especially in relation to the pre-modern period. To offer just one example, *Reform and Cultural Revolution* by James Simpson (2002), the second volume of *The Oxford English Literary History* (volume one was published in 2017), is a case in point, because even as it places later medieval canonical writers such as Chaucer and Langland alongside those less widely read today, it pays relatively little attention to women as writers or patrons.[12] The reasons for such exclusions are seldom articulated. When an explanation for the limited attention paid to women *is* provided, it is often along the lines of the lack of evidence, which may or may not be taken as indicative of a lack of literary activity by medieval women. David Wallace, the editor of *The Cambridge History of Medieval English Literature* (1999), justified a similar omission with the claim that 'a single chapter on medieval women writers might be disproportionately brief'.[13] The omission of medieval women from standard literary histories is also, more surprisingly, replicated in feminist literary histories. Although, in a text that is seen as foundational to the study of women's literary history, *A Room of One's Own* (1929), Virginia Woolf imaginatively reconstructed the life, and death, of Judith Shakespeare, a frustrated playwright every bit as talented as her brother but trapped by her circumstance and by society, many of the earliest scholarly accounts, such as those by Kate Millett, Ellen Moers, Elaine Showalter, Sandra M. Gilbert and Susan Gubar, and Janet Todd, looked to later periods – the eighteenth, nineteenth and twentieth centuries – for which the evidence of women writers is more overwhelming.[14] Indeed, Gilbert and Gubar, in the first edition of *The Norton Anthology of Literature by Women: the Traditions in English* (1985), a hugely influential anthology of primary text that has effectively constructed a 'canon' of women authors for generations of students, dismissed out of hand the relevance of the medieval and early modern period, calling it 'the Dark Ages' of the 'female imagination'.[15]

If many literary histories, traditional or feminist, pay scant attention to women's engagement with literary culture in the medieval period, even studies of medieval women's writing often effectively start in the twelfth to fourteenth centuries, for example Carole M. Meale's still crucially important edited volume *Women and Literature in Britain, 1150–1500* (1993), Summit's *Lost Property: The Woman Writer and English Literary History, 1380–1589* (2000), Jocelyn Wogan-Browne's *Saints' Lives and Women's Literary Culture c. 1150–1300: Virginity and its Authorizations* (2001), Carolyn Dinshaw and David Wallace's edited collection, *The Cambridge Companion to Medieval Women's Writing* (2003), and David Wallace's *Strong Women: Life, Text, and Territory 1347–1645* (2011).[16] These are all extremely valuable studies that have contributed hugely to our knowledge and understanding of women's roles in pre-modern literary culture, but what of the centuries before the twelfth century? A notable exception to this pattern is Laurie A. Finke's *Women's Writing in English: Medieval England* (1999), which does address both the early medieval and the post-Conquest periods.[17] Only eight years after the publication of Wallace's volume of *The Cambridge History of Medieval English Literature*, the third edition of Gilbert and Gubar's *Norton Anthology of Literature by Women* (2007) was expanded to include, finally, a few of the more famous later medieval women writers.[18] Nevertheless, if Gilbert and Gubar now acknowledge the importance of medieval (and early modern) women writers, they still regard the early medieval period as a wasteland of female creativity, holding fast to their position that 'we find no texts in the Old English period that have been definitively identified as composed by women'.[19]

One reason that early women's contribution to literary culture is rendered invisible in this way is that, for better or worse, English literary history is very much governed by periodization and teleology. The discipline is taught according to different eras – the Renaissance, the Eighteenth Century, the Nineteenth Century and so forth – and the boundaries between them are still quite strictly policed. Most researchers concentrate their expertise on one fairly narrowly defined period. To complicate matters further, within the study of medieval literature, there is a clear delineation between the early medieval period or Old English, and the later Middle Ages, or (early and late) Middle English. Relatively few scholars have the courage to bridge this divide. Two who do just this are Elaine Treharne, whose invigorating account of language and power, *Living Through Conquest* (2012), analyses texts produced in England between the early eleventh century and the early thirteenth century, and Elizabeth M. Tyler, whose recent study, *England in Europe* (2017), focuses on the eleventh century but has a much wider chronological range.[20] Treharne and Tyler are, however, exceptions that prove the rule. Work on women's literary culture from the twelfth century onwards rarely looks back to the early medieval period, and vice versa. Within early medieval English studies, work on women, gender and literary culture has been going on for some decades, as evidenced by volumes such as Jane Chance's *Woman as Hero in Anglo-Saxon Literature* (1986), *New Readings on Women in Old English Literature*, edited by Helen Damico and Alexandra Hennessey Olsen (1990), Shari Horner's *The Discourse of Enclosure* (2001), and *Sex and Sexuality in Anglo-Saxon England*, edited by Carol Braun Pasternack and Lisa M. C. Weston (2004).[21] Nevertheless studies of early medieval women's authorship have typically focused primarily on the anonymous women-voiced elegies.[22] In line with the pattern outlined above in relation to major surveys of literature in the later medieval period, early women's literary culture continues to be overlooked. Fortunately, this pattern of exclusion and marginalization has now begun to change, as witnessed by *The Oxford Handbook of Medieval Literature in English*, edited by Elaine Treharne and Greg Walker (2010), which covers both the early and later Middle Ages and includes a chapter on women, religion and authority, and also Clare A. Lees's edited volume, *The Cambridge History of Early Medieval English Literature* (2012), which includes chapters dedicated to both women's writing and to gender and sexuality.[23] From this we must conclude that the evidence *is* there, if we take the time to look for it. So why have critics been so loath to pay attention to women's engagement with literary culture in the early Middle Ages?

Judith M. Bennett, in her 2006 study *History Matters*, observes that as (sub) disciplines, women's and gender history have focused on the modern periods at the expense of the pre-modern, and argues that this is because of the greater challenges presented by studying what she calls 'the distant past'.[24] This is as true (if not more so) of the study of literary history. Indeed, it is ironic perhaps that Bennett entitles this chapter 'Who's Afraid of the Distant Past?' playing with title of the 1962 play by Edward Albee, *Who's Afraid of Virginia Woolf?* and also, more significantly, with the name of an author who was concerned so directly with the recovery of the lost women of literary history. While Bennett, in this specific chapter, is talking about history pre-1800, and most of the examples she provides in her book relate to the later Middle Ages, her arguments apply if anything all the more to what I think of as the 'deep' history of literature from the early Middle Ages.[25] Certainly, in order to understand the deep past of medieval women's literary culture, scholars are faced with very specific and sometimes daunting barriers, and these difficulties only intensify the further back in time we go. Often the evidence appears quite inaccessible in linguistic or historical terms, and is not easily accessible in print form or modern editions, although the availability of manuscripts or rare print materials in digital format has significantly changed this situation for the better in the last decade. Yet much of the surviving material is anonymous, and, as R. M. Liuzza has noted, survives only in fragmentary form,[26] making it hard to incorporate within a feminist literary history. But equally, mistaken assumptions about medieval women's illiteracy and lack of education, and about literary production, circulation and consumption, combined with a refusal to acknowledge the importance of writing in languages other than English (especially Latin) to the English literary tradition, has meant that a wealth of evidence about the deep past of early medieval women's literary history has been consistently overlooked.

Women, Writing and Religion, with its main focus on the pre-Conquest period, is the culmination of a project, or series of interconnected projects, that I have been working on for around fifteen years. It builds on the foundations of my previous study, *Medieval Women's Writing* (2007), which examined a range of texts and genres written in England in Latin, French and Middle-English, authored by women, by women and men together, and by men for women patrons or readers.[27] Having explored networks of textual production, reception and exchange, *Medieval Women's Writing* concluded that only by recognizing the collaborative nature of literary culture can the extent and nature of women's engagement with it be understood. My contention in this study is that the same can be said of the earlier period. *Women, Writing and Religion* is also connected to the volume *The History of British Women's Writing, 700–1500*, which I co-edited with Liz Herbert McAvoy (2012). It sought to extend significantly the scope of enquiry by placing a greater emphasis on the reception and influence in

England of works by continental women, and by giving consideration to writers in other parts of the British Isles, and to early medieval women.[28] Two essays in that volume are particularly relevant here: Lees and Gillian R. Overing's 'Women and the Origins of English Literature' and Catherine A. M. Clarke's 'Literary Production Before and After the Conquest'.[29] In the former essay, Lees and Overing urge scholars to pay greater attention to women's complex and often crucial participation in literary production and reception, stating, 'It's all a matter of rethinking the evidence'.[30] Clarke in turn argues that in order to understand women's engagement with literary culture in the period *c.* 980–1140, a period when the British Isles had strong linguistic, cultural and political connections to continental Europe and Scandinavia, attention must be paid to women's roles as patrons. She observes that 'sources rarely record female patronage in explicit, direct terms: instead, evidence for female agency is inscribed in complex, coded ways, often at the "edges" of texts in material such as dedicatory verses, prologues, and epistolary passages'.[31] Both of these essays have been influential on my reconceptualization of early medieval women's literary engagement, not least in their insistence on radically rethinking and *reviewing* material that may already seem familiar. *Women, Writing and Religion* also develops arguments initially proposed in my essay 'Literature in Pieces' in *The Cambridge History of Early Medieval English Literature*, ed. Lees (2012), where I discussed in some detail the omission of early women's literary culture from feminist literary histories, and suggested that in order to understand these absences, we need to consider the limitation of literary historiography itself, to look at the ways in which established paradigms and teleologies reify certain ideas of 'authorship' and 'literature' and exclude other forms of literary production.[32]

In setting out to trace evidence of women's engagement with texts and textual production that can be identified in the neglected earlier medieval period, *Women, Writing and Religion* bears comparison with an important early anthology, Peter Dronke's, *Women Writers of the Middle Ages* (1984), although that volume is European in focus and has a more sweeping chronological range.[33] In addition to the two essays in the *History of British Women's Writing*, edited by McAvoy and Watt, discussed above, this book builds on and develops the work of three book-length studies in particular: Stephanie Hollis's *Anglo-Saxon Women and the Church* (1992), Lees and Overing's *Double Agents* (2001) and *Writing the Wilton Women*, edited by Hollis, with W.R. Barnes, Rebecca Hayward, Kathleen Loncar and Michael Wright (2004).[34] Hollis's *Anglo-Saxon Women and the Church* offers a detailed examination of the status of elite women, queens and abbesses in the eighth and ninth centuries, drawing on the evidence of Latin clerical literature, and argues that the authoritative position of women was already in decline in the centuries before the Conquest. Lees and Overing's *Double Agents* also addresses the question of what the written record reveals about women and monastic culture. This crucially important, and carefully theorized, study focuses both on evidence of women's literacy and the feminine symbolic and female body in the historical documentary sources from poetry, riddles and saints' lives to wills and charters. Spanning the period from the seventh century through to the early eleventh century, it considers Old English as well as Latin texts, and examines not only the representation of women, paying particular attention to women's agency, but also their absence. Lees and Overing's study addresses some of the same texts as *Women, Writing and Religion*, such as the works of Bede and Aldhelm, but does not extend to cover the work of Goscelin of St Bertin, the subject of *Writing the Wilton Women*, edited by Hollis *et al.* This valuable work addresses the importance of Wilton Abbey as a centre of women's religious and literary culture at the very end of the early Middle Ages and in the decades immediately after the Conquest. Although there is overlap with the present study in the texts discussed, none of these books specifically examines broader questions of the interactions of women's literary and religious history throughout the early medieval period that are at the heart of my project. The project is also indebted to Jane Stevenson's monumental *Women Latin Poets* (2005), but while far narrower in chronological scope, it considers a much wider range of engagements with literary cultures and communities.[35] Clarke's *Writing Power in Anglo-Saxon England* (2012) and Tyler's *England in Europe* (2017) include analysis of key issues in relation to women and patronage, but do not focus on women as writers.[36] *Women, Writing and Religion*, in contrast, emphatically insists on the importance of recognizing the extent of early medieval women's engagement with textual production and reception in order to understand fully women's literary history as it continued into the second millennium.

Literary archaeology: Scope and methodology

This book participates in the ongoing project of writing women's English literary history, but in focusing on the early Middle Ages, it also seeks to reframe the debates. I began the research for this book by surveying the evidence of women's engagement with literary culture in the early medieval period. In order to do so, I had to work out the parameters of my field of study. The time frame was relatively easy to identify. The book would begin around the time of the earliest English poet whose name has been passed down to us, and who is therefore often seen as the point of origin in the history of English Literature: the Northumbrian poet Caedmon, who in the mid to late seventh century resided at Streonæshalch or Whitby, which was under the rule of Caedmon's patron Abbess Hild.[37] It would end before the so-called Barking Renaissance in the twelfth century, when the wealthy abbey of Barking became associated with flourishing literary and cultural activity. It would exclude the wealth of material written by women in the French of the English in the later twelfth century, including the works of Marie de France and the *Life of St Catherine* by Clemence of Barking (*fl.*1163–*c.* 1200), both of which I have already discussed in *Medieval Women's Writing*. However, I made the decision that it would include, in its coda, a short discussion of another twelfth-century woman, the English recluse Christina of Markyate (*c.* 1096–after 1155), who is discussed in *Medieval Women's Writing*, and whose *Life*, I argued, is indebted to the early medieval tradition of hagiographies of female abbesses. This discussion of Christina of Markyate would thus provide the connection between *Medieval Women's Writing* and *Women, Writing, and Religion*. The linguistic boundaries of this study also proved to be self-defining. Lees and Overing note in their introduction to early women's writing that 'no named woman writer is known to have been working in the vernacular language of Anglo-Saxon, or Old English, in the British Isles before 1150'.[38] Most of the texts discussed in this book are written in Latin, the language of religion and power in the European Middle Ages, and also a lingua franca that enabled communication across linguistic as well as geographical and political boundaries. Within this body of texts composed in Latin before 1100 we find prayers, hymns and verses, as well as letters and other longer works, such as saints' lives.[39] In comparison, far less Old English material can be ascribed with any degree of confidence to women. The geographical boundaries of this study were more difficult to define. While focusing primarily on 'English' literary and religious cultures, I am aware of course that the idea of an English nation is something of an anachronism throughout the centuries under consideration, that its borders do not correspond directly to those mapped out in present-day Britain, and that these borders were shifting and often porous. Like Tyler in *England in Europe*, I therefore adopted a 'wide view geographically', focusing not only on women's religious and literary cultures within England, but also looking *beyond*.[40] As noted at the beginning of this Introduction, some of women about whom I write, although of English birth or parentage, moved overseas in pursuit of spiritual fulfilment. Indeed, the named women writers whose works have survived from this period were all linked to St. Boniface's mission to Germany in the eighth century.[41] Finally, because so many of the works that I encountered in my research were visionary, hagiographical or devotional in nature, I made the decision to limit the focus of this book to religious women's literary culture.

As I progressed in my research, I came to think of my project as 'literary archaeology', inspired in part by Roberta Gilchrist's 1997 groundbreaking *Gender and Material Culture*, which offers a detailed and carefully substantiated evidence-based rebuttal of many prevailing assumptions about medieval women's religious houses.[42] I use the evidence I found in the surviving written record in order to reconstruct as fully as possible religious women's engagement with literary culture in the early Middle Ages, concentrating on identifying the following, sometimes overlapping, categories of material:

1. References to texts that have not survived but which were attributed to women writers.
2. Texts which are still extant, and that were written by women whose names have come down to us (in other words texts that are recognized to have been authored by women, in today's terms).
3. Anonymous and sometimes fragmentary texts for which a case for female authorship can be made.
4. Texts that acknowledge, directly or indirectly, their debts to female sources, oral as well as written.
5. Texts that acknowledge that they were written for female patrons and/or readers.

In relation to the first category, I identified references to texts attributed to women that have not survived from throughout the early medieval period, from a putative life of Hild (discussed in Chapter 1), a lost *liber* of Barking Abbey, letters and poetry sent from the nuns of Barking to Aldhelm, and a version of the vision of the monk of Much Wenlock authored by Abbess Hildelith of Barking herself (all discussed in Chapter 2) to lost lives of Wulfthryth and Edith of Wilton, a devotional manual written by Edith of Wilton and letters exchanged between Goscelin of St Bertin and Eve of Wilton (discussed in Chapters 5 and 6). Combined with the fact that letters, poems and hagiographies written by nuns linked to the mission of St Boniface have in fact survived (discussed in Chapters 3 and 4), the allusions provide compelling evidence to suggest that much more writing by women must have been produced and circulated in early medieval England. Aside from the texts discussed in this study, this would have included, for example, the eleventh- or early twelfth-century work, now lost, of

Muriel of Wilton, described as '*inclyta versificatrix*' [a celebrated woman poet].[43] Consideration of such writing provides me with a fuller understanding of early medieval women's literary culture located in the major abbeys, which were important centres of learning for women.

In analysing all of the texts which are still extant, including anonymous and fragmentary texts and texts that draw on female sources (looking at manuscripts, where possible, as well as modern printed or digital editions), I have paid particular attention to the gendered representation of authorship, authority and authorization and to the treatment of source material more generally, to the gendered representation of patrons, readers and audience, to the representation of women and their literacy, education and engagement in literary culture and other forms of religious cultural production, to visionary and prophetic voices, to the importance of origins and inheritance and matrilineage and female exemplary models and to the representation of kin and community and of friendships between women and between women and men. In my analyses of texts indebted to female sources in particular, I have attempted to identify, where possible, what has been derived from these sources and what changes may have been made to the source material, including what may have been omitted. This of course necessarily involves further speculative work, to some extent, but by paying close attention to what is actually written and by, where possible, comparing different versions of the same narrative, it is possible to make balanced and reasoned assessments about what may have been contained in the woman-authored texts that have not survived.

It is important to acknowledge what has, for pragmatic reasons alone, been left out of this book. Although it focuses on religious women and their books, we have to remember that throughout the medieval period the lines between religious and secular or religious and political were not necessarily distinct and it was in the elite institutions, the courts as well as the religious houses, that women gained skills in literacy and had access to resources such as libraries. These two institutions were closely interconnected with royal women educated in, and leading religious houses, or retiring to them later in life. The negative impact of the Benedictine Reform on women's religious authority and power in England has been well documented and the ninth and tenth centuries represent something of a hiatus in women's engagement in literary culture, especially in a monastic context.[44] Nevertheless, from the late ninth century on, royal and aristocratic women continued to play crucial roles as patrons of works memorializing their families in particular. In the last quarter of the ninth century, Matilda, abbess of Essen, for example commissioned her cousin

Æthelweard to produce a history of her English ancestors, and in response he produced a Latin adaptation of the *Anglo-Saxon Chronicle* which includes an address to her at the start of each book.[45] Other examples of women's patronage include the *Encomium Emmae Reginae,* written in praise of Emma of Normandy; the *Life of Edward the Confessor,* written for Edith of Wessex;[46] and the English gospel books commissioned by Judith of Flanders.[47] While these texts are not discussed in the current study, such examples of female patronage provide further evidence of women's involvement in literary culture, with these women exercising considerable control over the texts that they were commissioning.

A Case study: Ælfflæd, abbess of Whitby, and the overwriting of women's textual authority

The literary remains of Ælfflæd, abbess of Streonæshalch or Whitby (654–714), successor of Abbess Hild, provide a succinct case study that demonstrates my approach with some clarity. Ælfflæd's interest in fostering a vibrant literary culture at Whitby has been overlooked, perhaps because the importance of patronage in the production of texts has not been fully recognized. Writing about the later Middle Ages, Sarah McNamer has observed that 'there has been a curious reluctance to acknowledge the role of women readers and patrons at the point of origins'.[48] McNamer's comments have perhaps an even greater resonance when applied to the early Middle Ages. In Chapter 1, I will discuss Ælfflæd's contribution more fully in relation to her role as patron of the anonymous first *Life of Gregory the Great,* for which a case for female authorship can be made. Here I want to explore, briefly, other evidence that supports my claims about Ælfflæd's textual ambitions, beginning with an analysis of a passage that appears in Bede's prose *Life of Cuthbert* (c. 721).[49]

In the twenty-third chapter of the *Life,* Bede recounts a miracle relating to Ælfflæd that has resonances with the visions and miracles associated with early medieval holy abbesses that he himself relates in the *Ecclesiastical History,* such as those surrounding the illness and death of Torhtgyth of Barking (discussed in Chapter 2) and those recounted in Rudolf of Fulda's *Life of Leoba* (discussed in Chapter 4). Bede cites Ælfflæd's miracle as evidence of Cuthbert's ability to help others, even when physically removed from them. What is particularly significant about this passage, from our perspective, is that its authority lies in the claim that it is based on Ælfflæd's own first-hand account, albeit passed on to Bede via a male cleric:

Haec eo tempore sicut ipsa postea reuerentissimo Lindisfarnensis aecclesiae presbitero Herefrido et ille mihi referebat, graui percussa languore ac diu uexata, pene uisa est, peruenisse ad mortem.

At that time (as she [Ælfflæd] herself afterwards related to the most reverend priest Herefrith of the church of Lindisfarne, and he to me) she had been stricken by a grievous sickness and long afflicted, and seemed almost to have reached the point of death.

Bede, *Life of Cuthbert*, 230–1

Ælfflæd, we are told, endured a terrible illness that prevented her from walking and reduced her to crawling around on her hands and feet. Despite the intervention of physicians, it seemed impossible that she would survive it. However, remembering the example of Cuthbert, she prayed that she might obtain an object belonging to him that would heal her. The prayer itself is recounted here: 'Would that I had something belonging to my Cuthbert! I know well and believingly trust in God that I should speedily be healed' (Bede, *Life of Cuthbert*, 233). Her prayer was granted and she was presented with a 'linen girdle' sent by the saint. On binding it around herself, she recovered within three days. Ælfflæd then used the same girdle to heal a nun in her own abbey who was suffering from terrible headaches. The bestowal of the present of the linen girdle anticipates Rudolf's account of the cowl Boniface sent to Leoba before his death (see Chapter 4), although here the onus is very much on Ælfflæd as the receiver of a gift that she actively sought through her invocations. Ælfflæd herself takes the initiative to use the girdle to heal another nun in her community. As abbess, she recognizes her responsibility to share her blessings with the nuns in her care, and thus acknowledges that such miracles are not individual but shared and communal.

The episode does not appear in the other lives of Cuthbert, including Bede's own immediate if unacknowledged source, the life by an anonymous monk of Lindisfarne around 700.[50] Bede first drew on this source for his verse *Life of Cuthbert*, written around 716, and then revisited it five years later. He describes this process of rewriting in the prologue to the prose life, dedicated to Eadfrith, bishop of Lindisfarne, and to the monks in his care, explaining that as he was writing he showed his notes to Herefrith, and to others who had lived with Cuthbert 'so that they might read and revise it at their leisure' (Bede, *Life of Cuthbert*, 145), and in the light of their recommendations he made changes and expansions, adding ten new chapters, including the one based on Ælfflæd's recollections. The reason this particular inserted episode is so important is that it claims to be based on Ælfflæd's own narration, which is presumably an oral account, but could, conceivably have been written down. Furthermore, it has Ælfflæd's actual prayer embedded within it, suggesting that Ælfflæd wanted this narrative to be preserved and circulated.

Ælfflæd was undoubtedly an important and highly influential political figure in her age. The daughter of King Oswiu of Northumbria, and Eanflæd of Kent (626–after 685) with whom she initially shared the rule of Whitby, she was sister to Ecgfrith of Northumbria and half-sister to his successor, Aldfrith. In the anonymous *Life of Cuthbert*, the Lindisfarne author depicts Ælfflæd as the spiritual friend and trusted advisor of the sometime recluse, as one close enough to Cuthbert to be able to consult him about her concerns regarding the Northumbrian succession and to ask him about his own plans regarding his succession to the bishopric of Lindisfarne, as one to whom Cuthbert confides prophecies concerning his own death, and as one who is not only witness to his miracles, but also has a role to play in them. The Lindisfarne monk relates that one event is retold as 'the most faithful abbess Ælfflæd related to me' (Anonymous, *Life of Cuthbert*, 127). Like Herefrith, this monk cites Ælfflæd as his source in order to render his narrative more authoritative. As well as serving as the confidante of Cuthbert, Ælfflæd played a crucial role at the synod of Nidd in relation to the reinstatement of the controversial Bishop Wilfrid, and these events are recorded in Stephen of Ripon's *Life of Wilfrid*, written in the early eighth century.[51] Once again, Ælfflæd is cited as a source of authority: quoting Aldfrith's dying words, Stephen of Ripon states 'these words were heard by most faithful witnesses and told to us. Of these, one is the abbess and most prudent virgin Ælfflæd, who is indeed the daughter of a king' (*Life of Wilfrid*, 129). Ælfflæd testifies to the authenticity of Stephen of Ripon's account of Aldfrith's passing, just as in the following chapter she testifies at the synod of Nidd itself and thus crucially contributes to the restoration of Wilfrid's bishopric (*Life of Wilfrid*, 129–33). Taken together, this group of lives confirms not only that Ælfflæd's words counted in the court and ecclesiastical circles of her day – that she was a figure of great authority – but also that she was personally deeply invested in ensuring their transmission and preservation and ensured that she confided them to those responsible for producing the historical written record of the early church.

Returning to Bede's prose *Life of Cuthbert*, it is my contention that the representation of Ælfflæd within the linen girdle episode does not correspond to Bede's depiction of Ælfflæd elsewhere in his *Life of Cuthbert*, which is itself out of kilter with representations of Ælfflæd in his immediate source and elsewhere in the written record. Hollis undertakes a detailed comparison of the Anonymous *Life* and Bede's rewriting, pointing out that in Bede 'the friendship of Cuthbert and Ælfflæd [sic] has been rigorously transformed into a hierarchical relation in which Cuthbert's over-riding superiority is everywhere apparent'.[52] Certainly even in Bede's added episode concerning the linen girdle, Ælfflæd is described as one 'who always had a great affection for the man of God' but there is no indication in this that the feeling was equally reciprocated (Bede, *Life of Cuthbert*, 231). Hollis is uncompromising in her dismissal of Bede's account: 'Bede's rewriting of Ælfflæd's role in the *Life of Cuthbert* reflects, in its considerable hostility to her as an intimate of the bishop-saint, sharp competitive strains concerning women's participation in the ecclesiastical sphere'.[53] Hollis suggests that Bede included the linen girdle episode only because he 'was under an obligation to incorporate the additional information given to him by Herefrith of Lindisfarne'.[54] For her, it simply serves to illustrate 'the saint's god-like immanence'. As confirmation that Bede had no particular regard for Ælfflæd, it should be noted that Bede omits her completely from his accounts of the lives of Cuthbert and Wilfrid in the *Ecclesiastical History*.[55] However, disagreeing with Hollis on this one point, I suggest that in the episode of the linen girdle, the saintly piety of Cuthbert and that of Ælfflæd are imbricated in one another: if Cuthbert heals Ælfflæd, then Ælfflæd herself shares that miracle with a member of her own community. Ælfflæd is not simply cited, possibly with some bad grace, as an authority by Bede. Rather her story, and indeed her voice, in the prayer reported in the episode, are preserved. The discrepancy between the portrayal of Ælfflæd in this episode, and her depiction elsewhere in Bede's *Life of Cuthbert* supports the argument that the episode of the linen girdle has been inserted into Bede's text without being overwritten to the same extent that Bede altered the rest of his source material relating to Ælfflæd.

The example of Ælfflæd illustrates then the usefulness of examining in some detail texts that acknowledge their debts to female sources, whether those sources be oral or written. It shows that much is gained from paying attention to the gendered representation of authority and authorization, and the representation of female community and spiritual friendship between the sexes. In the case of Bede's prose *Life of Cuthbert*, we are in the fortunate position that the anonymous *Life of Cuthbert* still survives, and also that Bede himself described in some detail in his prologue the processes of composition, and in particular his decision to submit his draft material to monastic scrutiny and to add in additional chapters. It is therefore possible to look closely at Bede's treatment of his source, and also to compare this account of Cuthbert with another text that provides us with alternative perspectives on Ælfflæd, Stephen of Ripon's *Life of Wilfrid*, as well as to the version of Cuthbert's life in his own *Ecclesiastical History* in which Ælfflæd is marked by her absence. From this, we can see not only the extent to which Bede overwrote the authority of Ælfflæd, but also recognize that embedded within his *Life of Cuthbert* there survives a counter-narrative about Ælfflæd that is much more in line with her representation elsewhere. The very existence of this counter-narrative is indicative of the extent to which Ælfflæd herself, who, as already noted, also commissioned hagiographical writing, was concerned to ensure that her own words were enshrined within the written records being produced in her lifetime or shortly thereafter. It is possible therefore to recognize in Ælfflæd a powerful woman who recognized the value of, and actively fostered the literary culture that commemorated and memorialized the early English church.

Women, Writing and Religion

The six chapters of this book make the case that women's literary culture thrived throughout the early medieval period. Focusing on the religious houses of Ely and Whitby in the seventh and early eighth centuries, Chapter 1 reviews some of the surviving evidence of the earliest monastic women's writing. In so doing it re-examines the lives of the Abbesses Æthelthryth of Ely and Hild of Whitby found in the fourth book of Bede's *Ecclesiastical History* alongside the account of Hild found in the *Old English Martyrology* and the anonymous first *Life of Gregory the Great*. Taken together, what can be learnt from a study of these lives is that by focusing on texts associated with religious houses ruled by women, and by considering these texts to be the productions not of individuals but of communities, it is possible to get a fuller and more balanced understanding of women's writing in this earliest period of English literary history.

Chapter 2 focuses on Barking Abbey, a vital centre of learning in the early Middle Ages, and evidence relating to Minster-in-Thanet. Particular attention is given to the case of Abbess Hildelith, successor to the founding abbess of Barking, Æthelburh, and specifically to a lost *liber* or book, mentioned by Bede in his *Ecclesiastical History*. This text evidently recorded visions experienced by the nuns of Barking concerning the death of their founding abbess. Moving from Bede's appropriation of the lost book to a book of instruction, the chapter goes on to offer a detailed reading of Aldhelm's *De Virginitate*, written for Hildelith and her fellow nuns at Barking, outlining the further evidence of the engagement in scholarly literary activities of the nuns of Barking that the text provides before examining the dissonance between the texts and their intended audience. As *De Virginitate* indicates, Hildelith evidently was a keen scholar: she was a correspondent of Boniface as well as Aldhelm, and according to the former wrote an account of the vision of the monk of Much Wenlock, which Boniface himself overwrote with his own first-hand account based on the Monk's own testimony. The chapter speculates about why Boniface rejected Hildelith's version of the vision, and about the political functions it may have served for both Hildelith and her allies, and for Boniface. The final section of the chapter examines a fragmentary Old English *Life of Mildrith* and related material which may be derived from female-authored narratives.

Chapter 3 examines key letters by and to women, namely Ælfflæd, Ecgburg, Eadburg, Eangyth, Bugga and Berthgyth, and of course Leoba of Tauberbischofsheim, an example of whose poetry survives. Particularly striking here is the evidence provided in the letters of women's textual production. This chapter goes on to read letters of early medieval women, especially those of Berthgyth, alongside the more famous Old English elegies. It examines the epistolary explorations of emotions and memories of these early medieval nuns, including, but not only, women missionaries who migrated to Europe in order to convert others to their beliefs.

The work of women missionaries in Germany provides still further extraordinary examples of women's writing from the late eighth century: Hugeburc of Heidenheim's *Lives of Willibald and Wynnebald*. Hugeburc's *Hodoeporicon of St Willibald* offers an account of the saint's pilgrimage to the Holy Lands that is closely based on the saint's own oral account. Chapter 4 contrasts this text, with its self-depreciating depiction of the woman writer, with Rudolf of Fulda's ninth-century *Life of Leoba*. The *Life of Leoba* claims to be written from the somewhat garbled notes taken down by a monk, Mago, and supplemented by other written and oral accounts based on the memoirs of four named nuns. Rudolf's text is, then, in contrast to the lives by Hugeburc, considerably distanced from its subject's own life. Nevertheless, it provides us with further evidence of the scholarly and textual communities of early English women that existed both at home and abroad.

Chapter 5 explores Wilton in the eleventh century (following the Benedictine Reform) as a centre of women's scholarship and engagement with literary culture, comparable in some respects to Barking three centuries earlier. The chapter focuses on Goscelin of St Bertin's *Life of Edith*, which resonates in some respects with Bede's accounts of the early abbesses and their nuns, including in its shared focus on visions of death. Furthermore, like Bede's accounts, Goscelin's *Life* is written about an individual who is still well-remembered in her community. In writing, at least in part, for the female community at Wilton, Goscelin pays close attention in this text – and in his Barking hagiographies – to women's oral reports in particular. Goscelin, more than Bede, acknowledges women as authorities for his narratives.

Chapter 6 considers another work by Goscelin of St Bertin, the *Liber confortatorius*, written for Eve of Wilton around 1080 or shortly thereafter. This text takes the form of an extended letter offering advice to the recluse in her new spiritual life. The *Liber confortatorius* is significant because it is the earliest surviving guide for a female recluse in the English literary tradition. Other famous later examples of such works include the twelfth-century *De institutione inclusarum* by Ælred, abbot of Rievaulx, and the early-thirteenth-century *Ancrene Wisse* or *Guide for Anchoresses*. Goscelin's text is very different from these later examples, not least because, despite its form and avowed intention, its emphasis is far less on regulating the conduct of the recluse than on describing the author's sense of abandonment and loss. As a book of consolation, it is, arguably, directed more to the needs of the author-narrator than to those of the reader, whether Eve or any other individual seeking spiritual comfort. Indeed Eve herself, rather than appearing isolated, is depicted as a social recluse who continues to benefit from intimate relationships with other spiritual supporters.

The Coda draws out the ramifications of this study by exploring some of the texts associated with the twelfth-century prioress, Christina of Markyate, which look both backward to the early medieval period and forward to saints' lives and visionary writings of the later Middle Ages. The Coda thus reinforces the importance of exploring continuities across the divide between the early and late medieval periods. Together then, the chapters in this book reveal that the lively textual and religious cultures of early medieval women were intricately interconnected, and that it is possible to trace a tradition of English women's literary culture that extends throughout the early Middle Ages.

Women's Literary Communities at Ely and Whitby

Introduction

The first examples of the overwriting of women's literary culture come from the beginning of our period: Bede's *Ecclesiastical History*, completed in 731. Book four of the *Ecclesiastical History*, a work as a whole concerned with chronicling the foundation of the English church, includes the lives of three founding abbesses: Æthelburh (Ethelburga) of Barking (*fl.* 664); Æthelthryth (Etheldreda) of Ely (*c.* 636–679); and Hild of Whitby (614–680).[1] The lives of all three women, who wielded considerable political as well as religious power, suggest that early medieval female sanctity fitted into a long-standing tradition of women's visions and prophecy that originated in the pre-Christian era and continued to the Reformation and beyond.[2] Bede, like many of the influential churchmen who succeeded him, was divided in his motives: on the one hand, he wanted to honour and promote these early foundations by recording significant people and events associated with them; but on the other, he felt uncomfortable with, and therefore tried to contain textually, the degree of autonomy and power wielded by the early abbesses, autonomy and power which was subsequently circumscribed by monastic reform. Bede's accounts of these elite women elide their sources, which would certainly have included lives of the founding abbesses originally composed within their religious houses. While it is well known that Bede often failed to acknowledge his sources, whether he was writing about men or women (as is demonstrated in his rewriting of the anonymous *Life of Cuthbert*, discussed in the Introduction), the significance of this in relation to women's writing, where so little early evidence remains, is all the greater. In this chapter, I aim to explore in detail the traces that remain in the surviving record of the earliest monastic women's writing, focusing specifically on the religious houses of Ely and Whitby in the seventh and early eighth centuries. Further evidence of a tradition of women's writing in Latin emerging from the important religious house at Barking will be analysed in the following chapter, alongside evidence of writing emerging from the women's house at Minster-in-Thanet. I argue here that Bede 'overwrote' the women's lives in the sense that he wrote over, and thus partially obliterated accounts, whether written or oral, that had been produced in the abbesses' own monasteries. This chapter will focus initially on Bede's narratives of Æthelthryth and Hild. Æthelburh will be considered in Chapter 2 in the context of my exploration of the thriving literary culture at Barking.

The lives of the two important and powerful abbesses, Æthelthryth and Hild, stand in close proximity in the *Ecclesiastical History*, and Bede clearly intends them to be read together. Bede's life of Æthelthryth of Ely is given particular prominence in the *Ecclesiastical History* because it is accompanied by the *Hymn to Æthelthryth* which Bede himself composed. Æthelthryth is adopted by Bede as a representative of the ideal of female virginal piety, and Bede adapts her story to reinforce this point. In this chapter, I argue that traces of a different version of the life of Æthelthryth can nevertheless still be detected; an underlying narrative with a greater focus on the community at Ely and on a wider network of female religious, including a more pronounced emphasis on the role of Æthelthryth's sister Seaxburh. In writing his life of Hild, Bede faced a greater challenge. Hild, a patron of an educated scholarly community of women and men, as well as a powerful political figure in her own right, does not conform to Bede's model of virginal piety. In this case, not only does it seem likely that a lost life of Hild, written by her own community, once existed, which Bede drew upon, but it is also possible to reconstruct elements of this hagiography from another early text, in this case a version of the *Old English Martyrology*. Reading the *Old English Martyrology* alongside Bede's life of Hild provides further supporting evidence of the visionary concerns of the Whitby community. Furthermore, although lives of Æthelthryth and Hild, produced by their own communities, have not come down to us, one crucially important early Whitby text *has* survived: the anonymous first *Life of Gregory the Great*. This hagiography was produced at Whitby under the rule of Hild's successor Ælfflæd. It is a key text in the history of the conversion of the English, and another possible unacknowledged source of Bede's *Ecclesiastical History*. The Whitby *Life of Gregory* thus provides us with an example of the sort of underwriting or lost or unacknowledged source texts on which Bede drew, and, significantly it is one which may also have been female-authored.

Æthelthryth, Ely and Bede's *Hymn*

At the heart of the fourth book of *Ecclesiastical History* lies Bede's life of Æthelthryth, the founding abbess of Ely. Bede describes Æthelthryth's pious life and death and the translation of her body (*EH* 4.19), and composes his *Hymn* about her (*EH* 4.20).[3] This life would subsequently be incorporated along with a range of other sources (including possibly an Old English *vita*) into the *Liber Eliensis*, compiled in Ely in the late twelfth century.[4] Æthelthryth, who succeeded in remaining chaste through two marriages, represents for Bede the perfect state of virginity. Indeed Bede overwrites Æthelthryth's life in order to make it fit his ideal. His retelling of her narrative passes relatively quickly over her life as a devout wife: 'She had previously been married to an ealdorman of the South Gyrwe, named Tondberht. But he died shortly after the marriage and on his death she was given to King Ecgfrith. Though she lived with him for twelve years she still preserved the glory of perfect virginity' (*EH* 4.19, p. 391). In contrast, Bede pays far more attention to her life as a woman religious (her self-discipline, mortification of the flesh, and physical suffering), and especially to her death. As Virginia Blanton points out, Bede's treatment of Æthelthryth in *Ecclesiastical History* is exceptional: 'the story of Æthelthryth is fixated on her perfection.'[5] Æthelthryth plays such a central role in the fourth book of the *Ecclesiastical History* because she represents Bede's ideal of female sanctity.

Bede's *Hymn* to Æthelthryth is itself a remarkable document, celebrating as it does a form of heroic virginity that only partially fits Æthelthryth's own circumstances. Contrasting himself to Virgil ('Maro'), Bede asserts that he writes of peace rather than war, and of chastity rather than rape. Unexceptionally, Bede figures Æthelthryth as the bride of Christ and likens her to the Virgin Mary. Yet Bede also lists as examples of chastity the legendary virgin martyrs Agatha, Eulalia, Thecla, Euphemia, Agnes and Cecilia, who variously endured attempted seductions, imprisonment in brothels, and violent and often sexualized torture. While Æthelthryth's dedication of her virginity to God resonates with the vows of Agnes, Cecilia and Thecla, there are few other direct similarities. Æthelthryth's husbands do not rape her; she is not tortured; and she is not martyred. Indeed she dies of natural causes: as a victim of the plague, afflicted by 'a very large tumour beneath her jaw' (*EH* 4.19, p. 395). Bede forces Æthelthryth into a mould that she does not fit. By composing a hymn in praise of Æthelthryth alone out of all the abbesses, Bede bestows a unique status upon her, or rather (to use the evocative phrase of Clare A. Lees and Gillian R. Overing) upon her 'clean, chaste and dead body.'[6] It is her corpse, discovered to be incorrupt in the grave when it is dug up by her successor to be moved into the church, that is the final proof of her enduring virginity:

> Virginis alma caro est tumulata bis octo Nouembres,
>   nec putet in tumulo uirginis alma caro.

> [Veiled in the tomb sixteen Novembers lay,
>   Nor rots her virgin flesh veiled in the tomb.]

EH 4.20, 398–9

Note the emphatic repetition of '*virginis alma caro*' [nourishing virgin flesh] in these Latin lines (not rendered in the loose translation offered here, which inserts instead the repeated word 'veiled' not found in the original). There is a manifest tension between Bede's transcendental, panegyrical poetic rendering of Æthelthryth and the more earth-bound, pragmatic prose.[7] Yet both are part of the same prosimetrical text and neither takes precedence over, or overwrites, the other; rather the two aspects of the text counterbalance one another. Indeed, Bede's *Hymn* is perhaps the opposite of the fragment: if the fragment is 'a quotation taken out of context', the *Hymn*, like Æthelthryth's body, is safely enclosed within a larger whole, intact within its textual environment.[8]

If Bede uses Æthelthryth's life for his own ends, is it possible still to discern elements of the underwriting and to get a sense of the 'materials from here and there' (*EH* Preface, p. 5), the narratives oral and written, that he used as his sources? Such writings and traditions would have originated in Ely itself, under the headship of Seaxburh (*c.* 655–*c.* 700), Æthelthryth's own sister, and successor as abbess. Bede must certainly have had access to a life of the founding saint produced within her own monastery. One element that is common to Bede's accounts of Æthelthryth and Hild of Whitby, and also, as we will see in Chapter 2, Æthelburh of Barking, is a concern with visions and miracles of death that testify to the piety of the dead and of those who wish to honour them. It is Abbess Seaxburh herself who decides that Æthelthryth's tomb should be moved, and who sends out the monks to look for a new coffin. In initiating the translation of Æthelthryth's body, Seaxburh is fostering her sister's cult by announcing publically through this ritual her claim to sanctity, and thus attributing divine legitimacy to the abbey itself. Even within Bede's narrative women have key roles to play. While the whole community, monks as well as nuns, take part in the exhumation of Æthelthryth's corpse, it is the abbess and her sisters who open the old coffin with the intention of lifting the bones, and it is they who wash and re-clothe the body and carry it to its new resting place. Æthelthryth, who, we are told, in life did not wash herself but washed her fellow nuns, is here finally physically cleansed before being returned to the ground. This focus on the dead body of the saint, and on the roles played by her successor and the community of nuns in its translation, may well have been first memorialized by that very community.

What is so remarkable about Bede's account of Æthelthryth, however, is the extent to which, despite the centrality to it of Seaxburh and her community, it minimizes or overwrites the authority of women. Blanton suggests, for example, that Æthelthryth's speech (in *EH* 4.19, p. 397) may be derived from the lost life of Æthelthryth.[9] In this speech, the abbess described the illness that killed her as punishment for former vanity: 'I know well enough that I deserve to bear the weight of this affliction in my neck, for I remember that when I was a young girl I used to wear an unnecessary weight of necklaces' (*EH* 4.19, p. 397). Yet, in contrast to Bede's account of the death of Hild (which I will discuss in the next section of this chapter), there are in this narrative no visions of the saint's ascension experienced by the nuns of her monastery. Furthermore, although it was Seaxburh who, as noted above, was responsible for ordering the exhumation, it is Bishop Wilfrid, not Seaxburh, who testifies to Æthelthryth's virginity and who is named as a key witness to the preservation of Æthelthryth's corpse (*EH* 4.19, pp. 391–3 and 395). What is more, the physician Cynefrith, who attended the dying saint, is cited by Bede as the direct source of the story of the preservation of the corpse, and his words are taken as ultimate confirmation of the miracle (*EH* 4.19, p. 395). The incision that the physician had made in Æthelthryth's neck while she was still alive to drain a bubo on her neck has been replaced with an indistinct scar. This scar is the ultimate sign of her enduring purity. From Bede's perspective, the verification offered by these male commentators has a divinely endowed authority that far outweighs the evidence of women, which is implicitly viewed as partisan or unreliable.

Not only does Bede prefer male to female witnesses, he also distances Æthelthryth from her female kin. As Lees and Overing note 'the narrative process of isolating (in the cloister or the pedestal) the female saint obscures … her relationships with other women'.[10] Crucially, Bede makes no direct reference to Æthelthryth's familial ties to Hild, even though, as Blanton suggests, 'it is more than reasonable to believe that the women knew one another well and were in some way cognizant of their mutual work as leaders of monastic communities'.[11] While Bede does record that Æthelthryth entered the monastery of her aunt Æbbe (in *EH* 4.19, p. 393), this reference to Coldingham is somewhat troubling, and cannot be read straightforwardly as an implicit acknowledgement of female bonds of kinship. Later in the *Ecclesiastical History* (4.25), Bede describes how

Coldingham was subsequently destroyed by fire as a result of the sinfulness of its residents. Æbbe herself is implicated in this corruption in that she fails to control her communities, and the Coldingham reference scars the perfection of the narrative. Like the healed scar on the neck of Æthelthryth's corpse that replaced the bubo that killed her, this narrative scar signifies the corruption that threatens Æthelthryth's purity (comparable to her marriages, or the plague). In addition to isolating Æthelthryth from her wider female kin group, Bede also overlooks important information about Seaxburh. Rosalind C. Love points out that Bede makes no reference to Seaxburh's own foundation at Minster-in-Sheppey, or to her daughter Eormenhild.[12] Bede discusses the life, and death, of Seaxburh's other daughter, Earcongota, but only in another context (in *EH* 3.8). While Bede may do his best to marginalize Seaxburh, her continued presence in his life of Æthelthryth indicates how important she actually is to the preservation of her sister's history.

In thinking through the changes Bede made to his source material, it is also important to consider what may have been omitted. Missing from Bede's version of the early history of Ely is any detailed or specific information about the foundation of Ely itself. Bede simply records that a year after Æthelthryth's consecration 'she was herself appointed abbess' of Ely, and was responsible for the construction of the building, and for the instruction of her nuns (*EH* 4.19, p. 393). Only at the end of this hagiographical narrative does he provide more concrete information about the monastery, when he reports that Ely is part of the kingdom of the East Angles, that it covers some 600 hides of land, and that it is like an island in the fens. The significance of these facts is drawn out, albeit indirectly, when Bede goes on to say that Æthelthryth chose the location because she was herself of East Anglian descent, and also when he explains the etymology of the name 'Ely' which is taken from the number of eels in the surrounding fen. As daughter of Anna, king of the East Angles, Æthelthryth's legitimate claim to the substantial area of territory on which she has her monastery built is firmly established, while the future sustainability of the monastery, provided as it is with its own food supply, seems assured. This closing passage therefore serves an important function, but its meaning and implications are easily overlooked and Bede himself does not seem overly concerned with them. This lack of interest in the practicalities of the foundation of a religious house is typical of his approach more broadly, and not confined to the double monasteries governed by women. His sources would surely have placed the history of the monastery's foundation at the heart of the narrative rather than have appended it as a truncated postscript. Nevertheless, the underwriting shows through, revealing traces of the priorities and concerns of the Ely community itself.

In summary, Bede presents a heavily overwritten account of the foundation of Ely and the life of Æthelthryth. This is seen most clearly in his *Hymn*, which he had composed 'many years' before the prose life (*EH* 4.20, p. 397). As Blanton points out, however much Bede may attempt to disguise it, even in the prose life, with its emphasis on eyewitness testimonies, Bede has made 'deliberate choices about the presentation (shaping, editing, deleting)'.[13] Yet it is possible still to detect something of the underwriting that Bede drew upon: texts written to support the cult of Æthelthryth which her sister Seaxburh evidently fostered and which were produced by and in support of the Ely community as a community. It is important to acknowledge that the elision of broader collaborations in Bede's *Ecclesiastical History* is not limited to his accounts of holy women and their religious houses, but is a tendency demonstrated across his writing, including in relation to male figures. Despite the profession of the *Ecclesiastical History* to tell a shared, communal story of the English church and nation, Bede seems to work habitually by extracting characters as exemplars or key figures who embody ideals or transitions and changes, and in the process obscures wider processes and interactions. Yet, as we will also see in the case of Hild, the effect of this overwriting of the female community on women's history and literary history is particularly marked.

Hild and the literary culture of Whitby

As with the account of Æthelthryth in Bede's *Ecclesiastical History*, it is evident in his life of Hild (*EH* 4.23) that Bede was drawing on contemporary narratives about the abbess written by members of the religious community.[14] In this case it is reasonable to assume that Bede drew on a lost life of Hild from the double monastery at Streanaeshalch or Whitby.[15] One key factor that distinguishes Bede's life of Hild from his life of Æthelthryth is that, according to J. E. Cross, vestiges of a lost Whitby life can be traced in *The Old English Martyrology*, which dates back to the ninth century and is one of the earliest Old English prose texts to have survived.[16] It is also a text that could have been written by a woman, although its most recent editor and translator, Christine Rauer, is not convinced by earlier suggestions that it shows a marked interest in women's monasticism.[17] Cross's article was published in 1979, but the evidence presented there has not hitherto been re-examined in the light of more recent scholarship. By looking closely at the places where the entry on Hild in *The Old English Martyrology* diverges from Bede's life of Hild, it is possible to discern something of the concerns of the Whitby community itself. First, however, it is valuable once again to reflect upon the gaps and tensions within Bede's own narrative.

In failing – once more – to acknowledge his sources, Bede adapts Hild's life to fit his own agenda, part of which seems to be to remove surviving traces of Hild's own scholarly textual community.[18] This is vividly illustrated by the writing out of Hild's crucial role as patron of the poet Caedmon (in *EH* 4.24), which has been analysed by Lees and Overing.[19] Furthermore, although Bede, as we have seen in relation to Æthelthryth, is not overly concerned with recording the histories of the foundation of monasteries headed by women, he is particularly vague about the early years at Whitby, stating 'it happened that [Hild] undertook either to found or to set in order a monastery at a place called Streanaeshalch' (*EH* 4.23, p. 409). It seems quite remarkable, especially if we accept the possibility that Bede consulted the Whitby life of Hild, that Bede does not have access to more precise information about how much land was granted to the monastery and from where the land came. In fact in a slightly earlier passage, in describing Hild's return to Northumbria at the request of Bishop Aidan, Bede does state that Hild 'received a hide of land on the north side of the river Wear' when she lived for a year in a small community, possibly at South Shields (*EH* 4.23 p. 407). It is clear that Bede quite deliberately chooses not to record more information about Whitby's foundation. Indeed Hild's building of the monastery at Hackness in the year she died is also mentioned later only in passing (*EH* 4.23, p. 413). However, this is not the limit of Bede's agenda, as he also very deliberately excludes any mention of the Synod of Whitby, over which Hild herself presided (discussion of her role is limited to a couple of sentences in *EH* 3.25, where he mentions briefly that she took the Celtic side).[20] In his account of Hild's life, Bede emphasizes her personal devotion and her close association with Bishop Aidan and her role as spiritual mother of bishops, but without making it explicit that Hild was personally responsible for educating these men. The religious and political were profoundly imbricated in one another, as Hild's career illustrates. Yet Bede initiates a tendency to stress the religious over the political when discussing female saints and visionaries. Bede is also very selective in what he reveals about Hild's personal life. He certainly records, albeit in somewhat confusing terms, her royal family connections and her conversion, but reveals little more about the first half of her life, choosing instead to dwell on the events that followed her profession.[21] One argument that has been put forward to explain this is that Hild was a widow when she became a nun and that she did not conform comfortably to Bede's expectations of female sanctity.[22] However, in reconstructing Hild's early life and education and training, Helene Scheck and Virginia Blanton speculate that Hild may have been a single woman living a secular life at court, where she could have served as an advisor.[23] Indeed, Bede may have been unsettled by Hild's public and political life. In his account of her life and career, marked as it is by gaps and omissions, Bede effectively depoliticizes and decontextualizes Hild's sanctity, remoulding it to fit his own model.

What evidence, if any, remains of the underwriting, the life or lives that Bede drew on, the text or texts that more closely reflected the interests and concerns of Whitby itself and that may have been authored by Hild's fellow nuns? One point to note is that Bede does mention, at least in passing, some important figures in the early history of women's monasticism: Hild's own sister Hereswith in the monastery of Chelles, whom Hild wished to join; and Heiu, who founded the abbey at Heruteu or Hartlepool. Such women would surely have been celebrated in early writings by nuns. It also seems reasonable to assume that a version of Bede's narrative of the dream of a necklace experienced by Hild's mother Breguswith was found in the Whitby life. Indeed this dream does also appear in the *Old English Martyrology* although there are some significant differences.[24] Bede provides more background – explaining the absence of Hild's father Hereric as due to his exile – but locates the dream as having taken place after Hild's birth, and interprets the shining light of the necklace as representing the exemplary life Hild would go on to lead. The *Old English Martyrology* on the other hand renders this an annunciation vision. Hild is not yet born and the jewel signifies Hild's reputation:

> and þære meder wæs on slæpe ætywed, þa heo myd þam bearne wæs, þæt hyre man stunge ane syle on þone bosum ond seo ongunne scynan ofer ealle Brytene; Þæt tacnode þone hlysan þære fæmnan halignysse. And Sancta Hylda wæs þry and þrytig geara on læwedum hade and þry and þrytig geara under haligryfte, and heo þa gewat to Cryste.

> [and it had been revealed to the mother in her sleep, when she was with child, that a piece of jewellery would be pinned to her chest and it would begin to shine over the whole of Britain; that signified the fame of the virgin's sanctity. And St Hild lived for thirty-three years as a laywoman, and for thirty-three years after taking the veil, and she then migrated to Christ.]
>
> *Old English Martyrology*, 216–17

It is striking that, unlike Bede, the *Old English Martyrology* does explicitly refer to Hild as a virgin. The use of the rhetorical device of anaphora (the repetition of '*þry and þrytig geara*') is emphatic: the splitting of Hild's life in two parts at the age of thirty-three, the age of Christ when He was crucified, signifies that at this perfect age Hild herself was reborn. While Bede includes this symbolic detail, he does not link it to Breguswith's dream. Thus Bede avoids explicitly identifying Breguswith with the Virgin Mary and Hild with Christ. The version of Hild's life in the *Old English Martyrology* may well be much closer to the lost Whitby life or lives of the founding abbess.

As in the life of Æthelthryth, Bede is less concerned with the saintly woman's holy life than with her holy death. With the exception of Breguswith's dream, Bede reveals very little about the first half of Hild's life beyond the fact that it was spent 'very nobly in the secular habit' (*EH* 4.23, p. 407). But although men, whether as patrons (Bishop Aidan) or as sons of her religious house, are central to what Bede reveals of the second half of Hild's life, once she has taken the veil, women dominate the narrative of her death. Like Æthelthryth, Hild suffers agonizing illness for a prolonged period of time – she dies at cockcrow in the seventh year of her incapacity. That she struggled with ill health for seven years indicates that she achieved spiritual completion before leaving the world (seven signifies perfection in Biblical numerology). The reference to cockcrow may be to the third watch of the night in Mark 13.35: 'Watch ye therefor, (for ye know not when the master of the house cometh . . .)' rather than to Peter's denial of Christ in Matthew 26.34–75 and John 18.27. These Biblical references remain implicit rather than explicit in Bede's account. Again like Æthelthryth, Hild's death is marked by miracles and visions that ripple through the community and bring unity and joy. Breguswith's prophetic vision is mirrored in visions surrounding Hild's death witnessed by nuns at Whitby and its neighbouring house at Hackness (*EH* 4.23, pp. 413–14). Bede does in fact here acknowledge the authority of the female visionaries, from Breguswith to Begu (a nun at Hackness) and an anonymous Whitby novice. Indeed Bede even names another female witness to validate Begu's dream: Frigyth, who presided over Hackness. Begu, the nun at Hackness, sees in a dream the ascension of Hild's soul. Sleeping in the dormitory Begu is apparently awoken by a bell toll and watches in amazement as the roof opens and light pours into the room before seeing the abbess's soul carried upwards by angels. She rushes to share what she has seen with her prioress Frigyth, who summons her nuns to gather in the church to pray for Hild. The monks who later arrive with news of Hild's death find them thus. A nun at Whitby experiences a similar vision of the ascendance of Hild's soul. A single dream, which might correspond either to that of Begu or that of the anonymous Whitby nun, is also found in the *Old English Martyrology*:

And hyre Godes þeowa sum geseah hu englas hyre gast to heofonum læddon, and heo glytenode on þæra engla mydle swa scynende sunne oððe nigslycod hrægel. And seo ylce Godes þeowen gehyrde, on þa ylcan tyd þa heo gewat, wundorlicre bellan sweg on þære lyfte, and heo geseah eac þæt englas hofon up ongean hyre gast swyðe mycle and wundorlice Crystes rode, and seo scean swa heofenes tungol. And myd swylcere blysse Sancta Hyldan gast wæs gelæded on heofenas cyneþrym, þær heo nu a butan ende gesyhð urne Dryhten, þæs wyllan heo ær fremede þa hwyle heo on lyfe wunode on hyre lychaman.

[And one of her servants of God saw how angels took her soul to heaven, and it shone amid the angels like the bright sun or a new dress. And the same maid of God heard, at the same time as she died, the noise of a beautiful bell in the air, and she also saw that angels lifted up towards her soul a very large and marvellous Christian cross, and it shone like a star in the sky. And with such honour St. Hilda's soul was led into the royal majesty of heaven, where she can now look at our Lord always without end, whose will she had accomplished previously while she was alive in her body.]

Old English Martyrology, 216–17

There are a number of unique elements to the *Old English Martyrology* version. Cross draws our attention to the unusual simile of the '*nigslycod hrægel*' translated here simply as 'new dress', but which might be better read as the 'newly sleeked gown' or, according to Cross's own translation, the 'newly glossed garment'.[25] This may well reflect the perspective of a female author, although there are also echoes of the description of the Bride of the Lamb in Apocalypse 19.8: 'And it is granted to her that she should clothe herself with fine linen, glittering and white. For the fine linen are the justifications of saints.' The cross, shining like the jewel in Hild's mother's dream, is also absent in Bede's *Ecclesiastical History*. Once again, the *Old English Martyrology* presents Hild as Christ, and also in its final triumphant announcement of Hild's entry into heaven, as the Bride of Christ, and once again it includes additional details that may be derived from Whitby texts.

The Whitby *Earliest Life of Gregory*

Further evidence of the preoccupations and concerns of the Whitby community can be found in the eighth-century *Life of Gregory the Great*. In his account of the life of Hild in book four of his *History*, Bede makes no mention of her two powerful relatives and allies, who succeeded her as abbesses of Whitby, Ælfflæd (654–714) and her mother Eanflæd (626–after 685), despite discussing them elsewhere.[26] Yet the earliest Latin *Life of Gregory the Great* was clearly written under the patronage of Ælfflæd.[27] Andrew Breeze has made a convincing case for female authorship of the earliest *Life of Gregory*, produced at Whitby, [28] but it is also plausible that it was written not by a single nun, but by several. The *Life*, which was written between around 704 and 714, is uniquely preserved in a copy dating to the first quarter of the ninth century in St Gallen, Stiftsbibliothek, Codex Sangallensis [Cod. Sang.] 567, pp. 75–110 (see Figure 1.1).[29] Two scribes, both writing in a Rhaetian minuscule, were responsible for copying the *Life*, possibly in the scriptorium of Abbey of St Gall itself, a mid-eighth-century foundation that includes one of the oldest monastic libraries in the world, while a third corrected errors and omissions. Cod. Sang. 567 is collection of *vitae sanctum* [saints' lives] and related texts, including, alongside the *Life of Gregory the Great*, material relating to Pope Sylvester I (pp. 1–73), Hilary of Poitiers (pp. 111–33), Pope Lucius I (pp. 135–52), Ss Lonochilus and Agnofleda (pp. 155–63), and St Martin of Tours (pp. 164–70 and 172–99). It is made up for seven booklets copied at various times and locations between the early eighth and the late ninth centuries. Most of the items, including the *Life of Gregory the Great*, were bound together before the end of the ninth century, creating a hagiographic anthology, presumably specifically for monastic use (the lives of St Martin and related material were added later). It was then clearly a highly regarded and valued work, and as a biography of the so-called Apostle to the English it is also central to the early English tradition of religious writing, and would have been seen as such by contemporaries.

Critics are divided over the question of whether or not Bede drew on the Whitby *Life of Gregory* in writing his *Ecclesiastical History*.[30] The Whitby *Life* includes a crucial detail omitted by Bede: the name of Gregory's mother, Sylvia (*Earliest Life*, 73). The *Life of Gregory* establishes its connection to the Whitby abbesses: it refers to both Ælfflæd and Eanflæd in a key passage describing the miracles that surrounded the translation of the relics of Edwin of Northumbria to Whitby, which took place 'while Eanflæd was still living and in the monastic life' (*Earliest Life*, 103). Significantly, the narrative concerning the transfer of Edwin's bones is also not found in Bede's *Ecclesiastical History*. That those responsible for writing the earliest *Life of Gregory* are indeed members of the religious community at Whitby is apparent in the subsequent partisan description of the abbey as 'the well-known monastery of Ælfflæd, a most religious woman and the daughter of Queen Eanflæd, who was herself . . . the daughter of Edwin' (*Earliest Life*, 103). This crucial episode centres on a series of visions received by a priest called Trimma and is based in part on Trimma's own account (*Earliest*

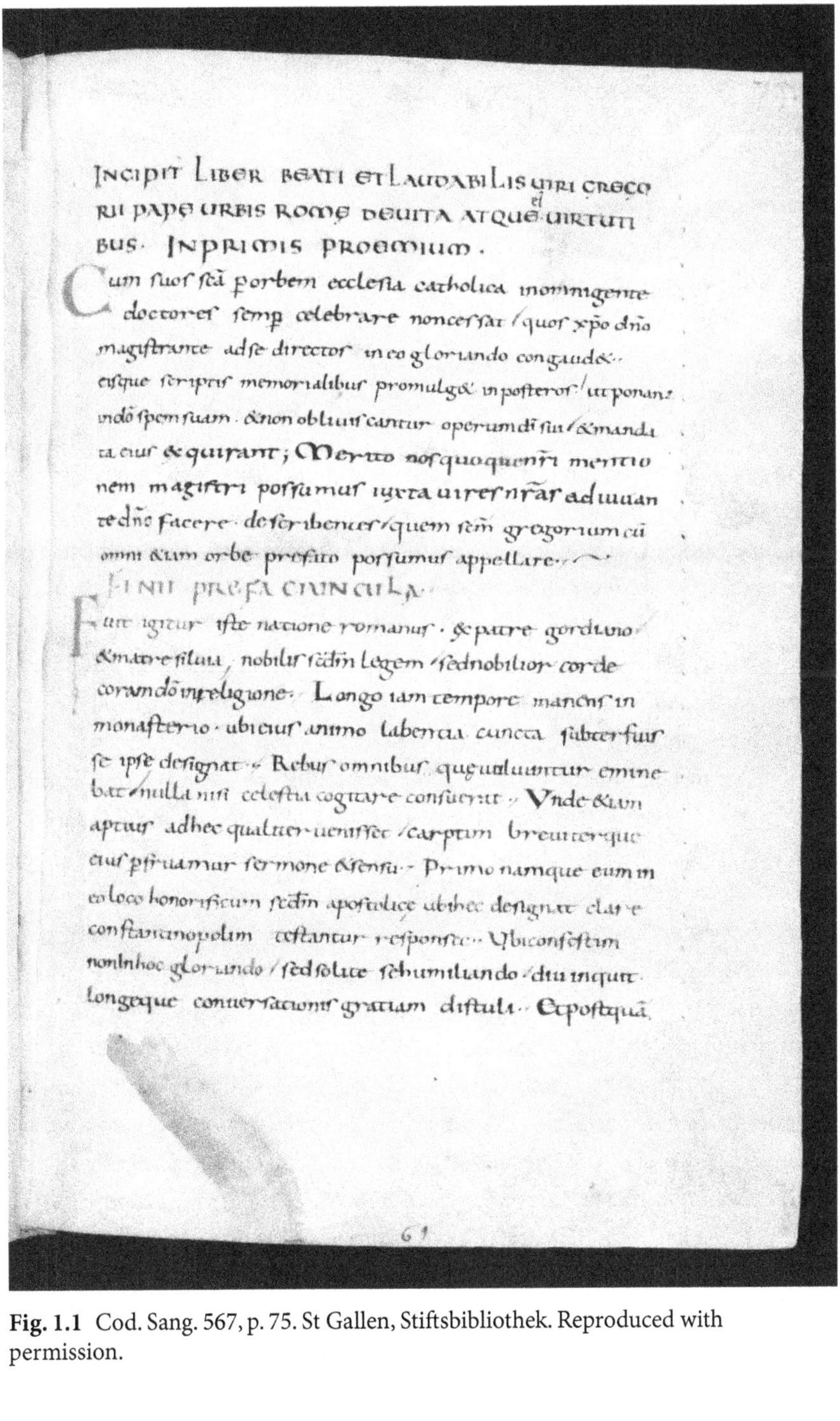
INCIPIT LIBER BEATI ET LAUDABILIS UIRI GREGO
RII PAPE URBIS ROME DE UITA ATQUE UIRTUTI
BUS. INPRIMIS PROEMIUM.
Cum suos scā p orbem ecclesia catholica inommigente
doctores semp celebrare noncessat / quos xpo dno
magistrante adse directos in eo gloriando congaudet
eisque scriptis memorialibus promulget in posteros / ut ponant
in do spem suam. et non obliuiscantur operum di sui / et manda
ta eius exquirant; Merito nos quoque nri mentio
nem magistri possumus iuxta uires nras ad iuuan
te dno facere. describentes / quem scm gregorium cu
omni et cum orbe profecto possumus appellare.
FINIT PREFACIUNCULA.
Fuit igitur iste natione romanus. ex patre gordiano
et matre silua, nobilis scdm legem / sed nobilior corde
coram do in religione. Longo iam tempore manens in
monasterio. ubi eius animo labentia cuncta subter fuis
se ipse designat. Rebus omnibus que uoluuntur emine
bat / nulla nisi celestia cogitare consueuit. Unde et cum
aptius adhec qualiter uenisset / carptim breuiterque
eius psuamur sermone et sensu. Primo namque eum in
eo loco honorificum scdm apostolice ubi hec designat clare
constantinopolim testantur responsa. Ubi consestim
non in hoc gloriando / sed solite se humiliando / diu inquit
longeque conuersationis gratiam distuli. Et postqua
61

Fig. 1.1 Cod. Sang. 567, p. 75. St Gallen, Stiftsbibliothek. Reproduced with permission.

Life, 105) and partly on that of 'our brother . . . who was a kinsman of the priest' (*Earliest Life*, 203). What is particularly striking about this description of Whitby and of its abbesses is that the text insists upon the royal credentials of the abbey, and on its connection with the St Edwin, described elsewhere in the text as 'our most Christian king' (*Earliest Life*, 99). The connection to Edwin, Hild's great-uncle, is clearly crucial to establishing the legitimacy of the abbey community and its female leaders, and therefore would have been of vital importance to the community that produced the text.

The importance of Edwin to the narrative becomes apparent when the account of Gregory's life is compared to the account given of Edwin's. While the *Life* begins the story of Gregory by describing with great confidence his parentage (even naming his mother, which Bede does not do), his early life, and the mission to convert the English, some doubt is cast over the authority of the final chapters, a doubt that is significant in considering the case for authorship of the text by the community of nuns at Whitby. Chapter 30 includes the instruction to those who find any mistakes in the *Life* that they must not 'nibble with critical teeth at this work of ours which has been diligently twisted into shape by love rather than knowledge' (*Earliest Life*, 129). The text misinterpreted by a censorious reader is likened to a manuscript gnawed by rodents, not digested but destroyed. Yet the act of writing is itself violent: the Latin verb *extorqueo* suggests a wrenching, wresting or forcing movement that is somewhat lost in the translation quoted here ('twisted'). The production of the text has been difficult, and the real barriers have had to be overcome. There follows an apology for any confusion in the relation of events, and for any potential mistakes and inaccuracies, and an acknowledgement that the work is based on third hand evidence: 'if anything we have written [*scripsimus*] did not concern this man – and, remember, we did not learn [*didicimus*] about them [the events] directly from those who saw and heard them but only by common report' (*Earliest Life*, 131–33). The use of the second person plural is a rhetorical convention, commonly found in homilies, for example, but in this context it is suggestive of the collaborative or communal authorship of the text. The *Life* tails off at its conclusion with that admission that the community which produced it does not know 'the form and fashion' of Gregory's death (*Earliest Life*, 139).

Yet even as the text appears to undermine its own authority it does so only ambivalently, echoing Matthew 13.17: 'many prophets and righteous men have desired to see the things that you see, and have not seen them, and to hear the things which you hear and have not heard them.' Such apologies should not be misunderstood simply as examples of humility topoi, whereby an author disclaims her or his abilities in highly conventional terms. Rather the *Life* makes it clear that there is temporal and geographic distance between the Roman pope and the Whitby community. This is not the case with Edwin, 'a man of this race of ours which is called the Humbrians' (*Earliest Life*, 95) whose own conversion is described.[31] Conversion is of course the key theme of the *Life of Gregory*: Gregory himself is responsible for the conversion of the English, but for the Whitby community it is Edwin who spreads the faith in the North. Indeed, according to John Edward Damon, in the Whitby *Life of Gregory*, 'Before his death in battle, Edwin's role in converting the Northumbrians represents his *only* claim to holiness.'[32] Furthermore, while we are told that the conversion of Edwin 'happened long before the days of any of those who are still alive' (*Earliest Life*, 99), it was 'related so sincerely by faithful witnesses' (*Earliest Life*, 99). In addition, the association of the translation of Edwin's body to Whitby with Eanflæd (*Earliest Life*, 103) establishes the authority of the account by intimating that it *is* based on eyewitness reports. The *Life* is far more confident in its handling of Edwin's life than it is in its handing of Gregory's death.

The most famous episode from the lives of Gregory is the story of Gregory's Roman encounter with the English youths. This narrative has its first iteration in the Whitby *Life*. A comparison of the Whitby version with that in Bede's *Ecclesiastical History* is extremely revealing, both about the relative perspectives of the Whitby author and of Bede, and about the linguistic competence of the Whitby author or authors. While Bertram Colgrave dismisses the Whitby author as 'no Latinist',[33] a revisionist analysis by Uppinder Mehan and David Townsend suggests that closer attention needs to be paid to the Whitby text.[34] Bede's version of the story is the one most widely known today: in this narrative Gregory encounters some beautiful slave boys for sale in the market place in Rome, and asks where they have come from; on discovering that they come from Britain, and following an elaborate play on words, Gregory resolves to convert the English (*EH* 2.1).[35] The Whitby version is rather different. In Colgrave's edition and translation it reads thus:

> Quod omnino non est tegendum silentio, quam spiritaliter ad Deum quomodoque ordis inconparabili speculo oculorum nostrum providendo propagavit ad Deum conversionem. Est igitur narratio fidelium, ante predictum eius pontificatum, Roman venisse quidam de nostra natione forma et crinibus candidati albis. Quos cum audisset venisse, iam dilexit vidisse eosque alme mentis intuitu sibi adscitos, recenti specie inconsueta suspensus et, quod maximum est, Deo intus admonente, cuius gentis fuissent, inquisivit. Quos quidam pulchros fuisse pueros dicunt et quidam vero crispos iuvenes et decoros.

Cumque responderent, 'Anguli dicuntur, illi de quibus sumus,' ille dixit, 'Angeli Dei.' Deinde dixit, 'Rex gentis illius, quomodo nominatur?' Et dixerunt, 'Aelli.' Et ille ait, 'Alleluia. Laus enim Dei esse debet illic.' Tribus quoque illius nomen de qua erant proprie requisivit. Et dixerunt, 'Deire.' Et ille dixit, 'De ira Dei confugientes ad fidem.'

[So we must not pass over in silence how, through the Spirit of God and with the incomparable discernment of his inward eye, he foresaw and made provision for our conversion to God. There is a story told by the faithful that, before he became Pope, there came to Rome certain people of our nation, fair-skinned and light-haired. When he heard of their arrival he was eager to see them; being prompted by a fortunate intuition, being puzzled by their new and unusual appearance, and, above all, being inspired by God, he received them and asked what race they belonged to. (Now some say they were beautiful boys while others say that they were curly-haired, handsome youths.) They answered, 'The people we belong to are called Angles.' 'Angels of God,' he replied. Then he asked further, 'What is the name of the king of that people?' They said, 'Ælli,' whereupon he said, 'Alleluia, God's praise must be heard there.' Then he asked the name of their own tribe, to which they answered, 'Deire,' and he replied, 'They shall flee from the wrath of God to the faith.']

Earliest Life, 90–1

The difficulty with Colgrave's translation of the Latin is not only that it inevitably loses the wordplay ascribed to Gregory in this famous episode (*Anguli/Angeli, Aelli/Alleluia, Deire/De ira*), but also that it irons out the grammatical complexities that characterize this particular version. Mehan and Townsend posit that rather than struggling linguistically, the Whitby author was an innovator, deliberately and self-consciously negotiating a linguistic and stylistic distance from metropolitan norms that mirror the distance of Northumbria from Rome.[36]

As Clare A. Lees points out, given the fact that the Angles in the story are from Northumbria, it 'should not surprise us' that this earliest *Life* of Gregory comes from Northumbria.[37] Certainly, the Whitby *Life* offers a partisan account. Read against Bede's overwriting of the narrative, it is possible to see the extent to which the writer identifies with the position of the young Deirans (what Breeze refers to as the text's 'Deiran patriotism').[38] In contrast to Bede's version, in the Whitby *Life* the Deirans are not slave boys being sold in the market but travellers to Rome; it is the Deirans, not a third party, who reply to Gregory's question about where they are from; and, crucially, the narrative alludes to an oral source or sources ('a relation of the faithful' and 'some say'), which may refer to narratives related by the Whitby community. Furthermore, the Whitby *Life* does not mention the paganism of the Deirans, which Bede chooses to emphasize: 'Alas that the author of darkness should have men so bright of face in his grip, and that minds devoid of inward grace should bear so graceful an outward form' (*EH* 2.1, p. 133). Whereas Bede has Gregory come upon the Deirans by chance, and articulates Gregory's gaze upon them in terms of desire ('as well as other merchandise he saw some boys put up for sale, with fair complexions, handsome faces, and lovely hair'),[39] the Whitby text states that Gregory sought out the Deirans, having heard of their arrival in Rome, and that his gaze was thus from the outset directed by God. The Whitby text shares with Bede's account the aim of representing the English people as chosen by God, but gives the Deirans – and thus implicitly and by extension the Whitby community itself – greater agency and self-determinacy. As in Bede's text, the Whitby text acknowledges the distance of Northumbria from Rome, but the experimental use of Latin gives the narrative a unique immediacy, even urgency.

To reiterate then, as is appropriate in a text produced at Whitby, the *Earliest Life of Gregory* pays considerable attention both to Gregory's English missions and to the role of Edwin of Northumbria, and it speaks directly to the Deirans with whom it closely identifies. However, the argument that a nun or a group of nuns of Whitby authored the *Life* is potentially undermined by one key element of its treatment of the English missions. We know from Bede's *Ecclesiastical History* that the role royal women played in the conversions of their husbands was crucial.[40] Bede records that the catalyst for the conversion of Edwin was the king's marriage to Æthelburg Tata (*EH* 2.9, p. 163). Here – in another key episode in the history of the conversion of the English – marriage to the already converted woman resulted in Edwin himself accepting Christianity, and in the missionary Paulinus, Æthelburg Tata's spiritual confidant, being consecrated bishop. Bede also discusses Eanflæd's birth in his account of Edwin and the fact that Edwin dedicated his young daughter to Christ, and placed her under Paulinus's care (*EH* 2.9, p. 167). The omission in the Whitby *Life of Gregory* of any account of Eanflæd's mother, or of Eanflæd's own consecration, is surprising, given the importance of Eanflæd in relation to the translation of Edwin's bones. It is all the more so given that the *Life* was produced under the rule of her daughter, Ælfflæd. Indeed Mechthild Gretsch argues convincingly that much of the material that forms the basis of the *Life* was circulated in oral form, and transmitted to Northumbria by Eanflæd's mother, and then Eanflæd herself (as she too moved from the South to the North).[41] However there is another telling omission, that of any mention of Hild, and Catherine E. Karkov suggests that this at least is motivated by Ælfflæd's desire to self-memorialize.[42]

Furthermore, despite the absence of any mention of Æthelburg Tata, the role of women in conversion is not completely ignored within the *Life*. Following the extended digressions on the conversion of the English and the life of Edwin and the translation of his bones to Whitby, the *Life* returns its focus to Gregory: 'Having brought these stories to an end, we will follow them up with some which rightly concern us' (*Earliest Life*, 105). The first of these narratives of Gregory's miracles to be recounted is the famous story of the unbelieving woman, which was later incorporated into the *Golden Legend*:[43]

> Nam antiquorum fertur esse narratio quia quedam Rome aliquando matrona sibi oblationes faciens, eas adtulisset, quas iam vir sanctus accipiens in sacrosancti corporis Christi sanctificavit agoniam. Cumque illa venisset eam communicare de manu Dei hominis atque illum audivit dicentem, 'Corpus Domini nostri Iesu Christi conservet animam tuam', subrisit. Quod vir Domini videns, clausit manum suam contra os eius, et nolens ei dare sanctum corpus Domini, posuit super altare eiusque vestimento ut sibi placuit abscondit. Missa vero peracta, eam sibi advocans interrogavit cur subrideret quando communicare debuit. Illa respondens ait, 'Ego ipsos panes meis feci manibus, et tu de illis dixisti quia corpus Domini essent.'

> [There is an ancient story that once a certain matron in Rome was making her oblations and had brought them to him; the saint received them and consecrated them into the most holy Body of Christ the Victim. When she came to receive it from the hands of the man of God and heard him say, 'The Body of our Lord Jesus Christ preserve thy soul', she began to smile. When the man of God saw this, he closed his hand as it reached her mouth, not wishing to give her the holy Body of the Lord; then he placed it on the altar and decided to hide it with his vestment. When mass was finished, he called her up and asked why she laughed when she should have communicated. She answered, 'I made those loaves with my own hands and you said they were the Body of the Lord'.]

> *Earliest Life*, 104–07

This episode can constructively be read as the counterpart of the story of Gregory's encounter with the Deiran youths. The figure of the Roman matron would especially resonate with aristocratic nuns of Whitby, many of who would have been married. The woman who cynically laughs at seeing the bread that she herself has made administered in communion, has her lack of belief challenged by Gregory, and in response to his prayers and those of the congregation, the bread of the host visibly transforms into a bloody finger part. This visual confirmation of the miracle of transubstantiation successfully overcomes the woman's incredulity. The narrative of transformation and conversion is highly didactic, and particularly appropriate in the context of the early English church, which needs continually to re-assert its new belief system. But it is also particularly appropriate to a community of royal and noble women, who themselves have come to an understanding that all aspects of their former lives, including the most domestic or mundane, have taken on a new meaning in the service of Christ.

Here then, in the Whitby *Life of Gregory the Great*, we have an example of the sort of unacknowledged underwriting that may lie behind Bede's *Ecclesiastical History*. As Breeze notes, this work 'displays evidence to suggest that a woman chose and shaped its narrative'.[44] Whether or not this experimental Latin Life was composed by a single nun or by a community of nuns, it was certainly written *for* the double house at Whitby, which included nuns as well as monks, and it was written under the rule of Abbess Ælfflæd.

Conclusion

Who, then, were the first women writers in the English literary tradition? The names of these women may not have come down to us, but we know about the communities in which they lived and worked and we know the names of the abbesses who commissioned their work and the work of their monastic brethren. If, in most cases, the works by women have not survived, traces can nevertheless still be discerned, albeit overwritten by male clerics. But in order to make sense of these traces, reading strategies have to be developed which take account of the full range of early women's engagement with literary culture. In reading the lives of Æthelthryth and Hild, it is possible to read *through* the narratives written by Bede, with, in the case of Hild's life, the assistance of another version found in the *Old English Martyrology*, in order to reconstruct something of the nature and concerns of the lost sources. In reading the anonymous Whitby *Life of Gregory*, there is certainly evidence of female patronage and readership, and, albeit more ambiguously, of female authorship. Taken together, however, what can be learnt from a study of these lives is that by focusing on texts associated with religious houses ruled by women, and by considering these texts to be the productions not of individuals but of communities, it is possible to obtain a fuller and more balanced understanding of women's writing in this earliest period of English literary history. Equally importantly, however, what can also be learnt from recuperating women's lost texts is the extent to which the earliest women's writing has been occluded from history and written out of literary history from the time of Bede to the end of the twentieth century and beyond.

Women Writing at Barking and Minster-in-Thanet

Introduction

Following on from the previous chapter's examination of the overwriting of women's authority in Bede's accounts in his *Ecclesiastical History* of the early double monasteries at Whitby and Ely, this chapter shifts the focus to literary evidence relating to the abbeys at Barking and Minster-in-Thanet. Barking Abbey, founded *c.* 666 or earlier, was a vital centre of early medieval learning with its own monastic school when it was under the rule of its second abbess, Hildelith, in the late seventh and early eighth century.[1] I pay particular attention to the intersection of lived practice at Barking and the literary record, focusing on three pieces of evidence: Bede's account of the early history of Barking in his *Ecclesiastical History*, completed in 731; Aldhelm's *De Virginitate* (*c.* 675–680), which was written for Hildelith and her fellow nuns; and a letter written by Boniface around 716 in which he relates the vision of the monk of Much Wenlock. Intriguingly Bede, in his *Ecclesiastical History*, specifically mentions a lost *liber* or book, which evidently recorded visions experienced by the nuns of Barking concerning the death of their founding abbess, Æthelburh. We cannot know for certain who wrote this book, whether a nun or monk at Barking or someone else, but it is reasonable to surmise it was commissioned by Æthelburh's successor, Hildelith. Boniface, in his epistolary recounting of the vision of the monk of Much Wenlock, alludes to a version of the narrative given to him by Abbess Hildelith herself. While it is usually assumed that this was an oral account, it is possible that it existed in written form, for example in another letter, now also lost. What are we to make of the fact that both Bede and Boniface refer to texts or accounts for or by nuns that they have overwritten in their own surviving work? The passing comment about Hildelith found in Boniface's letter takes on a greater significance when placed in the context of Bede's and Aldhelm's texts. At the very least, the evidence from Bede and Aldhelm suggests that, under

Hildelith's rule, there was at Barking considerable interest in the commissioning, production, reception and circulation of visionary accounts. That Barking was a centre of a specifically *literary* culture is revealed by Aldhelm's *De Virginitate*, which describes in detail the sheer extent of the nuns' engagement in scholarly activities. Taken together, the three texts reveal that, under the rule of the academically-minded Abbess Hildelith, Barking Abbey was at the centre of a vibrant network of textual exchange between the abbess and nuns and prominent churchmen and other religious communities.

Having explored the literary culture of Barking Abbey, I then turn to Minster-in-Thanet and from lost works by women, and from works written for women, to surviving Old English fragments of, or pertaining to, the legend of St Mildrith. The religious house in Minster-in-Thanet was founded in *c.* 670. St Mildrith (*fl.* 716–733) was the second abbess. The Mildrith legend probably dates back to the time of Mildrith's successor Eadburg (*c.* 732–751). Although the Old English fragments in question date to the eleventh century, it is perfectly plausible that they are derived from earlier female-authored material. In my reading of these fragmentary lives, I consider them in the light of the other hagiographies about or associated with the female monastic houses at Ely, Whitby and Barking, and note, for example, shared preoccupations with the supernatural and death and with female authority. These fragments illustrate just how important memorializing narratives explaining the origins of the female houses, which focus on the royal lineage of the founding abbesses and on their acquisition of land, must have been. These fragments are also significant for another reason: given that most of the works discussed in this study are written in Latin and the evidence of women's writing in Old English is so sparse, the survival of these few folios written in the vernacular is particularly remarkable.

The Barking Abbey *liber*

The connections between the monastic and literary communities at Barking are established within three texts which although very different in form share some common themes. Bede and Boniface are concerned with visions of the dying and the dead or with visions of the afterlife. Aldhelm too pays attention to death, in so far as *De Virginitate* dwells on the sufferings of virgin martyrs. Such preoccupations are not, perhaps, surprising: within Christianity death marks not an end but a transition. Intercession for the dead and their memorialization were key responsibilities of women, especially nuns. The idealized dead offered models of piety for the living to follow. Knowledge concerning the fate of the dead (whether their souls went to heaven or hell) endowed power on those who held it. For these early English Christians, death mattered. Visions concerning the dying and the dead certainly play a central role in Bede's account of the early history of Barking Abbey (*EH* 4.6–10).[2] In Bede's *Ecclesiastical History*, many prophecies and revelations of death and the otherworld are experienced by male visionaries, rulers, saints and sinners: Oswald, Fursa, Chad, Cuthbert, Dryhthelm and some whose names have not come down to us. But such visions were also circulated amongst *female* communities, and it seems that learned women as well as men were responsible for their transmission. One of these women was Hildelith of Barking (*fl. c.* 700).

Bede frankly acknowledges that the main source for his accounts in the *Ecclesiastical History* of the visions of Barking was a *liber* [book] or *libellus* [pamphlet] (*EH* 4.10, pp. 364–5) that had been compiled there:

> In hoc etenim monasterio plura uirtutum sunt signa patrata, quae et ad memoriam aedificationemque sequentium ab his qui nouere descripta habentur a multis; e quibus et nos aliqua historiae nostrae ecclesiasticae inserere curauimus.

> [In this monastery many signs and miracles were performed which have been written down by those who were acquainted with them as an edifying memorial for succeeding generations and copies are in the possession of many people. Some of these we have taken care to insert in this *History*.]
>
> *EH* 4.7, pp. 356–7

The writing of this *liber* would in all likelihood have been commissioned by Abbess Hildelith in order to foster the cult of Barking's foundress and thus to ensure the continuity of the monastery. Lisa M. C. Weston suggests that this *liber* was 'a hagiographical narrative transcribed from communal memory' and that it was produced at the time of Hildelith's translation of Æthelburh's body to the Abbey church (*EH* 4.10, pp. 363–5).[3] It also served to provide evidence of the links between the abbey and the East Saxon royal family. It was clearly intended for the instruction of future nuns and presumably also monks within the double house ('*ad memoriam aedificationemque sequentium*'). In the preface to the *Ecclesiastical History*, Bede names Abbot Albinus of Canterbury as a significant collaborator in the production of his work: Albinus gathered together materials which 'he then passed on ... through Nothhelm, a godly priest of the Church in London, either by writing or by word of mouth' (*EH* Preface, p. 5). As Weston points out, given that Bede states that it was Æthelburh's brother, Bishop

Eorcenwald of London, who first established Barking (*EH* 4.6, p. 355), it seems 'most likely' that Nothhelm provided Bede with the Barking *liber* or recounted to him its contents.[4]

It is also likely that the nuns themselves first recorded the 'signs and miracles' that took place in the early history of their Abbey, 'signs and miracles' which are explicitly recognized as a form of memorialization in the account by Bede quoted above. According to Bede, they were widely circulated. Indeed, circulation is surely a condition of the success of memorialization, which means precisely the construction of a more public, widespread memory. The Barking 'signs and miracles' recorded by Bede thus represent at least aspects of the lost book, the underwriting, that lies behind his version of the abbey's history, and consequently they should be given due consideration.[5] While Weston's interest, in analysing Bede's account of these events in Barking, is in what they reveal about relationships between women within the early monastic community, my focus is on what they can tell us about the literary concerns of the Barking nuns.

First and foremost, the lost *liber* of Barking Abbey celebrated the piety of Abbess Æthelburh. According to Bede, the death of Abbess Æthelburh was predicted by a vision, witnessed by the abbess's assistant Torhtgyth, who saw a body ascend to heaven, wrapped in a shroud and drawn upwards by golden cords (*EH* 4.9, p. 361). Realizing that she was seeing a portent of death, Torhtgyth correctly interpreted the golden cords as representing the virtuous deeds of the deceased. One striking aspect of this vision, and indeed of others that follow in the *Ecclesiastical History*, is its Marian quality: the ascension of Æthelburh resonates with the tradition of the Assumption of the Mother of God.[6] Æthelburh's exceptional piety is thus confirmed at the moment of her passing by the vision God gives to a member of her own convent.

The relationship between the visionary and the subject of her vision is a symbiotic one: the visionary testifies to, and thus authorizes the holiness of her subject, but in so doing she herself gains authority and her own piety becomes manifest. Furthermore, Bede anticipates the vision, and the good death of Æthelburh, by explaining that prior to the abbess's passing, Torhtgyth had experienced nine years of illness, which served to burn away 'any traces of sin remaining among her virtues through ignorance or carelessness' (*EH* 4.9, p. 361). The living Torhtgyth had to be purified to prepare her to receive divine revelation, but at the same time, she had to be prepared for her own good death and ascension to Heaven, which took place three years after that of Æthelburh (*EH* 4.9, p. 363). This was an equally miraculous event: Torhtgyth was paralysed for three days and nights (echoing the time between Christ's crucifixion and resurrection) and then suddenly awoke to engage in a conversation with an invisible person. This person was, as she explained to those around her, Æthelburh herself, who returned to call her to Heaven.

The events surrounding Torhtgyth's death can be read as supporting evidence of the saintliness of Æthelburh. Nonetheless, Æthelburh's holiness and the visionary blessings surrounding her death are not simply manifestations of a singular piety. Rather, both piety and revelatory experiences are shared by other members of the community. While Torhtgyth, as the abbess's staunch supporter in the convent, is singled out for special attention, less powerful figures also benefit. Another miracle recorded by Bede involves a disabled nun who, immediately following the abbess's death, asked to be carried to where the abbess's body lay in the church. Speaking to her 'as though she were addressing a living person', the nun hauntingly petitioned the abbess to intercede with Christ on her behalf to release her from her illness (*EH* 4.9, pp. 361–3). The nun's prayers were answered and twelve days later she died. While Bede tells us that the disabled nun was 'of noble family in this world' (*EH* 4.9, p. 361), others associated with visions of death in the time of plague include those of lesser rank, such as a three-year-old boy, one of the nuns responsible for teaching him called Edith, and an anonymous nun who was summonsed to God by a vision of a monk or priest (*EH* 4.8, p. 359). Through such visions, recorded in the Barking *liber*, and based on the nuns' own testimonies, the piety of the *whole* convent is recognized and authorized, and their connection to the wider community is established.

As Ian Wood has established, the lost Barking *liber* was heavily influenced by Jonas of Bobbio's *Life of St Columbanus* (*c.* 640).[7] The second book of the *Vita Columbani* with its account of the Merovingian double monastery of Faremoutiers, which Wood describes as 'one of the chief influences on female monasticism in seventh-century England',[8] includes very similar visions to those described as taking place at Barking. This literary dependency is significant because it reveals the close connections and cultural contact that existed at the time between Barking and the continent.[9] Although these sorts of deathbed miracles were not limited to female houses, they were often connected to them.[10] This sequence of visions is framed in Bede's *Ecclesiastical History* by what appears to be a specific and localised conflict concerning the location of the nuns' cemetery at Barking. As Jocelyn Wogan-Browne has noted, the nuns' cemetery clearly had great significance as the 'locus of memory and continuity and an ever-present theatre of events'.[11] Æthelburh, the founding abbess, was uncertain where to locate it, until she received divine guidance that it should be separate from that of the monks (*EH* 4.7, pp. 357–9). However, her successor at Barking, Hildelith, subsequently resolved that due to constraints of space 'the bones of the servants and handmaidens of Christ which had been buried there should all be taken up and transferred to the church of the blessed Mother of God and buried there in one place' (*EH* 4.10, pp. 363–5). Stephanie Hollis contextualizes these events more broadly in terms of theological debates about the validity of double monasteries: significantly Theodore's *Penitential*, which dates to the mid eighth century, prohibited interring monks and nuns in the same burial ground.[12] But it is important to recognize that *both* Æthelburh's and Hildelith's decisions receive divine authorization through visions and miracles shared by the community. This is more marked in the case of Æthelburh, because her initial hesitation was answered by a vision of light which Bede recorded was experienced by the nuns of Barking, who at the time were praying by the monks' graves, and which was also partially witnessed by two of their brethren, an older monk and a younger one, who were inside the oratory (*EH* 4.7, pp. 357–9). It is possible to explain away Bede's inclusion of the testimony of the two monks in terms of the gendering of authority, clerical male eyewitnesses being perceived to be more reliable than female eyewitnesses, even women religious, and therefore being necessary for the story to be fully convincing.[13] Yet, this is not the whole picture. For, again, what emerges from this miracle is a sense of the shared nature of such revelations. This vision concerning the positioning of the cemetery radiates outwards to all parts of the community like the divine light that identifies the blessed place where the bodies of the deceased nuns are to lie. It connects the living nuns and monks, just as the souls of their companions are chastely united in death.

In summary, it is evident that the lost *liber* of Barking Abbey must have drawn on the testimonies of many of the nuns, as well as monks, and would therefore have been very much a communal production, aimed at helping secure the future of the foundation as a whole. Hildelith, as the second abbess of Barking, is likely to have commissioned the production of this *liber* to coincide with the translation of her predecessor's body, and we must entertain the possibility that she may also have played a role in its writing. Bede does not consider it necessary to acknowledge the authorship of, or to provide any further information about, the *liber* to which he is so indebted. Equally, he makes no mention of Hildelith's engagement with literary culture in his discussion of her in *EH* 4.10, nor does he describe her intellectual prowess. Yet, as noted above, there is strong evidence of continental monastic influence on Barking, which renders plausible the claim in later hagiographic accounts that Hildelith had received a monastic education in France and was specifically invited to join Barking in order to set up the school there.[14] While we cannot prove that the lost *liber* of Barking Abbey was written by Hildelith or her nuns, there is compelling evidence to suggest that the nuns were actively engaged in literary activity, in a variety of ways. The primary evidence is of course Aldhelm's *De Virginitate*, which reveals that Barking under Hildelith was a centre of literary culture and scholarship.

Aldhelm's *De Virginitate*

Aldhelm's prose treatise, *De Virginitate*, which was indebted to the *De Virginitate* of the sixth-century Merovingian Latin poet Venantius Fortunatus, was written for, and at the request of, Hildelith and her nuns and eulogizes their letter-writing talents.[15] Aldhelm (*c.* 639–709) was abbot of Malmesbury and bishop of Sherborne.[16] His subsequent poetic version of the treatise on virginity was also written in response to the request of the nuns, although it omits the opening and closing material found in the prose text which addresses the nuns directly, and in this respect is of less interest.[17] Such a complex and difficult text would only have been accessible to highly educated readers. It is vital therefore to give full consideration here to what Aldhelm's work explicitly reveals about the literacy of the nuns of Barking, and also to what it *implies*. In re-examining the ways in which sexuality and gender interact within the text, I argue here that while Aldhelm's admiration of the literary and scholarly activity of his Barking patrons was authentic, *De Virginitate* betrays a level of anxiety about women's monastic life in England and beyond which sits uncomfortably with its implied, actual and intended readers: the Barking nuns. In *De Virginitate* we find compelling evidence of the extent of the literary activity at Barking, which supports the claim that the lost *liber* was produced by the community of women, and also evidence that the representation of women's monastic life was markedly different in a text commissioned but not written by the nuns themselves.

De Virginitate opens with an address to Hildelith, 'teacher of the regular discipline and of the monastic way of life' (*De Virginitate*, 59) and her fellow nuns Justina, Cuthburg, Osburg, Aldgith, Scholastica, Hidburg, Berngith, Eulalia, and Thecla.[18] One of these nuns, Osburg, is described by Aldhelm as being 'related (to me) by family bonds of kinship' (*De Virginitate*, 59). Michael Lapidge offers the suggestion that Osburg was Aldhelm's sister.[19] Certainly Aldhelm is keen to establish a close connection between himself and his immediate audience. Aldhelm goes on to describe his pleasure at receiving letters from Barking; correspondence which, unfortunately, has not survived.[20] These letters profoundly impressed him:

Quo stilo non solum ecclesiastica promissorum uotorum foedera, quae fida pollicitatione spopondistis, ubertim claruerunt, uerum etiam melliflua diuinarum studia scripturarum sagacissima sermonum serie patuerunt.

Prosa De Virginitate 29–31

[In your writing not only were the ecclesiastical compacts of (your) sworn vows – which you had pledged with a solemn promise – abundantly clear, but also the mellifluous studies of the Holy Scriptures were manifest in the extremely subtle sequence of your discourse.]

De Virginitate, 59

According to Aldhelm, then, the letters reflect the chaste virtue of the nuns, and their scholarship.

Aldhelm proceeds to praise the 'rich verbal eloquence' of the writing of the Barking nuns which, although coupled with an 'innocent expression of sophistication' (*De Virginitate*, 59), is nevertheless seen to emerge from intense academic activity. In an extended metaphorical discussion, Aldhelm praises the nuns as spiritual athletes, 'who, traversing the special race-courses of the Scriptures, are known to exercise the most subtle industry of their minds and the quality of (their) lively intelligence through assiduous perseverance in reading' (*De Virginitate*, 61). Aldhelm records that the Barking sisters read widely and were interested in histories and chronicles as well as Scripture and Biblical commentaries (*De Virginitate*, 61–2). While some notes of warning have been sounded against making too much of Aldhelm's hyperbolic eulogies about the learning of the Barking nuns, it is manifest that this was a religious house that prided itself on its intellectual achievements.[21]

Aldhelm not only commends the scholarship of the nuns but he also acknowledges that the nuns themselves wrote verse:

Nunc grammaticorum regulas et ortograforum disciplinas tonis temporibus trutinatas, pedibus poeticis compactas, per cola et commata hoc est pentimemeren et eptimemeren diremptas, immo centenis metrorum generibus sequestratim discretas sagaciter inquirendo.

Prosa De Virginitate, 61

[Now, sagaciously inquiring into the rules of the grammarians and the teachings of experts on spelling and the rules of metrics (as they are) measured out into accents (and) times, fitted into poetic feet, broken up into cola and commata – that is into pentimemeres and eptimemeres – and indeed, divided into a hundred kinds of metre.]

De Virginitate, 62

While this poetry has not come down to us, Aldhelm's reference to the practicalities of repeated sequences and patterns, line length and punctuation, indicate that it was technically accomplished.[22] There is good reason to believe that he was not overstating the literary activities of early medieval nuns in England, given that poetry from their later counterparts on the continent has survived.[23] The poetic achievements of the Barking nuns are echoed closely later in the text, in the discussion of Alexander, bishop of Alexandria, tutor of Athanasius (296–373) 'who taught him in a kindly manner the written characters which scribes use, as well as the periods of the grammarians, distinguished separately by cola and commata' (*De Virginitate*, 93). The education of the Barking nuns is thus implicitly likened to that received by one of the Church Fathers, or even vice versa – the education of Athanasius is likened to that of the Barking nuns. Aldhelm uses similar language in his elaborate metaphor of the house built of metrical verse which he uses to describe the labour of composing the poetic version of his treatise on virginity (*De Virginitate*, 130–1). In this highly elaborate ending to the text, Aldhelm explicitly represents himself not as the patron of the nuns, but as one who benefits from their patronage, and waits anxiously to hear whether or not his text pleases them (*De Virginitate*, 131). For Aldhelm, then, the Barking nuns are not only patrons, responsible for commissioning his work for their own edification, but they are his literary equals, a vital part of his own textual community.

Yet, while Aldhelm praises the literacy and learning of the Barking nuns, Clare A. Lees and Gillian R. Overing make the case that his text nevertheless presents a complex and somewhat fraught account of the women's monastic vocation, showing considerable anxiety over their practices.[24] Many of the nuns for whom Aldhelm was writing would themselves have been widows rather than virgins, and some may well, following a recognized early medieval practice but one with which many churchmen felt uncomfortable, have left their marriages in order to pursue a monastic life. It is possible that Hildelith herself was previously married, while the Cuthburg or Cuthburh who is cited in Aldhelm's opening address can be conjecturally identified as the sister of Ine, king of Wessex, in the *Anglo-Saxon Chronicle* entry for 718: 'And Cuthburh founded the monastery at Wimborne. She had been married to Aldfrith, king of the Northumbrians, and they separated during their lifetime.'[25] Aldhelm follows the established scheme of praising virginity, chastity and marriage, while recognizing virginity as the ideal, seeing chastity as the secondary state and acknowledging the virtue and necessity of marriage and procreation, but placing it at the bottom of the hierarchy (*De Virginitate*, 66). Aldhelm, no doubt fully cognisant of his audience's background, is careful to define chastity in such a way that it includes not only widows, but also women who have separated from their husbands or are divorced, and to emphasize the importance of spirituality in conceptualising virginity.[26] However, for Aldhelm, the married woman is still open to attack as worldly:

> Ista collum lunulis et lacertos dextralibus ornari ac gemmiferis digitorum anulis comi concupiscit … ista tortis cincinnorum crinibus calamistro crispantibus dilicate componi et rubro coloris stibio genas ac mandibulas suatim fucare satagit …istat stolidis ornamentorum pompis indruticans adinstar illius mulieris aureo calice prostibuli poculum letiferum propinantis, quam Apocalipsis super bestiam sedisse describit, composita pulchrum pariter et perniciosum cernentibus spectaculum praestat.…

Prosa De Virginitate, 199–203

> [The latter strives that her neck be decorated with necklaces and her arms with bracelets and that she be adorned with gem-studded rings on her fingers … [She] is busy being alluringly coiffed with the twisted curls of her ringlets curling round the tongs, and to paint her cheeks and lips after her own fashion with the scarlet rouge of artificial colour … parading with the senseless pomp of her ornaments—in the likeness of that woman offering the lethal drink of the brothel in a golden chalice, whom the *Apocalypse* describes as having sat on the beast—when turned out offers a sight which is equally pleasing and harmful to the spectators.]

De Virginitate, 73

These lines, with their allusion to the whore of Babylon of Apocalypse 17, are damning in their treatment of married women, and thus, implicitly, of the *former* lives of at least some of the women whom Aldhelm is directly addressing. The focus on hair styling, cosmetics and adornments sits uncomfortably with surviving archaeological evidence from Barking in the Saxon period that includes combs, manicure sets and jewellery.[27]

In his later account of the militant widow Judith, who, with the assistance of her handmaiden, overcame Holofernes, the tyrannous leader of the Assyrians – an account which would seem on the surface to offer a much more positive exemplum to many of the nuns of Barking than the virgin saints which are Aldhelm's main focus –Aldhelm returns to attack violently and at length the practices of adornment, in this case of both women *and* men, which he once again associates with vanity and wantonness (*De Virginitate*, 127–8). In his account of Judith's conquest, Aldhelm falls back on biblical commonplaces about the dangerously seductive nature of women's beauty, even likening Judith to 'the stubborn and insolent woman in Proverbs who ... in the trappings of a harlot and with alluring luxury, is described as having enticed a foolish young man' (*De Virginitate*, 127). Heide Estes's analysis of Aldhelm's portrayal of Judith in both the prose and poetic version highlights the ambivalence inherent in his depiction of militant chaste widowhood.[28]

Aldhelm follows one of his principal sources, Ambrose's *De Virginibus ad Marcellum* ['On Virgins'], in taking the Virgin Mary as the example of holy female virginity par excellence, but he goes on to provide his own lengthy catalogue of saintly women who rejected marriage beginning with Cecilia, Agatha, Lucy, Justina and Eugenia.[29] Aldhelm's descriptions of the sufferings of these martyrs could not differ more from Bede's descriptions of the visions surrounding the deaths of Æthelburh and her supporters. Yet, Aldhelm also differs from Ambrose in that he introduces extensive lists of male virgin saints, who are also subjected to temptations and assaults, including, for example, Paul the Hermit, who had to endure being 'prostituted from the first immaturity of adolescence' (*De Virginitate*, 87) and Babilas and his pupils, who were, respectively, flayed and flogged, before being beheaded (*De Virginitate*, 94–5). The prevailing critical explanation for Aldhelm's innovative inclusion of male saints is that even though the nuns of Barking are cited as having commissioned this work and are clearly the implied audience of the text, because Barking itself was a double monastery, Aldhelm's intended audience must have been made up of men as well as women (*De Virginitate*, 57). These virgin martyrs, then, are to serve as a model of piety to both the nuns and monks of Barking, whatever their background.

However, the assumption that Aldhelm was writing for a mixed audience may offer too easy an explanation for his inclusion of male as well as female saints. Aldhelm finds himself continually drawn to ornate, if highly conventional, masculine metaphors of athletes or warriors.[30] Thus, for example, in his opening praise of 'the catholic maidservants of Christ' he moves from exalting them as the 'adoptive daughters of regenerative grace brought forth from the fecund womb of ecclesiastical conception' to comparing them with admiration to the Olympian who 'smeared with the ointment of (some) slippery liquid, strives dexterously with his partner to work out the strenuous routines of wrestlers, sweating with the sinuous writhings of their flanks in the burning centre of the wrestling-pit' (*De Virginitate*, 59–60). The pleasure Aldhelm takes from developing what is an extended and highly homoerotic description of male sporting activities can be contrasted with his damning condemnation of other queer sexual desire. In relating the story of the learned cross-dressing saint Eugenia, who disguised herself as a man in order to escape marriage and enter a monastery, he viciously attacks Melanthia 'who, forgetful of her own matronly modesty, deceitfully tried to force upon the same Eugenia the false debauchery of the bawdy-house and the wickedness of the polluted brothel' (*De Virginitate*, 111). While Aldhelm feels able to celebrate sporting contests between men, alternative queer forms of desire are condemned in an angry tirade.

In another, particularly elaborate, metaphor, Aldhelm compares the nuns to bees, which are seen to reproduce 'innocent of the lascivious coupling of marriage' (*De Virginitate*, 62). Yet while this comparison of the Barking women drawing others to the religious life to the breeding of worker bees (gendered female) seems entirely conventional, even here there is blurring of gender roles as the bees are also described as carrying 'their fertile booty in numerous loadings of their thighs and hips' (*De Virginitate*, 61). Once again, Aldhelm struggles to accommodate the masculine authority of the Barking nuns within his text about virginity. More specifically he also struggles to contain the active roles that these nuns play, as is illustrated in the following passage:

> Quamdiu enim antiquas inhabitare sedes et exigua fouere tuguria gracillimis contexta uiminibus seu cauatis consuta codicibus ille, qui inter ceteras magistratus officio fungitur, decreuerit, nulla ex immense multitudine fugitiuis discursibus et passiuis uolatibus per aethera uagatur . . . .
>
> *Prosa De Virginitate*, 67–9

> [For as long as that bee who among the others discharges the office of magistrate, shall decree that they should inhabit their ancient dwellings and care for their little cottages woven with slender cane or knitted together with hollow stems, no bee from the immense multitude roams through the air on wandering routes or with undirected flights . . . .]
>
> *De Virginitate*, 62–3[31]

In going on to praise those who nevertheless, when required by necessity, 'set out for foreign parts (in search) of a residence more willingly than they would remain at home in their cells (where they are) used to domestic comforts and content with subservient tranquillity' (*De Virginitate*, 62–3), Aldhelm anticipates, in positive terms, the early medieval nuns who subsequently travelled to the continent as missionaries (whose writings are discussed in Chapters 3 and 4), and who put the care of others above their own ease and security. At the same time, however, by simply evoking the idea of 'wandering routes' and 'undirected flights', Aldhelm warns against unjustified and pointless journeys, and implies that the proper place for nuns is an enclosed community under the authority of a suitable spiritual leader.

While then, in *De Virginitate*, Aldhelm presents a very positive picture of Barking as a scholarly community, in contrast to the lost Barking *liber*, as transmitted by Bede, he does not offer an empowering account of the lived religious practices of the Barking community and he reveals his disquiet about the conduct of women, especially widows. Aldhelm's portrayals of the spiritual endeavours of the Barking nuns repeatedly draw upon masculine metaphors of warfare and sport. In *De Virginitate*, the most acceptable relationships for women are those between holy men and women, either as chaste marriages or close spiritual friendships. The latter in particular are based on patronage and scholarship. Aldhelm provides a variety of examples of such bonds, such as the celibate partnerships of Chrysanthus and Daria, and Julian and Basilissa (*De Virginitate*, 96–9, and 99–102) or the alliance between St Jerome, Paula and Eustochium (*De Virginitate*, 115–16). This last example provides a model for Aldhelm's own relationship with Hildelith and her nuns, and indeed he breaks off his account of them to comment, 'I think that these (commentaries) are in no way unknown to the wisdom of your intelligence, racing curiously through the wide-open fields of books' (*De Virginitate*, 116). Their spiritual friendship is, in a sense, a metaphor for the textual network that centred on Barking under Hildelith's leadership, but which radiated throughout the early English church more generally, that brought together churchmen and women with a shared love of scholarship and books, and that fostered women's active engagement with literary culture.

Hildelith and the vision of the monk of Much Wenlock

Further contexts for the Barking Abbey *liber* are the visions of the dead found in other early medieval sources, which have not hitherto been explored in the context of discussions of the nuns' engagement with literary culture. As noted above, while the Barking Abbey *liber* functioned specifically to authorize the entire monastery, rather than simply to testify to the piety of exceptional individuals, it was nevertheless in many ways typical of the sort of revelatory texts in circulation in the seventh and eighth centuries.

Around 716 Boniface wrote to one of his female followers, the Abbess Eadburg (probably of Wimborne rather than Minster-in-Thanet):

> Rogabas me, soror carissimae, ut admirandas visiones de illo redivivo, qui nuper in monasterio Milburge abbatissae mortuus est et revixit, quae ei ostensae sunt,

scribendo intimare et transmittere curarem, quemadmodum istas veneranda abbatissa Hildelida referente didici.

[You have asked me, my dear sister, to describe to you in writing the marvelous visions of the man who recently died and came to life again in the convent of the Abbess Milburga [Mildburg, abbess of Much Wenlock], as they were revealed to him and were related to me by the venerable Abbess Hildelida [Hildelith].][32]

Many historians and critics assume that Boniface is alluding to an oral account, but this (albeit fleeting) reference may indicate that Hildelith had written down a now lost text of the vision, which she then passed on to others.[33] Whether written or oral, Hildelith had certainly provided her own version of the vision of the monk of Much Wenlock, which no doubt differed from Boniface's, and which may have been based on one given to her by Mildburg, abbess of Much Wenlock. Furthermore, this confirms that Hildelith was part of Boniface's textual community, a community in which knowledge and books were exchanged and shared, as we will see in the following chapter.

Unfortunately, Boniface did not record Hildelith's account of the vision of the monk of Much Wenlock, preferring the testimony of the visionary himself: 'because I myself spoke recently with the aforesaid resurrected brother when he returned to this country from beyond the seas.' Boniface prefers to draw on the first-hand eyewitness account by the male visionary ('related to me in his own words'), rejecting the second-hand account by a woman, albeit an abbess, stating that he is thus 'able to fulfill your wish more fully and more accurately'. At the end of the letter, he emphasizes further that the authenticity of his own version can be testified to by male authorities: 'I have written down these things at your earnest request as he told them to me in the presence of three pious and most venerable brethren, who are known to be trustworthy witnesses and vouchers.' Boniface is determined to assert the authority of his own account over that of Hildelith.

Once again, despite Boniface's rejection of Hildelith's version of the vision of the monk of Much Wenlock, something of the literary interests of the abbess of Barking and her sisters can be derived from the surviving evidence. The anonymous visionary monk of Much Wenlock had fallen seriously ill when suddenly he was released from his suffering body and raised high into the sky by angels. From there the monk could look down at the world encircled with flames, and could see evil spirits and demons arguing over the souls of the dead and the dying. He heard his own sins speak of his ill deeds, and the testimony of a man he had once physically wounded, before then hearing the defence offered by his virtues. He saw the torments of hell and the beauty of paradise, and the heavenly Jerusalem. He was able to see the victory of the angels in winning the soul of a former abbot, and the suffering of a brother whose kinsman did not carry out his dying wishes, but he also gained insight into the secrets of individuals still living, including a girl who had stolen a distaff, and a woman who had yet to make satisfaction for her sins. As testimony to the accuracy of his vision he was also required to confess his own sins to a priest, Begga, and Begga's own undisclosed act of ascetic piety – the wearing of an iron girdle – was revealed to him. With its focus on suffering, sin and penance, the narrative is highly conventional.[34] As with the visions of the dead found in the lost Barking *liber*, the monk of Much Wenlock's revelation owes a great deal to Western European visionary traditions.[35]

One aspect of the vision of the monk of Much Wenlock stands out in particular. Within Boniface's account of the vision, the 'multitude of horrible crimes' of Ceolred, king of Mercia, was revealed to the monk. Although Ceolred was at the time of the vision still alive, the monk saw Ceolred attacked by demons and tortured 'with indescribable cruelties'. This vision is itself conventional and echoes in part a revelation recorded about the fate of King Coenred of Mercia (*fl.* 675–709), Ceolred's predecessor.[36] Nevertheless, for Boniface, the authority of the vision was demonstrated by the testimony of the priest Begga, to whom the monk of Much Wenlock confessed, although the ultimate proof of the vision lay in the subsequent 'death of the wicked king', which demonstrated beyond doubt 'that what he had seen of him was the truth'. Ceolred died in 716, so Boniface's letter describing this vision must have been written immediately after his death, and also that of Abbess Mildburg (*d.* 715).

Ceolred's surviving reputation is overwhelmingly a negative one: he is seen as a king who wrongly appropriated monastic resources and cruelly persecuted Æthelbald (*d.* 757). According to Felix's *Life of St Guthlac* (730–740), Guthlac not only prophesied to Æthelbald that he would succeed to the throne, but also predicted Ceolred's death:

> Cervices inimicorum tuorum subtus calcaneum tuum rediget, et possessiones eorum possidebis, et fugient a facie tua qui te oderunt, et terga eorum videbis, et gladius tuus vincet adversarios tuos. . . . Non in praeda nec in rapina regnum tibi dabitur, sed de manu Domini obtinebis; exspecta eum, cuius dies defeccerunt, quia manus Domini opprimit illum, cuius spes in maligno posita est, et dies illius velut umbra pertransibunt.

> [He will bow down the necks of your enemies beneath your heel and you shall own their possessions; those who hate you shall flee from your face and you shall

see their backs; and your sword shall overcome your foes. . . . Not as booty nor as spoil shall the kingdom be granted you, but you shall obtain it from the hand of God; wait for him whose life has been shortened, because the hand of the Lord oppresses him whose hope lies in wickedness, and whose days shall pass away like a shadow.][37]

The terms of this prophecy, with its focus on divine retribution and punishment resonates with the account of Ceolred's suffering recorded by Boniface. It is clear that Boniface shared Guthlac's view of Ceolred. Writing a joint letter in 746 or 747 to King Æthelbald (some thirty years after he recounted the vision of the monk), Boniface and his fellow bishops expressed concern about rumours of ill-conduct, and reminded Æthelbald of the fate of Ceolred, who along with Osred I of Northumbria (*d.* 716) was guilty of the 'two deadliest of sins . . . namely lust and adultery with nuns and the destruction of monasteries' and who consequently was 'surprised by an early and terrible death. . . [and] plunged into the depths of hell and the bottom of the abyss'.[38] The letter goes on to describe in more detail the events surrounding Ceolred's death:

Nam Ceolredum, precessorem venerande celsitudinis tuae, ut testate sunt qui presentes fuerant apud comites suos splendide epulantem malignus spiritus, qui eum ad fiduciam dampnande legis Dei suandendo pellexit, peccantem subito in insaniam mentis convertit, ut sine penitentia et confessione furibundus et amens et cum diabolis sermocinans et Dei sacerdotes abhominans de hac luce sine dubio ad tormenta inferni migravit.

[For while Ceolred, your worthy highness' predecessor — as those who were present testify — was feasting splendidly among his nobles, an evil spirit, which by its persuasions had seduced him into the audacious course of breaking the law of God, suddenly turned him in his sin to madness; so that without penitence and confession, insane and distraught, conversing with the devils and cursing the priests of God, he departed from this light assuredly to the torments of hell.][39]

Here more details are provided about Ceolred's terrible fate, including that Ceolred lost his mind before his demise and did not repent his sins. Boniface's opinion of Ceolred could not be more negative.

For Patrick Sims-Williams, the visionary content alone is sufficient to explain Hildelith of Barking's interest in the monk of Much Wenlock, but this is over-simplistic.[40] The inclusion of the specific revelation concerning Ceolred may explain Boniface's decision to cross-examine the monk himself, and to produce his own account. Boniface must have recognized the value of the vision of the monk of Much Wenlock as propaganda against a king whom he stridently opposed. But while Boniface was forthright in his condemnation of Ceolred, it is far from clear that Mildburg, as abbess of Much Wenlock, would have shared Boniface's views on the Mercian king. Indeed Mildburg clearly benefited from Ceolred's patronage, having received from him a grant of four 'manentes' [or hides, a unit of land] at Wyre Piddle in Worcestershire.[41] Sims-Williams notes that Much Wenlock is in fact the only monastic house recorded to have been granted a royal charter by Ceolred.[42] It would hardly have been in Mildburg's interest, then, to publicize a vision that damned Ceolred. Hildelith's version of the vision of the monk of Much Wenlock, oral or written, may well have been rather more circumspect than that of Boniface. Intriguingly, the subsequent Old English translation of Boniface's letter completely omits the attack on Ceolred.[43] Without the condemnation of Ceolred, the vision of the monk of Much Wenlock is not less political than that recorded by Boniface, but its political import is quite different, serving to reinforce rather than potentially to undermine the status of Mildburg's monastic house in the fragile early decades after its foundation in *c.* 680.

That such a vision of hell could be used as a tool to discredit an opponent is illustrated further by another hell vision, dated to after 757, which exists in the Bonifatian correspondence. Here an anonymous monk sees the suffering of a number of individuals, such as Æthelbald, as well as a number of other men, women, and even unbaptized children:

> Et in ipsis poenalibus puteis Cuthburgam simulque Uuialan quondam reginali potestate fruentes demersas. Alteram usque ad ascellas, id est Cuthburg, capite autem humeroque preclaram ceteris membris maculis consparsam, alteriusque, id est Uuialan, supra caput flammam extendere totamque animam simul cremari intuebatur. Ipsos autem poenarum ministros in facies illarum proprias carnales voluptates quasi lutum ferventem inicere. Et horribilem ululatum, quem quasi per totum mundum resonasse miserabiliter vocibus earum audiebat.

> [In the penitential pits were plunged Cuthburga [Cuthburg] and Wiala [Wialan], once crowned with queenly power—one, Cuthburga, up to the armpits, her head and shoulders clear, her other members covered with spots. Above the head of the other—that is, Wiala—he saw a flame spreading and burning the whole soul at once. The tormentors themselves threw the carnal sins of these women in their faces like boiling mud, and he heard the horrible howls resounding, as it were, through the whole world.][44]

Is this the same Cuthburg of Barking Abbey mentioned in the opening of Aldhelm's *De Virginitate*, the Cuthburg who was earlier tentatively identified as the future abbess of Wimborne? If so, then Cuthburg (and Wialan), whose *'horribilem ululatum'* resonate across the earth, must have made powerful enemies who set out to destroy their reputations and the reputations of the houses with which they were associated through the dissemination of such visions.

Visions of the dead, such as the vision of the monk of Much Wenlock or the anonymous monk's vision of Cuthburg and Wialan, although very much part of larger European traditions, are quite different from those which Bede reports were found in the Barking Abbey *liber*. Whereas the visions of the good deaths of the holy abbess and of her closest supporter serve to validate an entire community, and could be utilized to secure the future of the abbey, revelations of a female religious leader and her associate suffering in hell were potentially powerful weapons that could be used to undermine the status of an entire religious house. Yet if one aim of circulating the vision of Cuthburg was indeed to undermine the houses at Barking or Wimborne, it does not seem to have succeeded. Bede's overwriting of the Barking *liber* did secure the preservation and dissemination of the visions and reputations of the Barking nuns.

Fragmentary lives and Mildrith of Minster-in-Thanet

My analyses in Chapter 1 and in the first section of this chapter of the lives of Æthelthryth of Ely, Hild of Whitby and Æthelburg of Barking in the fourth book of Bede's *Ecclesiastical History* read alongside other textual traces of writings associated with early medieval women suggest, then, that lives of the founding abbesses of Barking, Ely and Whitby were produced by their communities, and that these lives focus in particular on the deaths of the abbesses and the visions and miracles that surrounded them. This raises the question: have any similar narratives by nuns actually survived? In fact narratives derived from versions that may have been originally authored by women do exist, including most notably Old English fragmentary lives apparently pertaining to the life of St Mildrith of Minster-in-Thanet, sister of Mildburg of Much Wenlock. Fragments are very much the staple of the vernacular early medieval literary tradition, and pose quite specific problems to the modern reader. R.M. Liuzza describes the tradition of Old English literature that has been passed down to us as 'the flotsam and jetsam of a vanished world, manuscripts and fragments of texts divorced from their original context, most of them second- or third hand copies of unknown originals, many of them saved from oblivion only by chance or neglect' and justifiably complains that 'it is sometimes difficult to imagine how to move from these discontinuous scraps to a reconstructed reality'.[45] In this section, I examine three such 'scraps' for further evidence of early medieval monastic women's writing.

As noted earlier, the legend of Mildrith dates to the time of Mildrith's successor, Eadburg of Minster-in-Thanet, who translated Mildrith's remains and fostered her cult.[46] Eadburg probably commissioned the writing down of the earliest version of this legend, or she may have written it herself. The longest Old English fragment survives in London, British Library, MS Cotton Caligula A.XIV, fols 121v–124v (see Figure 2.1).[47] It occupies seven leaves of a composite manuscript that also contains the 'Caligula Troper' (fols 1r–36v), a fragmentary eleventh-century liturgical chant book with musical notation and very striking illuminations. The Mildrith fragment was also copied in the mid-eleventh century and is found at the end of the manuscript. It appears, quite literally, in the midst of two other mid eleventh-century copies of earlier hagiographical works written in what seems to be the same hand: Ælfric's life of St Martin of Tours, also incomplete (fols 93r–111v and 125r–130v), and his life of St Thomas the Apostle (fols 111v–121v).

Bede did not include Mildrith's biography in his *Ecclesiastical History*, and as a result direct comparisons are not possible. Hollis, however, in making the case for an Old English Mildrith tradition that was 'created by monastic women', contends that the main functions of St Mildrith's *Life* were 'commemoration of the founder-abbess of Thanet and continued possession of the monastery's land'.[48] Minster-in-Thanet was a seventh-century royal foundation, and remained a prosperous economic and cultural centre for the next couple of centuries, so much so that it even had its own small fleet of ships in the mid eighth century.[49] The Mildrith tradition celebrates and legitimates the granting of land to the religious house. Whether or not we agree that this text constitutes a foundation narrative, there are certainly parallels between this legend and those sources overwritten by Bede concerning the foundations at Ely, Whitby and Barking: in all cases the memorialization of the founding abbess is associated with a desire to establish the legitimacy of the religious houses and to ensure their future. Yet Bede's versions do not pay close attention to the establishment of the religious houses themselves, but concentrate rather on the lives – and deaths – of the abbesses, and on the visions shared by the communities. Bede does not state how the founding abbesses came into possession of their land, with the exception of Æthelthryth of Barking (who was given it by her brother).[50] In contrast, as we will see, the Mildrith narrative in the Cotton manuscript is more centrally

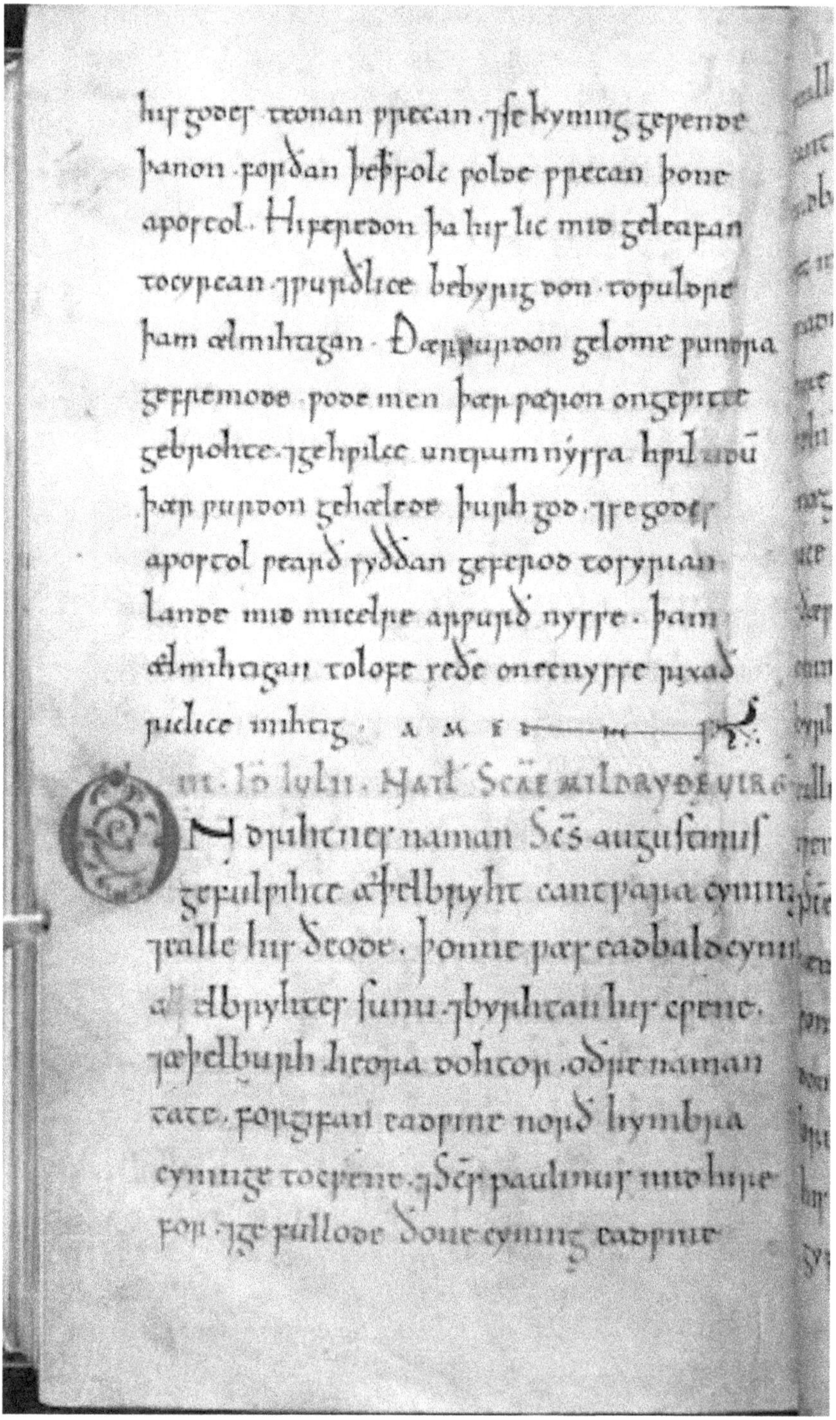

Fig. 2.1 Cotton Caligula A.XIV, fol. 121v. © The British Library Board.

concerned with the legality of the establishment. To what extent these differences reflect actual differences between the texts and to what extent they simply reflect the differing nature of the texts as they have been transmitted to us (whether in fragmentary form or as overwritten texts where the sources have been lost) is impossible to say for certain. It is likely that the conventions for writing the lives of founding abbesses were not fixed and that different lives focused on or foregrounded different issues.

The Mildrith legend, as David Rollason outlines in his study, is recorded in a number of different versions in various states of completeness, including three Latin lives (one by Goscelin of St. Bertin, some of whose work is discussed in Chapters 5 and 6).[51] This Old English version differs, however, in significant respects from the Latin lives in its emphasis on the significance of women. What is immediately striking about the Old English fragment in the Cotton manuscript is that it is headed 'IDUS IULII, NATALE SANCTAE MILDRYDAE VIRGINIS' [13TH JULY. THE BIRTH OF ST. MILDRITH, VIRGIN] but breaks off *before* it reaches Mildrith's own story. Only the first part of the narrative, as it is found in the other versions, has survived in this fragment. This opening section provides an account of the miraculous foundation of the monastery at Thanet by St Mildrith's mother, referred to in this text as 'Domne Eafe' [Lady Eve] (*f.* 689–697). It is preceded by a summary of the royal lineage of Domne Eafe and Mildrith, explaining their descent from the kings of Kent. The genealogy relates that Domne Eafe was married to Merewald of Mercia, and that the couple had three sainted children, 'and then after that, for the love of God and this world, they separated and gave their children and their worldly possessions to God' ('A Fragmentary Life', 18). The genealogy also refers back to Augustine's conversion of Æthelberht of Kent and his son Eadbald, and, in contrast to the Whitby *Life of Gregory* (discussed in Chapter 1) it outlines the part played by Æthelberht's daughter, Æthelburg Tata, in the conversion of Edwin of Northumbria, recording that Paulinus travelled with her to baptize the king and his people, and that following Edwin's death he returned with her to Canterbury. In contrast also to the account of Æthelburg Tata in Bede's *Ecclesiastical History*, discussed in the previous chapter, Æthelburg Tata here demonstrates considerable autonomy, choosing, once she becomes a widow, to endow the church with her own wealth, in return for commemorative masses for her father and herself ('A Fragmentary Life', 17). The opening genealogy finishes with a brief description of where the bodies of Mildrith and her sister Mildgyth lie, and the explanation that the third of Domne Eafe's daughters, St Merefin, died in infancy. The focus thus remains on the female line.

Having rooted Thanet's history firmly within that of the first Christian English kings, and within the history of saintly women, the narrative proceeds to relate the story of the dreadful murder of Domne Eafe's brothers by Thunor, the councillor of their cousin Ecgberht, king of Kent, who was guardian to the boys. The narrative in the Cotton fragment does its best to make Thunor, who is described as motivated by jealousy of the boys and their close relationship to the king, solely responsible for their deaths. Ecgberht himself is described as unwilling to countenance such a crime against his own kin,[52] and on discovering it he determines, after consultation, to offer compensation to Domne Eafe according to her wishes and those of 'her closest friends' ('A Fragmentary Life', 20). At this point in the narrative, Domne Eafe, like Æthelburg Tata in the earlier episode, has an active role. The fragmentary life stresses that, 'with God's assistance [Domne Eafe] so arranged it that she chose that compensation in the island which is called Thanet: that is, the eighty hides of land she received there from the king' ('A Fragmentary Life', 20). While the extent of the land which Domne Eafe secures does not compare favourably with the 600 hides owned by Ely (according to Bede), this narrative is unique in that it describes a woman's role in securing the land on which the abbey is built rather than the generosity of a male benefactor.[53]

The episode that follows, in which the amount of wergild or compensation is decided, is striking because of its rich symbolism.

> And hit ða swa gelamp þa se cyning and hio Domne Eafe ærest þæt land geceas, and hi ofer þa ea comon, þa cwæð se cyning to hire hwylcne dæl þæs landes hio onfon wolde hyre broðrum to wergilde. Hio him andsworode and cwæð þæt hio his na maran ne gyrnde þonne hire hind utan ymbe yrnan wolde, þe hire ealne weg beforan arn ðonne hio on rade wæs. Cwæð þæt hire þæt getyðed wære þæt hio swa myceles his onfon sceolde swa seo hind hire gewisede. He ða se cyning hire geandsworode and cwæð þæt he þæt lustlice fægnian wolde. And hio ða hind swa dyde þæt hio him beforan hleapende wæs, & hi hyre æfter filigende wæron, oðþæt hi comon to ðære stowe þe is nu gecwedon Þunores Hlæwe.
>
> 'A Fragmentary Life', 25–6

[And thus it happened that when the king and Lady Eve first chose the land and came across the river, then the king asked her what piece of the territory she wished to take as compensation for her brothers. She answered him and said that she desired no more of his [territory] than her hind (which always ran before her when she was out riding) would run around. She said that it was granted to her that she should take as much of his [territory] as the hind indicated to her. Then the king answered her and said that he would welcome that with pleasure. And then the hind so acted that it leaped in front of them, and they followed after it, until they came to the place which is now called Thunor's Mount.]

'A Fragmentary Life', 20

Joshua Davies points out the 'only the version preserved in the Cotton text suggests that Domne Eafe exploited her knowledge of her tame hind's behaviour to maximize the amount of land the king awarded her'.[54] The fragmentary Old English life breaks off just after this point, when Thunor challenges the king's decision and the earth suddenly opens up, but the conclusion is forgone: in an act of divine justice, Thunor will be swallowed up into the ground. As Hollis's analysis reveals, the episode has strong Celtic folktale elements: the king's rash promise, the supernatural deer, the otherworld beneath the surface of the earth.[55] These are combined with Christian hagiographical motifs such as the deer as a symbol of Christ (see Song of Songs 2.8–10 and also the Old English life of St Giles).[56] The name, 'Þunores Hlæwe' ['Thunor's Mount', or more accurately 'Thunor's Low'], indicates that the place at the outer boundary of the foundation's territory was a burial mound.[57] The representation of the earth swallowing the murderer evokes endless representations of penitential pits and the sort of hellish suffering experienced by Ceolred in the vision of the monk of Much Wenlock or by Æthelbald, Cuthburg and Wialan in the vision of the anonymous monk.

The demise of Thunor – struck down by the hand of God – mirrors the earlier scene in the episode in which the corpses of the murdered princes, hidden in the king's hall, are miraculously revealed to the king:

ðurh Godes mihte hi þanon gecydde wurdon, emne swa ðæs leohtes leoma stod up þurh þære healle hrof up to heofonum. And he ða se cyning sylf embe forman hancred ut gangende wæs, and he þa him sylf geseonde wæs þæt wundor.

'A Fragmentary Life', 25

[they were made known there by the power of God, inasmuch as a beam of light rose up towards heaven, up through the roof of the hall. And then when the king himself was going out about first cock-crow, he witnessed the miracle himself]

'A Fragmentary Life', 20

The supernatural light ('leohtes leoma') and the dawn revelation resonate with visions of the dead that characterize Bede's accounts of the lives – and deaths – of the founding abbesses of Ely, Whitby and Barking. In all cases, such visions are associated with validating the authority, as well as establishing the sanctity and piety, of the early abbesses and thus, if only indirectly, with legitimizing their monasteries' divinely inspired claims to their landholdings. Domne Eafe's family have been the victims of persecution, and the king, according to the codes of early medieval law, has granted to her the land on which she founds the house at Thanet but it is the intervention of God that ensures that justice is done.

Two other fragments of Old English lives of or related to Mildrith have also survived. These are found in London, Lambeth Palace, MS 427, fols 210r–210v and 211r–211v.[58] They appear at the end of the composite manuscript that includes the so-called Lambeth Psalter, which is renowned for its interlinear Old English glosses. The fragments are written in a single neat hand that is distinct from that of the principal scribe of the manuscript and on leaves that are slightly darker and fractional bigger than the folios that precede them. Stitch marks reveal that they were originally part of the manuscript binding and stubs of parchment after fol. 211 indicate that some leaves are missing. Their appearance suggests that these two folios are non-contiguous parts of the same text, although the relationship of these fragments to that found in the Cotton manuscript, or indeed to each other, remains uncertain. Mary Dockray-Miller, for example, concludes that 'the two Lambeth folios have some sort of a textual relationship with the Cotton text, but not necessarily a close one'.[59] The fragment that begins on fol. 211r of the Lambeth Palace manuscript is similar in some respects to the Cotton fragment in terms of content and form and may also be derived from a female monastic tradition, whether originating from Minster-in-Thanet, as Hollis contends,[60] or elsewhere (most obviously, as we will see, Minster-in-Sheppey). Admittedly the short section that remains focuses on the activities of Seaxburh (the sister of Æthelthryth of Ely), but a brief mention of Mildrith at the start indicates that an account of her life may have preceded the text in its current form. The fragment begins half way through a sentence, which evidently alludes to the miracles that continue to be performed, presumably at Mildrith's tomb, before going on to state that Eadburg succeeded Mildrith as abbess, and that she was responsible for the construction of the church at Thanet. A break in the narrative follows, and a summary of Æthelthryth's two marriages, the miraculous preservation of her virginity and her choice of her own burial place provides the introduction to the Seaxburh's story, which focuses on events prior to her move to Ely.

This fragmentary account of Seaxburh's life parallels that of Mildrith in the Cotton manuscript in a number of important respects.[61] First, it too starts with an account of royal and saintly lineage. Anna, king of the East Anglians, has three daughters: Seaxburh, Æthelthryth and Wihtburh. This is followed by a matrilineal line of piety, or, to borrow Dockray-Miller's term, a 'matrilineal genealogy'.[62]

While Æthelthryth, of course, was childless, Seaxburh married Eorcenberht of Kent and one of her children was Eormenhild, who in turn married Wulfhere of Mercia. Eormenhild in turn gave birth of Werburh. Second, the account describes, in unusual legalistic detail, the foundation by Seaxburh of the monastery of Minster-in-Sheppey on the island of Sheppey in Kent, which is 'three miles broad and seven miles long' ('A Fragmentary Life', 23).[63] The construction by slaves lasted thirty years, during which period Seaxburh 'held the kingdom on behalf of her son Hlothhere'. ('A Fragmentary Life', 23–4). While the text smoothes over the struggle for succession that ensued after the death of Hlothhere's older brother Ecgberht in 673, only alluding to Seaxburh's role as effective regent, it does establish clearly that Seaxburh purchased the land on which Minster-in-Sheppey was built: Seaxburh 'then bought his share of the territory from him and enfranchised it to the minster for as long as Christianity should be maintained in England' ('A Fragmentary Life', 24). This account is much more pragmatic and naturalistic than the more fantastic description of how the land on which Minster-in-Thanet was established was obtained, but the effect is similar: the legitimacy of the monastery's claim on its territory is established. Furthermore, as with the Thanet story, there is divine authorization of the establishment of the monastery in the form of a prophetic revelation:

> Ða þæt mynster getimbrod wæs, ða com hyre to Godes engel on nihtlicre gesihðe, and hire bodode þæt ær feala gearum hæðene leod sceolde ðas þeode gewinnan.

> [Then, when the minster was built, an angel of God came to her [Seaxburh] in a vision at night and announced to her that before many years a heathen people should conquer this nation.]

> 'A Fragmentary Life', 27 and 23

By linking the completion of the construction of the church to Seaxburh's divine foreknowledge of the Danish invasions, the text establishes a powerful, almost eschatological, connection between the establishment of the religious house and the unfolding of the history of the nation. The Seaxburh who appears here is a far more powerful figure than the one who appears in Bede's version of the life of her sister, Æthelthryth of Ely, in the *Eccesiastical History*, which makes no mention of her as foundress of Minster-in-Sheppey.

These two fragments differ quite markedly from the third, also found in the Lambeth Palace manuscript, on fol. 210r–v. As the two fragments previously discussed make clear, the representation of a dynastic line of female sanctity was a key element of the early lives of the abbesses of the first English monasteries.

Succession between family members was common, and created a sense of divinely authorized stability. The rule might pass from mother to daughter, as in the case of Domne Eafe and Mildrith, or from sister to sister. In the fragment that begins on fol. 210r of the Lambeth Palace manuscript, however, is found a unique description of the admission of a child as a nun:

> Ða hyre modor hi mid þyssere bletsunge hyre ðus onfangen hæfde, heo hy aþenedum limum ætforan þam halgan wefode astrehte, and hy mid teara agotennysse to Drihtne gebæd. Ða heo hyre gebed geendod hæfde, heo up astod and to hyre modor cneowum onbeah. And heo hy ða mid sibbe cosse gegrette, and ealle ða geferrædene samod. And hy hire wæter to handa bæron, æfter regollicre wisan.
>
> 'A Fragmentary Life', 26

> [When her mother had thus received her with this blessing, she stretched herself out before the holy altar with extended limbs, and with a flood of tears prayed to the Lord. When she had finished her prayer she stood up and bowed before her mother's knees. And then she greeted her and the whole congregation together, with the kiss of peace. And in the manner of the Rule, they brought her water for her hands.]
>
> 'A Fragmentary Life', 22

The mother here receives her daughter, taking on roles that would subsequently become the privilege of the male clergy. She proceeds to sing three verses to the congregation and a comparison is made to and Anna and Simeon, who witnessed the dedication of Christ in the temple (Luke 2:25–38). The mother then 'earnestly instructed' her daughter ('A Fragmentary Life', 22), who in turn lived up to the trust and faith placed in her: 'She was the benefactor of widows and orphans and the comforter of all the wretched and afflicted, and in all respects humble and gentle' ('A Fragmentary Life', 23). The bonds between mother and daughter, teacher and pupil, abbess and successor, are recognized and celebrated by the whole community, which shares in the rituals of consecration. According to Hollis, this allusive fragment appears, remarkably, to describe the admission or consecration of Mildrith by her mother, Domne Eafe, but as Dockray-Miller has noted, it could refer to any mother offering her daughter as an oblate.[64] A reading such as Dockray-Miller's pays greater attention to the indeterminacy of the fragment form, which continually frustrates any expectations of narrative completion. In its surviving form, the fragment on fol. 210r–v of the Lambeth Palace manuscript includes neither a genealogy nor an account of the early history of a religious foundation, and it makes no reference by name to any women saints, but despite its obliqueness, it too addresses the concerns of monastic women, and should therefore also be understood as a product of monastic women's engagement with literary culture.

Conclusion

The exploration of the literary culture of Barking Abbey in the seventh and early eighth centuries illustrates the extent to which women were actively involved in the production of texts. It demonstrates that in his account of the miracles at Barking Abbey, Bede drew on pre-existing literary accounts of the visions of the nuns, accounts written for and quite plausibly by the nuns themselves which were then circulated more widely in order to secure the future of their house and the continuing female governance of the abbey. Hildelith, as successor to the founding abbess Æthelburh, may have played a key role in the production of these accounts, collected together in the Barking *liber*, either as commissioner or even as author.

The evidence of Aldhelm's *De Virginitate* indicates the extent to which the nuns of Barking were fully engaged in literary culture, as producers as well as consumers. There exists a real relationship between Aldhelm's implied and his actual audience: monks and nuns were part of the same intellectual and interpretative communities and literary networks, books were lent and borrowed, and the exchange of letters and other forms of literary composition, including poetry, was not one way, but was very much reciprocal. Yet at the same time, Aldhelm's *De Virginitate* illustrates how, even within a text written at their behest, and addressing them directly, the Barking nuns' religious practices might be critiqued, undermined and overwritten, just as Bede's *Ecclesiastical History* overwrites their words.

The vision of the monk of Much Wenlock provides a further example of the appropriation or overwriting of a woman's narrative, in this case an account, oral or written, provided by Abbess Hildelith herself. Boniface's version of the vision of the monk of Much Wenlock clearly had its own political agenda, which Hildelith may not have shared, and one not dissimilar to that of those writers who circulated the vision of Cuthburg in order, possibly, to undermine the women's houses at Barking or Wimborne. Taken as a whole, the surviving evidence suggests that, even in the first decades after the foundation of their abbey, the Barking nuns were highly literate, that they valued and cultivated scholarship and learning, and that they fully understood the political as well as religious power of visionary writings.

Women's engagement with literary culture beyond the major foundations at Ely, Whitby and Barking is revealed by looking at other sorts of evidence. The fragmentary lives of and pertaining to Mildrith and the histories of Minster-in-Thanet and Minster-in-Sheppey pose very different problems to the contemporary reader than do Bede's *Ecclesiastical History*, the Whitby *Life of Gregory* or Boniface's account of the vision of the monk of Much Wenlock, texts which are complete in themselves and are also located firmly within a larger context that limits and controls their meaning. These fragmentary texts do however provide us with examples of material written in the vernacular rather than in Latin. A credible case for female monastic composition can be made here based on the dual foci on genealogies of women and on female authority and power. The fragments support the argument that early medieval nuns were invested in composing as well as preserving the histories of their foundations. Taken together, these texts, including those which survive only in a handful of leaves, offer tantalizing insights into women's writing in the earliest period of literary history.

Missionary Women's Letters and Poetry

Introduction

This chapter explores some of the earliest surviving writing unquestionably attributable to named English women: the letters of early nuns found in the collections that have come to be known as the Boniface correspondence. In all, there are ten letters in the correspondence written by nuns and abbesses: a letter from Ælfflæd, probably the abbess of Whitby; a letter from the nun Ecgburg; a letter from the abbess Eangyth with her daughter Bugga or Heahburg; a letter from Bugga herself; a letter from Leoba, future abbess of Tauberbischofsheim; a letter from Cneuburg with abbot Ealdhun and her fellow abbess Cenburg; a letter from Cena; and three letters from the nun Berthgyth. These letters are significant in their own rights and also because some contain the earliest surviving examples of poetry by English women: verses written by Leoba and Berthgyth. All of the letters are preserved in one manuscript: Vienna, Österreichische Nationalbibliothek, Cod. Lat. Vindobonensis 751 (the Vienna Boniface Codex), which dates to the second half of the ninth century.[1] This collection of letters relating to St Boniface (672–754) and his follower Lul (c. 710–786) is therefore one of the most significant manuscripts in the history of English women's literary history. Two other early codices of the Boniface correspondence are Munich, Bayerische Staatsbibliothek, Codex latinus monacensis 8112 (dating to around 800) and Karlsruhe, Badische Landesbibliothek, Codex Rastatt 22 (mid- or late ninth century). The contents of these codices are not identical and the Vienna Boniface Codex, while lacking the historically important papal correspondence found in the other two codices, contains unique copies of over fifty letters, including, most pertinently in this context, a number by women that are not included in the other two codices or found anywhere else. The Vienna Boniface Codex is made up of four manuscripts that were bound together sometime before the mid-sixteenth century. Alongside the Boniface correspondence, there are some books

from the New Testament, a German biblical glossary, and a selection of other
religious and legal material, such as some poems by Aldhelm, including the
only surviving copy of his *Carmen Rhythmicum*. As discussed in Chapter 2,
Aldhelm is also known to have corresponded with women, and the Boniface
correspondence in the Vienna Codex itself includes one letter from Aldhelm
to a woman, Sygegyð (fol. 33v). The Boniface correspondence is the first item
in the codex (it appears in fols 1r–77r) and, except for the final couple of
pages, it has been copied by a single scribe. The hand is a mid ninth-century
Carolingian minuscule. Like the Munich and Karlsruhe texts, the manuscript
was copied in Mainz (in modern-day Germany), where Boniface had been
appointed archbishop a century earlier. All three manuscripts of the Boniface
correspondence are thought to be ultimately descended from a single lost
archetype, with the collection found in the Vienna Boniface Codex being closer
to that archetype than the versions found in either the Munich or Karlsruhe
codices but significantly supplemented from the collection of original drafts and
letters kept in Mainz.[2]

It is likely that the larger collection of letters relating to Boniface and his
followers was put together, possibly by Lul, not simply to preserve the contents
of the letters, but also for formal reasons, as a guide to letter writing.[3] Nevertheless,
the authorship of the letters was evidently important, as the collection clearly
celebrates the missionary saint and his circle. In the Vienna Boniface Codex,
there are two main groupings of letters by women: those from Eangyth and
Bugga (*c.* 719–722), Bugga (*c.* 720). Leoba (*c.* 732) and Cena (*c.* 723–*c.* 755)
appear on fols 20v–23v, while those from Ælfflæd (*c.* 713), Cneuburg, Ealdhun
and Cenburg (*c.* 729–*c.* 744) and Berthgyth (possibly datable to after her kinsman
Lul's death in 786)[4] appear on fols 32r–35v (see Figure 3.1). Ecgburg's letter
(*c.* 716/718) is the outlier on fols. 64r–65r, located in the supplementary letters.
It therefore does not appear to have been included in the earlier manuscript
from which the Vienna Boniface Codex was copied. The marginalization of the
women's letters within the collection is fairly recent. As Felice Lifshitz has
pointed out, the letters to and from women occupy far more prominent positions
in the Vienna Boniface Codex than they do in Michael Tangl's early twentieth-
century edition (1915), which is the most recent edition and is still widely
regarded as definitive.[5] Furthermore, twentieth-century translations, such as
those by Edward Kylie (1911) and Ephraim Emerton (1940) do not include all of
the women's letters, and some of the women's letters – namely those of the nun
Berthgyth – have only recently been published in translated form in their
entirety.[6]

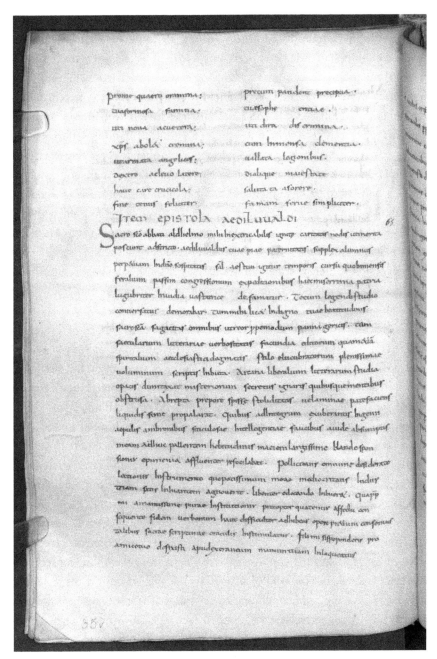

Fig. 3.1 Cod. Lat. Vindobonensis 751, fol. 35v. Vienna, Österreichische Nationalbibliothek. Reproduced with permission.

These letters, some written by women religious to Boniface and his fellow missionaries in Germany, and others written by those who had themselves travelled to Europe in order to convert others to their beliefs, are revealing about the cultural productivity and exchange that was associated with this early missionary movement.[7] The surviving letters of these women represent only a fragment of what must have been a much larger archive; indeed in *De Virginitate*, Aldhelm refers to letters written to him by the nuns of Barking, letters that no longer exist. However, if their immediate context is often lost, reading the letters by women in the Boniface collection in relation to those that are addressed by Boniface and Lul to these women and to other nuns (most notably to Eadburg, also discussed in Chapter 2), and in relation to those between men, provides valuable insights into the shared activities and interests of the scattered community of missionaries and their supporters, and also into the different experiences of women and men. In its analyses of these letters, this chapter will examine the cultural and religious practices that they describe and from which they emerge.

The English missionary narratives are framed as discourses of power, as outlined in Nicholas Howe's important study of migration in early medieval England.[8] As Howe explains, for Boniface and his supporters, life itself was perceived as a pilgrimage, and the missionary's journey to convert the Germanic people was understood in typological terms, as the fulfilment of events foreshadowed in the Book of Exodus. Boniface referred to himself in one letter as 'an exile in Germany',[9] and many of the women, both in Germany and in England, describe themselves in similar terms. Figuring Boniface's circle as an English diaspora may be productive although it should not be forgotten that the activities of the missionaries and their supporters were those of colonizers and even of slave owners. The letters in the Boniface collection are only part of the surviving evidence of the circuits of reception and production that extended between England and the continent. As will be seen in the following sections, this evidence, taken as a whole, testifies to the importance to this religious network of fostering and maintaining affective as well as spiritual bonds through shared knowledge and creative and cultural exchange. Howe notes, 'against great obstacles of distance and culture, the *ecclesia* as community could be preserved through letters',[10] but it could also be preserved through the production and exchange of books and through activities such as prayer, pilgrimage and composing and sharing poetry.

According to Jane Stevenson, women 'bore serious responsibilities' in Boniface's mission to convert the pagans, and their role as educators was vital.[11]

A number of the women's letters in the collection, whether written by nuns in England or on the continent, are overtly concerned with this topic. Another key recurring theme is the importance of friendship, and the extent to which it is celebrated within these letters can also not be overstated.[12] Nevertheless, some of these nuns left behind personal testimonies in their poems and letters of their own experiences of isolation and distress, and these will also be examined in this chapter. These were women who, because of pilgrimage or missionary migration, found themselves separated from their mothers and fathers, sisters and brothers, sons and daughters, and other more distant kin, and from their close spiritual friends. As Andy Orchard and Lisa M. C. Weston have both shown, despite its diffuse nature, the correspondence is characterized by intense intertextuality and a common literary or epistolary language, and also by shared emotional values centred on experiences of solitude and isolation (experiences which can seem at odds with the missionary fervour demonstrated elsewhere in the collection).[13] I will demonstrate later in this chapter that these are similar values to those found in Old English verse in famous elegies such as *The Wanderer, The Seafarer*, and especially in the women's elegies, *Wulf and Eadwacer* and *The Wife's Lament*, poems that disclose seemingly private emotions of grief and melancholy, nostalgia and longing stimulated by experiences of exile, abandonment and loss of kin and community.[14] Some of the early medieval women's letters, while distinct in key respects, bear certain similarities to these elegies, in terms of the temporalities they explore, the emotions they evoke, and the kinships that they forge.[15]

The English diaspora, and cultural production and exchange

An important form of cultural production amongst the missionary diaspora was the composition and exchange of poetry. Aldhelm wrote the poetic as well as the prose treatise on virginity for the nuns at Barking Abbey. In the Boniface correspondence in turn, there is further evidence that churchmen composed poetry specifically for the edification of religious women, even (or perhaps especially) when they were separated from them by considerable distance. Lul addresses one letter to two women religious in which he describes how they cared for him in his sickness and he sends them poetry in thanks, with the qualification, 'But if you find anything unsuited to the work, anything involved or contrary to the rules of the grammatical art, this remember to polish, taking a file from the shop of the grammarians.'[16] These lines indicate the collaborative nature of such poetry whereby both writer and recipient share their knowledge and learning, and the recipient is invited not only to read but also to rework and improve the verses. Clare A. Lees and Gillian Overing describe this sort of phenomenon as 'communal literacy'.[17] As noted in the previous chapter, according to Aldhelm, the nuns of Barking were technically accomplished in the writing of poetry. Although none of that poetry has been preserved, some verses embedded within the letters by women in the Boniface correspondence has.

Leoba, one of Boniface's key supporters, wrote the earliest surviving example when she was still a nun of Wimborne, in the early 730s:

> Vale, vivens aevo longiore, vita feliciore, interpellans pro me.
>> Arbiter omnipotens, solus qui cuncta creavit,
>> In regno patris semper qui lumine fulget,
>> Qua iugiter flagrans sic regnat gloria Christi,
>> Inlesum servet semper te iure perenni.

> [Farewell, and may you live long and happily, making intercession for me.
>> The omnipotent Ruler who alone created everything,
>> He who shines in splendor forever in His Father's kingdom,
>> The perpetual fire by which the glory of Christ reigns,
>> May preserve you forever in perennial right.][18]

For Lees and Overing, Leoba's 'sonorous Latin' is wrongly dismissed 'as a poor imitation of Aldhelm's style', yet, arguably, it is the very formulaicity of this letter and the poetry embedded within it that renders it radical.[19] This is because, in borrowing the language and phraseology of Aldhelm, Leoba forges her own literary identity, appropriating for herself an elite masculine authority, which, according to Weston, enables her 'to "speak" as it were in public, to write and to exchange texts and textual bodies in the synthetic kinship of literacy and monasticism'.[20] Certainly, these lines of poetry in praise of the Creation and Christian justice should be read as integral to Leoba's valediction to Boniface, who was her kinsman. She urges him to pray for her, and thus seeks to establish an enduring relationship with him, which, if it does not place them on equal footing, certainly invites Boniface to act as her spiritual protector.

The letter within which Leoba's verse is embedded provides significant information about why the relationship with male kin in particular was so important and also about the education and possible career trajectories of English nuns. The letter is Leoba's first to Boniface. She uses the verse as a means of introducing herself to her relative, and, it seems, as a means of encouraging him to allow her to join his mission. She stresses their familial connection: not only is her mother Æbbe related to Boniface, but also her late father Dynne was his good friend. Her parents having died, Leoba represents herself as a woman who, in the absence of kinsmen, is isolated and vulnerable. Nevertheless the tone of Leoba's letter is assertive rather than plaintive. She appeals to Boniface as her closest, or at any rate most trustworthy, male relative, and therefore as one whose duty it is to protect her and to protect her interests.

Leoba anticipates a positive response, and crucially figures as a learning experience the exchange of letters with Boniface which she hopes will follow:

> Illud etiam peto, ut rusticitatem huius epistolae digneris emendare; et mihi aliqua verba tuae affabilitatis exempli gratia transmittere non recusses, quae inhianter audire satago.
>
> Istos autem subter scriptos versiculos conponere nitebar secundum poeticae traditionis disciplinam, non audacia confidens, sed gracilis ingenioli rudimenta exercitare cupiens et tuo auxilio indigens.

> [I beg you also to be so kind as to correct the unskilled style of this letter and to send me, by way of example, a few kind words which I greatly long to hear.
>
> I have composed the following verses according to the rules of poetic art, not trusting to my own presumption, but trying only to exercise my little talents and needing your assistance.][21]

Leoba states that she learnt the art of poetry from her teacher Eadburg, who was, as we saw in Chapter 2, a correspondent of Boniface and who may have encouraged Leoba to write this letter. Leoba implies that she has learnt as much as possible at Wimborne and now feels it is time to progress her education further. She wishes to advance from the convent instruction she received from Eadburg to a higher level, which she believes can only be achieved with male patronage. Boniface was clearly impressed by Leoba's correspondence and invited her to join him. Boniface entrusted her with leading the nuns in his mission and subsequently Leoba became abbess of Tauberbischofsheim in Francia.

Although no further letters from Leoba survive, three letters to her do, one from Lul and two from Boniface. They date to Leoba's time in Francia, and are concerned with offering and requesting spiritual support and with the writers' and recipients' common focus on learning and conversion. Lul writes to encourage Leoba in adversity, and to affirm their spiritual friendship, emphasizing that he has not forgotten her, but that he has been battling with troubles of his own.[22] The first of Boniface's letters to Leoba is very brief.[23] In it he grants a request for permission to educate a girl in her care. The second is a letter addressed not only to Leoba, but also to two of her fellow nuns, her kinswoman and disciple Thecla, and Cynehild, aunt of Lul and mother of another writer in the collection, Berthgyth. In this letter, Boniface requests their prayers for their shared missionary activities and describes his frustration with his converts and his fears in the face of 'heretics and schismatics and hypocrites'.[24] With their emphasis on learning and the need for spiritual support, albeit from afar, the letters provide further evidence of the cultural practices of the English diaspora.

The letters between Boniface and the abbesses and nuns in England and on the continent illustrate the importance to this diaspora of the reciprocal exchange of books between male and female religious. Stevenson points out that 'both in England and on the Continent, nuns produced many volumes of vitally necessary books for the missionaries, a serious commitment of both time and money'.[25] Indeed, such textual exchange was endowed with great spiritual and emotional significance. The name of Leoba's teacher, Eadburg, recurs in the Boniface correspondence; in all, five letters – four by Boniface and one by Lul – are addressed to Eadburg. In the previous chapter we saw that Boniface's account of the vision of the monk of Much Wenlock was addressed to Eadburg, who evidently had already encountered, directly or indirectly, Hildelith of Barking's version of the same revelation. As noted in Chapter 2, while it has often been assumed that this Eadburg can be identified as Eadburg, abbess of Minster-in-Thanet (successor to Mildrith), it is more likely, as Barbara Yorke argues, that Leoba's teacher and Boniface's correspondent was a nun and possibly later abbess of Wimborne, where Leoba was cloistered before she moved to Germany.[26] Yorke also posits that Boniface had educated Eadburg before he left England.

The other letters addressed to Eadburg, who remained in England, were written some twenty or thirty years after the one concerning the vision of Much Wenlock, and in one Boniface explains that literary gift-giving was an important form of support for the missionaries: 'she has consoled with spiritual light by the gift of sacred books an exile in Germany'.[27] In another widely cited letter, Boniface reminds Eadburg that she has comforted him with 'the solace of books and the comfort of . . . garments' and continues:

> Sic et adhuc deprecor, ut augeas quod coepisti, id est, ut mihi cum auro conscribas epistolas domini mei, sancti Petri apostoli, ad honorem et reverentiam sanctarum scripturarum ante oculos carnalium in praedicando.

> [And I beg you further to add to what you have done already by making a copy written in gold of the Epistles of my master, St. Peter the Apostle, to impress honor and reverence for the Sacred Scriptures visibly upon the carnally minded to whom I preach.][28]

It is clear from this that Eadburg herself must have been trained as a scribe and that there was a scriptorium at Wimborne. The ornate manuscript she is asked to produce is a copy for display rather than for everyday use; it will be designed to be gazed upon with awe and reverence. Although in this letter Boniface links the different gifts (*librorum, vestimentorum*) he has received, John-Henry Wilson Clay points out the importance of distinguishing books from other forms of gift: 'Gifts were symbols … of great importance in creating and maintaining social relations. Books meanwhile – at least books of Scripture – belonged to the world of the sacred.'[29] The gold inscribed copy of the letters of St Peter, written in Eadburg's own hand, is requested not only because of its material value, but because of its spiritual worth; it will be used to impress the heathens as well as to convey to them the Christian message. As a gift from and produced by Boniface's close friend, it has an almost talismanic value: implicitly the book offers Boniface protection. Indeed, in another letter, he goes on to describe to Eadburg the very real dangers he faces, seeking her intercession with God on his behalf in order to preserve his safety and ensure the success of his mission.[30]

Friendship is crucial throughout these epistolary exchanges. In his letter to Eadburg, Lul sends 'a silver styl[us], and some incense [storax] and cinnamon' in exchange for her prayers and a letter, and writes about the charitable love 'which joins us in spiritual kinship'.[31] A number of letters survive to and from another nun in England, Bugga (Heahburg).[32] Writing to Boniface following his early mission to Frisia, Bugga applauded his success in converting the pagans, requested masses for a relative, sent him fifty shillings and an altar cover, and apologized for failing to send him a text which he had requested:

> Simulque sciat caritas tua, quod passiones martyrum, quas petisti tibi transmitti, adhuc minime potui impetrare. Sed, dum valeam, faciam. Et tu, mi carissimus, dirige meae parvitati ad consolationem, quod per dulcissimas litteras tuas promisisti, id est congregationes aliquas sanctarum scripturarum.

> [Know also that the Sufferings of the Martyrs which you asked me to send you I have not yet been able to get, but as soon as I can I shall send it. And you, my best beloved, comfort my insignificance by sending me, as you promised in your dear letter, some collection of the sacred writings.][33]

Given the extent to which patient endurance of hardship and isolation figures in this correspondence, the consolatory value of *The Sufferings of the Martyrs* is self-evident, and indeed Boniface did die for his cause. Bugga's own request that her gifts and prayers be reciprocated with a letter containing Biblical verses indicates the productively cyclic nature of the exchanges: every gift or present invites, often explicitly, a response, whether that be a reply, a prayer or another gift.

The exact nature of the presents being exchanged is not always clear, as is the case in a letter from a nun, Cena, which states that it accompanies unspecified 'little gifts' and 'tokens of affection' and promises Boniface that he will be remembered in her prayers, and also that she will offer hospitality and assistance 'if any of your people should ever come to this country'.[34] Similarly, the joint letter from Abbess Cneuburg of Inkberrow near Worcester written to Cengisl, abbot of Glastonbury, another abbot, Ingeld, and a priest of Glastonbury, Wiehtberht, refers somewhat obliquely to the exchange of prayers for one woman for their intercession on behalf of the souls of other women:

> Libenter nanque atque gratanter vestrae salutationis munuscula suscepimus Deoque adiuvante isdem digna reconpensare disideramus et eam, quam circa nos scripsistis habere in orationibus, communionem bono animo et pura fide erga vos indesinenter habere horis, quibus intimastis, consentimus. Nomina quoque nostrarum defunctarum sororum ego Cneuburg memorialiter te habere, o Wiehtberhte presbiter fidelis, deprecor et omnibus circumquaque amicis transmittere.

> [Willingly and gratefully we received the little gifts of your greeting and with God's help we desire to repay them worthily and we consent to have her, whom you wrote about, in our prayers and communion with good spirit and pure faith towards you at the hours you suggested, incessantly. And I Cneuburg beg you, o faithful priest Wigbert [Wiehtberht] to keep the names of our dead sisters in your memory, and transmit them to our friends all around.][35]

Here the rhetorical switch from first person plural to singular (*ego Cneuburg*) has the effect of making the letter seem more intimate and urgent as Cneuburg entrusts one specific recipient with the responsibility of ensuring that the names and lives of her familial and monastic sisters are commemorated by the scattered community of Christians.

In some cases the gifts are not poems, books or prayers, but people. A letter from Lul and two of his fellow missionaries, Denehard and Burchard (who became bishop of Würtzburg), to Cneuburg includes a request that she send two recently freed slaves to join their mission.[36] Alongside trade, invasion, missionary activity and pilgrimage, human trafficking was a major component of migration in this period in history, as illustrated in the story of Gregory the Great and the Deirans discussed in Chapter 1.[37] This brief reference to the practice of slavery stands in marked contrast to the explorations of individual isolation and sadness that we will see are found in other letters: there is a clear division between the lives that count, emotionally as well as legally (the lives of the missionaries), and lives that do not (the lives of former slaves, whose voices are lost).[38] Nevertheless the request is qualified with the words 'if this should be their free act and if they are within your jurisdiction', suggesting that the former slaves are granted at least some choice about whether or not they comply.[39] The letter to Cneuburg is, additionally, significant for another reason: in it, Cneuburg is deferred to as an abbess and a noblewoman (*domina*) and her protection is sought: 'if any one of us should happen to visit Britain we should not prefer the obedience and government of any man to subjection under your good-will'.[40] Here, the economic power of the woman, and the dependence on her of Lul and his colleagues, places her in a position of authority that is effectively gendered masculine. Discussing this letter, Fell reminds the reader of lament for the 'hlaford' or 'lord' in *The Wanderer* and observes that: 'a traveller from abroad might choose to put himself in the protection or overlordship of an abbess . . . a "lordless" man might choose an abbess as his *hlaford*, and . . . she would then have the full responsibility for him'.[41] Cneuburg may well have been the teacher of the three men before they left for Francia. Within the unsettled world of the German mission, the gendered lines of authority and power could be and were crossed and re-crossed, as poems, gifts, books, prayers, humans and hospitality were exchanged between men and women.

Migratory desires: Pilgrimages and prisons

Alongside prayer, poetry and gift-giving, pilgrimage was another vital religious and cultural practice that connected the missionary diaspora. It is the topic of the single letter to survive in the Bonifatian correspondence written by one woman to another, a letter that, possibly coincidentally, is also the earliest by a woman in the collection. This is authored by one Ælfflæd. She may possibly be identified with the second abbess of Whitby, who commissioned the earliest *Life of Gregory the Great* which was produced at the abbey. Ælfflæd's letter does not fit so easily into the collection, as it is not addressed either to Boniface or to Lul but rather to one Adolana or Adela, usually identified as the abbess of Pfalzel, whom Ælfflæd has not met in person but whose reputation has so impressed her that she declares that 'love for you seized me in the depths of my being'.[42] In this letter, Ælfflæd introduces another abbess, 'our dearest and most faithful daughter from the years of her youth', who is finally able to set off on a longed-for pilgrimage to Rome, and she requests that Adolana offer assistance, hospitality and directions to this woman and her travelling companions in order that they may reach their destination safely.

Within the context of pilgrimage, connections between women, who are able to give practical advice on travel specifically for women, were evidently very important. A pilgrim nun, Wethburg, is mentioned in another early letter written by Ecgburg who (as may also have been the case with Eadburg) studied under Boniface. Ecgburg wrote to Boniface describing her grief brought about by the death of her beloved brother Oshere. Anticipating Leoba's appeal to Boniface's friendship with her father, Ecgburg describes how Boniface became for her 'both father and brother' in the place of Oshere, and how her trust in him is based on the 'friendship which you surely had for my brother'.[43] It is, however, Ecgburg's immense grief at her separation from her sister Wethburg which sets this letter apart, uniquely describing, as it does, such a close bond between women:

> Et postquam mihi simul carissima soror Wethburg, quasi inflicto vulnere iteratoque dolore, subito ab oculis evanuit, cum qua adolevi, cum qua adoravi idem nutricum sinus; una mater ambobus in Domino et dereliquid; Iesum testor: ubique dolor, ubique pavor, ubique mortis imago. Malui mori, si sic Deo auspice, cui arcana non latent, placuisset, vel tarda Mors non tricaverit.
>
> Sed quid dicam nunc? Ante inprovida tandem nos non amara mors, sed amarior divisio separavit ab invicem; illam, ut reor, felicem; me vero infelicem, quasi quoddam depositum, huic saeculo servire permisit, sciens enim, quantum illam dilexi, quantum amavi, quam nunc, ut audio, Romana carcer includit.
>
> [And when at the same time my dearest sister Wethburga vanished from my sight – a new wound and a new grief; she with whom I had grown up, whom I adored and who was nursed at the same mother's breast – Christ be my witness, everywhere was grief and terror and the dread of death. Gladly would I have died if it had so pleased God from whom no secrets are hid, or if slow-coming death had not deceived me.
>
> But what shall I say now? It was not bitter death but a still more bitter and unexpected separation that divided us one from the other, leaving her, as I think, the happier and me the unhappy one to go on, like something cast aside, in my earthly service, while she, whom, as you know, I loved so tenderly, is reported to be in a Roman cell as a recluse.][44]

The shock of Wethburg's departure on pilgrimage is vividly captured: Ecgburg feared that her sister would not survive the journey, but she had not anticipated Wethburg's decision to live in strict isolation in the Holy City. Within the letter, Ecgburg incorporates sacred, learned and literary allusions (including references to Jerome's letters and the *Aeneid*) alongside an image of the 'storm-tossed sailor' that Boniface uses elsewhere to describe himself, but she combines this image with that of the 'anxious mother' waiting for her son's return from the sea. Ecgburg thus ascribes to herself roles that are, as Weston notes, both 'active male and passive female'.[45] While she still hold out hopes that they may be reunited, Ecgburg is so overwhelmed by feelings of grief for the loss of Wethburg that she mourns the sister who is still alive as if she had already died in her self-imposed imprisonment in exile.

This letter draws the reader's attention to a further example of layering of authorship within the collection. It contains a postscript by the male scribe of the letter. It was of course common, indeed expected, for literate men as well as women to make use of scribes in their correspondence and other writing, but this addendum is a timely reminder of the collaborative nature of authorship throughout the Middle Ages, where writers and scribes worked together in the production of texts. The scribe is also part of the missionary diaspora, and reminds Boniface that he promised to pray for him so that 'though we are separated in the body, may we be united in our memories'. For the scribe, if not for Ecgburg herself in this case, practices such as prayer and letter writing can bridge the physical distance that separates two people.

Another early letter to Boniface, jointly written by Bugga and her mother Eangyth, echoes closely the language of Boniface's own correspondence in which he describes at length his own suffering when mother and daughter complain that they are afflicted by 'a load of misery and . . . a crushing burden of worldly distractions'.[46] They relate their concern for the souls of the monks in their care in their double monastery (the identity of which is unknown, although Yorke suggests that it was in Kent),[47] the poverty that they have to endure, and their troubles at the hands of the king and his servants. Their situation bears similarities to that of Leoba in her first letter to Boniface as they go on to lament 'the loss of friends and compatriots, the crowd of relatives and the company of our kinsfolk':

> Non habemus filium neque fratrem, patrem aut patruum, nisi tantum unicam filiam penitus destitutam omnibus caris in hoc saeculo, praeter unam tantum sororem eius et matrem valde vetulam et filium fratris earum, et illum valde infelicem propter ipsius mentis et quia rex noster eius gentem multum exosam habet.

> [We have neither son nor brother, father nor uncle, only one daughter, whom death has robbed of all her dear ones, excepting one sister, a very aged mother, and a son of a brother, a man rendered unhappy because of his folly and also because our king has an especial grudge against his people.][48]

There is a riddling quality to this letter in which the identities of the two women of different generations merge and the reader is required to unravel the web of relationships:[49] neither woman has a brother, father or son; the daughter is Bugga; the aged mother Eangyth. The sister, Eangyth's, is passed over without comment – her worth seems minimal. The brother's son (Bugga's cousin) is named subsequently as Denewald; he too is considering joining Boniface's mission, and thus their isolation will be even greater. Even though these two women remain in their monastery, the metaphors they use to describe their sense of their own abandonment are those associated with the trauma of migration. The pains of the mother and daughter draw on imagery of waves crashing against rocks and boats that capsize and break up in the storm. The seasonal rhythms are disrupted – the women allude to the months of July and August when the days 'should lengthen out the hours of summer' but of course the days actually shorten after the mid-summer solstice. The women share this experience of nature's asynchrony, this feeling of being out of time, of being, as Carolyn Dinshaw puts it in *How Soon is Now?*, 'out of sync with the ordinarily linear measurements of everyday life'.[50] Summer brings no solace: the women find that existence exhausts them 'and it is almost a burden to live'. This suffering inspires the women to seek out Boniface as a friend who can be trusted to give good counsel. Boniface is likened to Habbakuk, sent by angels to feed Daniel in the lions' den (Daniel 14.33–8) and Philip, who taught the Ethiopian eunuch in the desert (Acts 8.26–39).

It is in this letter by Eangyth and Bugga that the parallels with the Old English elegies can begin to be seen. The women's account in this letter of their personal trauma bears comparison with the elegiac poems *The Wanderer* and *The Seafarer* in which the speakers meditate on their solitary existences, having found themselves without their lords, protective kinsmen, companions and confidants. Eangyth and Bugga also explain their own isolation as itself a form of exile even though, paradoxically, it is they who remain at home in England. Their kin have either died or travelled abroad on pilgrimage. Yet, although separated from Boniface 'by a wide expanse of sea and land and the borders of many states',[51] this distance can be traversed by letters, and also physically. Howe comments that, 'when Boniface describes himself ... as being tossed on the stormy seas of Germanic heathendom, we hear not simply a Christian speaking but an Anglo-Saxon Christian whose religious destiny has been marked by his people's history'.[52] Eangyth and Bugga deliberately draw on Boniface's own metaphor with similar effect, and in so doing, they attribute to themselves a spiritual virility that seems on closer examination somewhat at odds with their own situation, at home in England. The composite 'we' briefly switches to 'I' when Eangyth writes about her long-felt desire to visit Rome that originated when 'my only daughter [was] too young at that time to share my longing'.[53] Together, mother and daughter seek Boniface's intercession and ask for clear guidance about whether to undertake this journey. Pilgrimage is often thought of as a form of voluntary exile,[54] whereby in leaving home pilgrims find their true spiritual home, but, in the context of the Boniface correspondence, pilgrimage is also a significant cultural practice amongst the religious diaspora. Rome rather than England or Germany is for the women, as it is for Boniface, the central point of the Christian map. It is for advice on this matter that Bugga and Eangyth have greatest need of a friend.

The topic of pilgrimage recurs in a later letter from Boniface to Bugga, in which he discusses the merits of travelling to Rome.[55] Boniface is circumspect in his recommendation, and elsewhere both Boniface and Lul fall back on antifeminist stereotypes when they write about women pilgrims who end up in prostitution or living immoral lives.[56] Here, however, Boniface merely alludes to Bugga's concerns about other male and female religious and suggests to Bugga that the journey will be advantageous if, in remaining where she is, she is unable to enjoy 'freedom and a quiet mind'. He also recommends that she get in touch with Wethburg, whose absence is so mourned by her sister Ecgburg, because she has previously made the pilgrimage to Rome and has not returned. Boniface tells Bugga that he has already contacted Wethburg himself to discuss Bugga's predicament and notes that Wethburg advises against travelling while Rome is under threat from the Saracens. Another later letter from Bugga's kinsman, Æthelberht II, king of Kent, indicates that Bugga did make the journey to Rome where she spent time in prayer and discussion with Boniface, and where 'reminded as it were by the ties of our blood relationship', she interceded with Boniface on his behalf.[57] Once again the ties of kinship, whether spiritual or biological, figure strongly in the shared language of this community: during her visit to Rome, Bugga was finally united in person with the man whose friendship she and her mother sought so urgently.

A last surviving letter from Boniface to Bugga, sent, it seems, towards the end of her life, when she had retired from her role as a monastic leader, indicates that the difficulties Bugga had faced throughout her spiritual journey did not diminish over time.[58] Bugga, like Wethburg, ultimately chose to become a recluse, and thus, in a sense, to live once again as an exile, but her isolation was disturbed. In his letter, Boniface sympathises with her because of the 'storms of troubles which with God's permission have befallen you in your old age'.[59] This 'brotherly letter of comfort and exhortation' draws heavily on quotations from Scripture, as one would expect, as Boniface reiterates that tribulation is a divine gift and that those who suffer on earth will be rewarded in heaven, but it succeeds in evoking the deep emotional connection that has developed over the long course of their 'ancient friendship'.[60] Boniface reminds Bugga that 'all soldiers of Christ of either sex have despised temporal troubles and tempests and have held the frailties of this world as naught'.[61] There are, once again, echoes of *The Wanderer*, which laments the loss of a beloved lord, although here it is the anticipated death of a spiritual supporter that is described. But whereas in the second half of *The Seafarer*, old age is mourned because it brings grief and isolation,[62] in Boniface's elegiac letter the sufferings and pains of Bugga's final years are to be welcomed as a test of faith: 'rejoicing in the hope of a heavenly fatherland, hold the shield of faith and patience against all adversity of mind or body'.[63] Boniface's letter reads as a final farewell to a much-loved spiritual sister, and as a celebration of the spiritual lost origins that this community of monks and nuns hope to reclaim in the afterlife.

Diasporic loss

The writer of two early Latin poems embedded within three elegiac letters in the Boniface correspondence is Berthgyth, daughter of Cynehild and kinswoman of Lul, and, like her mother, she was an English woman missionary in Thuringia.[64] She is mentioned in Otloh's *Life of Boniface*, where she is described as being highly educated and as having been given the role of teacher in Thuringia.[65] Her high levels of literacy are confirmed by her letters and poems, which were written following the death of her mother, and which describe her loneliness in vivid terms.

In the first surviving letter Berthgyth beseechingly asks her brother Baltheard, in rhythmic prose, why he has not visited her:

> Quid est, frater mi, quod tam longum tempus intermisisti, quod venire tardasti? ... O frater, o frater mi, cur potes mentem parvitatis meae adsiduae merore fletu atque tristitia die noctuque caritatis tuae absentia adfligere?

> [Why is it, my brother, that you have let so long a time pass, that you have delayed to come? ... O brother, o my brother, for what reason can you afflict my mind with grief, tears and sadness about my constant insignificance day and night, through the absence of your love?][66]

Peter Dronke first pointed out the similarities between Berthgyth's descriptions of her love-longing for the absent Baltheard, and the anxious laments for exiled or distant lovers expressed in the two surviving female-voiced Old English elegies: *Wulf and Eadwacer* and *The Wife's Lament*.[67] The speaker of the former poem for example, cries out:

Wulf, min Wulf,   wena me þine
seoce gedydon,   þine seldcymas,
murnende mod . . .

[Wulf, my Wulf, my hopes of you
have made me sick, your rare visits,
a mourning mind . . .][68]

On the surface Berthgyth's situation seems somewhat different from that of the speaking voice in *Wulf and Eadwacer*, and, of course, she writes in Latin, the language of power and of conversion. Furthermore it is clear that her isolation from her brother is a consequence of her circumstance, as an English nun living in Germany (whether or not that circumstance was her choice). The nature of the speaker's loss in *Wulf and Eadwacer*, and indeed her identity (whether wife, adulterous woman, woman separated from or grieving her husband or lover, or mother lamenting a lost or dead child) is obscure, but the separation being mourned is clearly imposed upon her by others.[69] Nevertheless despite these differences, the parallels are striking, with the emphatic repetitions and urgent questionings, and of course, the idea of death evoked to capture the intense suffering that the separation has caused the speakers.

Berthgyth's second letter draws on the metaphor of the sea also found in *Wulf and Eadwacer* and *The Wife's Lament* as well as in the male-voiced exile poems, *The Wanderer* and of course *The Seafarer*:

Multae sunt aquarum congregationes inter me et te, tamen caritate iungamur; quia vera caritas numquam locorum limite frangitur.

[Many are the congregations of waters between me and you, yet let us be joined in love because true love is never divided by the borders between places.][70]

'The congregation of waters' that God created in Genesis 1.10 (*congregationesque aquarum appellavit maria*) is more than the sea that creates a physical barrier between Berthgyth and Baltheard. It is also witness to the 'caritas' or 'true love' that unites sister and brother in their spiritual marriage. The relationship between brother and sister was one of the strongest and most intimate kinship bonds of the time, and the intensity of Berthgyth's feelings are manifest. The metaphor of the sea or other waterways standing for enforced separation is also found in the elegies. In *Wulf and Eadwacer*, the speaker is separated from the elusive Wulf by the mire:

> Wulf is on iege,   Ic on oþerre.
> Fæst is þæt eglond,   fenne biworpen
>
> [Wulf is on an island, I on another.
> That island is secure, surrounded by fen.][71]

In *The Wife's Lament* the speaker has been left behind by her departed lord:

> Ærest min hlaford gewat   heonan of leodum
> ofer yþa gelac
>
> [First my lord went away from the people
> over tossing waves.][72]

The sea, waterways and storms are significant in these Old English poems and Latin letters that memorialize the traumas of migration and separation, whether written by or in the voice of those who feel or find themselves compelled to set out on a journey, or by or in the voice of those left behind. Yet their significance changes according to the gender of the speaker. For Boniface himself, in his own letters, as for the speaker in *The Seafarer*, travelling across the sea is, to use Howe's term, 'a Christian act'.[73] In contrast, according to Stacy S. Klein, 'the female speakers [of the elegies] . . . envision exile as being trapped in place and consigned to interminable stasis'.[74] Certainly the speaker in *Wulf and Eadwacer* is unable to escape her fastness, and can only wait for Wulf's 'seldcymas' [rare visits], while the speaker in *The Wife's Lament* is confined in isolation 'in þam eorðscræfe' [in the earth-cave].[75] Berthgyth too represents herself as constrained spatially and temporally, unable to return to her homeland and her beloved brother. For all the Biblical references, and despite her own active role as a missionary, Berthgyth represents herself quite differently to Boniface. Whatever the reality behind her situation, she figures herself not as one who has chosen exile in fulfilment of the divine plan, but as one who has exile forced upon her.

Of all the letters in the Boniface collection, Berthgyth's are the ones that can be most read as individual testimonies. They are infused with Biblical allusions, and she presents herself as Job-like in her suffering. At the same time, her love-laments for her absent brother resonate with the language of the Song of Songs: the reader is again and again forced to confront and question the sheer intensity of her feelings towards her sibling. As with *Wulf and Eadwacer* and *The Wife's Lament*, where the identities of the speakers, the circumstances of their exile, and the nature of their relationships are all ambiguous, there is again something enigmatic about Berthgyth's writing. The second letter ends with ten lines of rhyming octosyllabic verse written in a style that mirrors the alliterative half-lines of Old English poetry and an invocation that seems to be intended to end her separation from her brother:

> Valeamus angelicis victrices iungi milibus,
> Paradisi perpetuis perdurantes in gaudiis.
> Elonqueel et Michael, Acaddai, Adonai, Alleuatia, alleluia.

> [May we thrive, victresses joined with the angelic thousands,
> Living forever in the perpetual joys of Paradise,
> Elonqueel and Michael, Acaddai, Adonai, Alleuatia, Alleluia.][76]

Stevenson observes that Berthgyth 'underlines the vehemence of her plea for her and her brother's safety and salvation with a string of magical names (mostly names for God in garbled Hebrew) which she may have thought of as ensuring that her prayer would be heeded'.[77] Berthygyth seeks divine assistance to find relief from her internal torments. Berthgyth's hope that she might be united with her brother in heaven seems highly conventional, but elsewhere Stevenson draws our attention to a gender confusion in these lines – the Latin feminine plural noun *vitrices* is used to describe Berthgyth and her brother rather than the masculine *victores* – that may indicate that the poem was first written for another woman rather than for Berthgyth's brother and only subsequently incorporated into the letter.[78] Weston adds, 'If so, it is perhaps interesting that a female–female bond of purely synthetic monastic kinship offers [Berthgyth] a less conflicted space for the reconstruction of self than the female-male bonds she shares with her brother in blood and in faith'.[79] However this conclusion is, perhaps, too easy – why should 'synthetic' same-sex kinship be assumed to be 'less conflicted' than a biological sibling relationship between a woman and man? The gender confusion points to a gap between the ostensible object of longing in the poem identified as the recipient of the letter (Berthgyth's brother) and an alternative, unnamed object, gendered female. *The Wife's Lament* opens with the statement:

> Ic þis giedd wrece   bi me ful geomorre,
> minre sylfre sið

> [I relate this mournful riddle about myself,
> about my own journey.][80]

The riddle of Berthgyth's poem, in contrast, is not who is the speaker or what has happened to her. Rather, as in *Wulf and Eadwacer*, where the identity of Wulf in particular is unclear, to the extent that we cannot even be sure that he is a man rather than a beast,[81] the unanswered question in Berthgyth's poem is: whom does the speaker really desire?

The third letter, written in response to a reply from Baltheard that does not seem to have been entirely satisfactory, is less elaborate in its language, but it too ends with a short poem, which, like the earlier one, shows the influence of Aldhelm in its composition. Although the verses seem to offer hope, as Christ 'abolishes sins, cruel hazards, both new and old',[82] the overall tone of the letter is similar to the earlier one, and the theme of exile remains. Berthgyth complains that 'When I see and hear other women going to travel to their friends' then she remembers how 'I was abandoned by my parents in my youth and I remain here alone',[83] and she continues to plead to Baltheard that he come to her. The concluding lines of *The Wife's Lament* certainly resonate with Berthgyth's poetry and prose:

> Wa bið þam þe sceal
> of langoðe leofes abidan
> [It is misery for those, who, longing,
> have to wait for a loved one.][84]

In this her final surviving letter, Berthgyth describes how it is her wish that she should be able to visit the graves of her parents where she can end this '*temporalem vitam*' or 'transitory life',[85] a commonplace that nevertheless reminds us of the laments of the Wanderer and of the Seafarer.[86] The desire to be united in her death with her dead parents found in Berthgyth's final surviving letter resonates too with modern diasporic nostalgia or a '"diaspora aesthetic"', which Stuart Hall describes in these terms: 'the endless desire to return to "lost origins," to be one again with the mother, to go back to the beginning'.[87] Berthgyth, despairing of being with her brother, at least while she remains in this life, also wishes to 'go back to the beginning'.

Conclusion

The women's letters in the Boniface correspondence are connected by cultural practices and productions as well as emotions that centre on the conversion mission, and which function to keep alive connections between the religious diaspora; practices and productions that include copying and exchanging books, present-giving, education and scholarship, exchange of people, pilgrimage, spiritual friendship and support, and the composition and sharing of poetry. Biological and spiritual kinships were vital to the forging of strong links between those who saw themselves in exile abroad and those at home. A striking recurring focus of these letters, and of the poetry embedded within them, is loss and isolation. Many letters are concerned with describing the writers' traumatic experiences that result from the death or absence of kin. The pain they describe is closely tied to the missionary activities of the nuns and of their family and friends. These are women who endured the trauma of being left behind when others migrated overseas, or who in travelling away from their homeland, found themselves alone in an alien environment. In testifying in their letters to their private traumas, they contributed to a developing public discourse that is at times closely aligned to the elegiac form of celebrated Old English poetry. These letters, which comprise some of the earliest surviving writings definitively written by English women, are a testimony to the impressive scholarship of these early nuns, which extended from studying scripture to instructing and teaching, and from copying manuscripts to composing sophisticated, evocative and often emotive prose and verse.

Exemplary Missionary Lives

Introduction

The women missionaries in Germany provide still further extraordinary examples of women's writing in the *Lives* of two brothers, Willibald and Wynnebald, authored by the late eighth-century nun, Hugeburc or Hygeburg (*fl.* 760–80).[1] This chapter focuses on the former, Hugeburc's *Hodoeporicon* or voyage narrative of St Willibald, which offers an account of the saint's life and of his pilgrimage to the Holy Land in the 730s that is based closely on the saint's own oral account, which he dictated to her some forty years later in 778, and which is therefore very much the product of collaborative authorship.[2] Hugeburc was a nun of the monastery of Heidenheim, founded by Wynnebald in 752. Walburg, sister of Willibald and Wynnebald, became abbess following Wynnebald's death in 761, and at that point Heidenheim became a double monastery.[3] Hugeburc joined at the same time. Hugeburc was related to this powerful missionary family both biologically and spiritually and was deeply personally invested in her hagiographical writings. Pauline Head describes Hugeburc as possibly 'the only woman of her time to write biographies of male saints'.[4] The earliest surviving manuscript of Hugeburc's two hagiographies is Munich, Bayerische Staatsbibliothek, Codex latinus monacensis (Clm) 1086, which also includes Willibald's own life of Boniface.[5] Written in a Carolingian miniscule, it is usually dated to the early ninth century and assumed to have been copied at Willibald's own monastery of Eichstätt.[6] But the lives by Hugeburc in this manuscript seem to be very closely related to her original version, and Andreas Bauch even suggests they could have been copied in Hugeburc's own lifetime, in the late eighth century, at Heidenheim itself.[7] The life of Wynnebald is on fols 44v–71v and the life of Willibald on fols 71v–102r. This chapter contrasts Hugeburc's text with its self-deprecating depiction of the woman writer with Rudolf of Fulda's ninth-century *Life of Leoba* (written *c.* 836, over fifty years after Leoba's death).[8] The *Life of Leoba*, commissioned by the abbot of Fulda, Hrabanus Maurus (*c.* 780–856), shortly before the translation of Leoba's body and in support of her cult,[9] provides further evidence of the scholarly and textual communities of early medieval women that existed both at home and abroad, communities which in this case were closely linked to Fulda, a major centre of learning and monastic book production.[10] Indeed, Leoba's monastery in Tauberbischofsheim may well have had a scriptorium where the nuns routinely copied books for their own use and also for others.[11] A case can be made for female collaboration in the writing of this hagiography, including (as with Hugeburc's text) some dependency on the saint's own words and self-fashioning, and indeed Rudolf claims that his text reworks the somewhat garbled notes taken down by a monk, Mago, notes which were in turn based on the memoirs of four named nuns. However, as Rudolf is more distanced from his subject than Hugeburc is from hers, he has more opportunity to rework his raw materials. The *Life of Leoba* thus also provides a further example of male monastic overwriting of women's authority and female sources.

Travels with her kin: Hugeburc's *Hodoeporicon of St Willibald*

Hugeburc introduces herself at the start of her life of Willibald as an '*indigna Saxonica*' [unworthy Saxon Woman] ('Vita Willibaldi', 86; translation my own) seemingly deflecting attention away from herself and onto actual and future readers, whom she identifies as men of the Church (monks, priests, deacons and abbots). Hugeburc asserts that she is motivated to write by a desire to preserve the memory of Willibald for posterity. Such protestations are commonplace in hagiographic writing. Sulpicius Severus, in the preface to his fourth-century *Life of St Martin*, for example, justifies writing an account of his pious contemporary by explaining that he did not do so with the intention that it would be publically circulated:

> Ego quidem, frater unanimis, libellum quem de vita sancti Martini scripseram, scheda sua premere et intra domesticos parietes cohibere decreveram, quia, ut sum natura infirmissimus, iudicia humana vitabam, ne, quod fore arbitror, sermo incultior legentibus displiceret omniumque reprehensionis dignissimus iudicarer, qui materiem disertis merito scriptoribus reservandam impudens occupassem: sed petenti tibi saepius negare non potui.

> [I had determined, my like-minded brother, to keep private, and confine within the walls of my own house, the little treatise which I had written concerning the life of St. Martin. I did so, as I am not gifted with much talent, and shrank from the criticisms of the world, lest (as I think will be the case) my somewhat

unpolished style should displease my readers, and I should be deemed highly worthy of general reprehension for having too boldly laid hold of a subject which ought to have been reserved for truly eloquent writers. But I have not been able to refuse your request again and again presented.]¹²

Sulpicius Severus claims in quite conventional terms that he lacks rhetorical ability, but states that he is motivated to record and share this narrative in order that 'he should not remain unknown who was a man worthy of imitation'. Like Hugeburc, he is inspired to write by the sanctity of his subject.

In contrast Hugeburc apologizes specifically because, as she says, she is *'feminea fragilique sexus inbecillitate corruptibilia, nulla prerogativa sapientiae suffultus aut magnarum virium industria elata'* [corruptible by the feminine frailty of the fragile sex, neither supported by the prerogative of wisdom nor elevated by the industry of great strength] ('Vita Willibaldi', 86; translation my own). She responds to Church anxieties concerning women's teaching (1 Timothy 2.12: 'But I suffer not a woman to teach, nor to use authority over the man: but to be in silence') by emphasizing that she is aware that she lacks the authority and experience required for writing the life and miracles of her subject. Indeed as with the anonymous Whitby *Life of Gregory* (discussed in Chapter 1), critics have commented on her difficult and somewhat flawed Latin, which nevertheless has been described in more positive terms as 'ambitious'.¹³ Once again, what is understood as evidence of more limited linguistic competence by one reader might be interpreted as innovation and experimentation by another. Hugeburc may, of course, hope to deflect negative criticism that she fears her presumption in undertaking such a novel task may engender. Yet even as Hugeburc apologizes for her apparent boldness, which she recognizes might seem inappropriate in a woman, she asserts that it is the very male clerical authority that might otherwise oppose her undertaking that encourages it, through its generosity and wisdom. Her confidence in the support of her male counterparts may well reflect her experience as a nun within a double monastery, where men and women worked side by side in the service of God.

Hugeburc's disclaimer that she is a conduit of divine will and that it is the grace of God that inspires her is itself conventional. Her dismissal of her role as hagiographer anticipates by several hundred years the famous apology offered by the fourteenth-century woman visionary Julian of Norwich:

Botte God forbede that ye shulde saye or take it so that I am a techere. For I meene nought so, no I mente nevere so. For I am a woman, lewed, febille, and freylle.

[But God forbid that you should say or understand that I am a teacher. Because that is not what I mean, nor did I ever mean thus. For I am a woman, uneducated, feeble, and frail.][14]

There is something of an inevitable paradox in Hugeburc's adoption of the humility topos, because even as she directs her readers away from herself, she makes them very aware of her identity: a female religious from a saintly Saxon family. And indeed within the text of MS Clm 1086 at fol. 71v, she encrypts a sentence containing her own name by substituting the vowels with abbreviations for ordinal numbers. She thus ensures that, like the narrative she recounts, her name is preserved for posterity, and her role as writer is acknowledged even as it is disguised (see Figure 4.1). Unencrypted, the Latin reads: '*Ego una Saxonica nomine Hugeburc ordinando hec scribebam*' [I, a Saxon nun named Hugeburc, wrote this].[15] In so doing, as Pauline Head points out, Hugeburc, fits into a tradition of overt as well as 'covert expressions of identity and the desire to be recognized and remembered' that includes not only monks of Fulda, but also anticipates the ninth-century English poet Cynewulf, and the writer Dhuoda (*c.* 803–*c.* 843), whose *Liber manualis* was addressed to her son, William of Septimania.[16]

Later in her text, Hugeburc authorizes her own narration further by embedding within it Willibald's own retelling of his adventures to Pope Gregory III when he finally returns to Rome (*Hodoeporicon*, 173). Hugeburc's account of Willibald's wanderings, which are described at such length, is here recounted in brief, reduced to his travels to Bethlehem and the Jordan and to the four visits to Jerusalem. This story is given the seal of approval by the Pontiff himself. Hugeburc then reiterates that she is basing her account on Willibald's own words, and that the accuracy of her text can be attested to by male religious authorities:

Transacto atque terminato prolixa iteneris meatu Willibaldi, quam ille sagax in 7 annorum indutia lustrando adiebat, illa nunc reperta et ex ritu rimata explanare intimareque conavimus, et non ab alio reperta nisi ab ipso audita et ex illius ore dictata perscripsimus in monasterio Heidanheim, testibus mihi diaconis eius et aliis nonnullis iunioris eius. Ideo dico hoc, ut nullus iterum dicat frivolum fuisse.
'Vita Willibaldi', 105

[The long course of Willibald's travels and sightseeing on which he had spent seven long years was now over and gone. We have tried to set down and make known all the facts which have been ascertained and thoroughly investigated. These facts were not learned from anyone else but heard from Willibald himself; and having received them from his own lips, we have taken them down and written them in the Monastery of Heidenheim, as his deacons and other

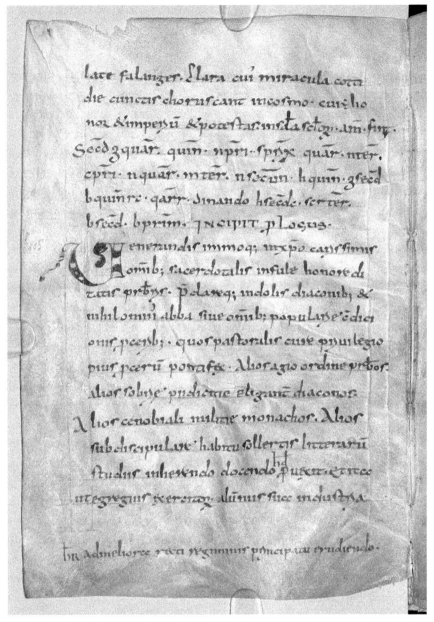

Fig. 4.1 Codex latinus monacensis (Clm) 1086, fol. 71v. Bayerische Staatsbibliothek München. Reproduced with permission.

subordinates can testify. I say this so that no one may afterwards say that it was an idle tale.]

Hodoeporicon, 175

The very place in which the life has been written adds to its credibility. Hugeburc draws an implicit but crucial distinction between a fiction or fable based on lies and fabrication and her own divinely sanctioned narrative rooted in truth and written to instruct in line with Romans 15.4: 'for what things soever were written were written for our learning.'

At the same time as Hugeburc defers to the authority of God, the authority of her subject Willibald, and the authority of the male clergy, she also assumes an authority of her own, not as a woman, but as a *kins*woman, or as she puts it, a 'humble relative' of Willibald himself (*Hodoeporicon*, 153). As we saw in the previous chapter in relation to the women correspondents in Boniface's circle, bonds of kin were extremely significant amongst the English missionaries. As Lisa M. C. Weston explains, 'premodern identities – including gender and sexual identities – are not so much personal and individual as they are constructed in relation to community, and especially to kin-group'.[17] Indeed Hugeburc implies that it is this bond of kinship that ultimately justifies her assumption of the responsibility of recording Willibald's adventures over the claims of the more educated male clergy. Certainly bonds of kinship are emphasized throughout the narrative that Hugeburc relates. Willibald's parents are portrayed as acting on the advice of their kin when making the decision that he should become a child oblate (*Hodoeporicon*, 155). Hugeburc represents Willibald's pilgrimage as an exile, a separation from the security of wealth, homeland and kin (*Hodoeporicon*, 156), even though Willibald himself insists that his father and his brother Wynnebald should accompany him on his pilgrimage in the face of his father's own initial resistance to being separated from the rest of his family.[18] As Aidan Conti notes, Hugeburc's writings 'help elevate her male relations to saintly status within a region in which her extended family acted as settlers (and people intent on changing indigenous customs to conform to those of the dominant ideology of Christianity)'.[19]

Following her opening preamble, Hugeburc goes on to explain that she will structure her account of Willibald's life and travels in terms of the four ages of man, beginning with his infancy, before moving onto his life as a young man, and from there to his maturity and old age (*Hodoeporicon*, 154; and *cf.* 156).[20] Willibald's early childhood is marked by a paralysing illness, which brought him close to death. The age when he is struck down – only three years old – is symbolic, mirroring the three days between the Crucifixion and the Resurrection. As soon as Willibald's parents vow to dedicate the sick infant to a religious life, he is instantly miraculously cured. By the age of five, Willibald is portrayed as beginning to demonstrate reason as he begins his monastic education at Bishops Waltham. Even as a child Willibald dedicated himself to assiduous study and to contemplation, but it was when he reached his young manhood that he began to forge his own destiny, as he formed the resolution to undertake his pilgrimage to the shrine of St Peter in Rome. Willibald is now depicted as a Christian soldier, dedicated to his cause.

Significantly, Willibald's young manhood is also marked by critical illness when he and his brother fall ill in Rome only to be healed again by divine grace (*Hodoeporicon*, 159). Willibald also falls ill at the moment of his arrival at the Church of the Holy Sepulchre in Jerusalem (*Hodoeporicon*, 166), and when he starts to recover he visits Solomon's Porch, which he identifies with the Pool of Bethesda and the curing of the paralysed man in John 5.2–8. Subsequently, when he is travelling from Bethlehem back into Gaza, he visits a church where he attends mass, and temporarily goes blind, only to be cured once more a couple of months later when he returns to the Church of the Holy Sepulchre in Jerusalem (*Hodoeporicon*, 168). This disability, with its clear resonances of the conversion of St Paul, signals a key moment in his spiritual development. Indeed Willibald's next recorded illness occurs as he travels around Syria, before returning to Damascus (*Hodoeporicon*, 169).

At the same time as Willibald's life is structured according to the ages of man, his development is also figured in terms of the exemplary lives of the saints. The text is punctuated with allusions to pious role models, such as Martin of Tours (*Hodoeporicon*, 158; and *cf.* 166). Like Willibald, St Martin was also inspired to follow the monastic life from early in his life:

> nam cum esset annorum decem, invitis parentibus ad ecclesiam confugit seque catechumenum fieri postulavit. mox mirum in modum totus in Dei opere conversus, cum esset annorum duodecim, eremum concupivit, fecissetque votis satis, si aetatis infirmitas non obstitisset. animus tamen aut circa monasteria aut circa ecclesiam semper intentus meditabatur adhuc in aetate puerili, quod postea devotus implevit.

> [For, when he was of the age of ten years, he betook himself, against the wish of his parents, to the Church, and begged that he might become a catechumen [*ie* be instructed in preparation for baptism]. Soon afterwards, becoming in a wonderful manner completely devoted to the service of God, when he was

twelve years old, he desired to enter on the life of a hermit; and he would have followed up that desire with the necessary vows, had not his as yet too youthful age prevented. His mind, however, being always engaged on matters pertaining to the monasteries or the Church, already meditated in his boyish years what he afterwards, as a professed servant of Christ, fulfilled.][21]

A former soldier, this saint travelled widely before becoming bishop of Tours and founding the Abbey of Marmoutier. His life thus anticipates Willibald's own consecration as bishop at Salzburg, and the founding of the monastery at Eichstätt, a point that is underlined when Willibald's consecration is dated to 'three weeks before the Feast of St. Martin' (*Hodoeporicon*, 175). Throughout the narrative, saints are mentioned either in relation to their feast days, as in the case of Martin of Tours, or in relation to the shrines and tombs visited by Willibald on his travels. Nevertheless, their significance may well extend further, as may be the case in relation to his visits to the shrines of St Agatha of Sicily, who died in prison, and the Seven Sleepers of Ephesus, who were entrapped within a cave (*Hodoeporicon*, 160). The imprisonments of these saints anticipate Willibald's own tribulations: Hugeburc goes on to describe at some length two occasions when Willibald and his companions are arrested and imprisoned as spies in Syria, and brought before a Saracen leader who may have been Umayyad Caliph Yazid bin Abd al-Malik (Yazid II), and who is referred to by Willibald as *Myrmumni*, a corruption of 'Amir al-Mu'minin' (Arabic أمير المؤمنين) [Leader of the Faithful] ('Vita Willibaldi', 95; cf. *Hodoeporicon*, 163). Another example of a saint whose experiences resonate with those of Willibald is St Apollinaris. Willibald's ordination is dated to the Feast of Mary Magdalene, but also to the Feast of Apollinaris, the Syrian saint and martyr, who became the first bishop of Ravenna (*Hodoeporicon*, 175). Given Willibald's pilgrimages through Italy and Syria, it is likely that Apollinaris would have been another figure with whom he closely identified. Female saints as well as male saints are considered worthy of veneration and emulation: St Helena, for example, is mentioned twice; once in the context of the discovery of the True Cross (*Hodoeporicon*, 165), and also in the context of her church building (*Hodoeporicon*, 161). St Eustochium is also mentioned, in relation to the monastery which she built between Jericho and Jerusalem (*Hodoeporicon*, 165).

Hugeburc only returns to the ages of man structure after the lengthy account of Willibald's pilgrimage. She offers a developmental narrative of Willibald's subsequent career as a monk in St Benedict's monastery in Monte Cassino, recounting that he spent a year as sacristan, a year as dean and eight years as porter (*Hodoeporicon*, 172–3), and records his progression from being ordained as a priest to being consecrated as a bishop (*Hodoeporicon*, 175). Indeed, Willibald's consecration is explicitly represented as the apex of his life. Twice we are told that Willibald is forty-one years old when he is made a bishop, and Hugeburc states at this age he was 'already mature and middle-aged' (*Hodoeporicon*, 175). However, at this point Hugeburc silently abandons the structure she set out at the start, choosing not to conclude with Willibald's frail old age (he was in his late seventies when he related his travels to Hugeburc). Instead, Hugeburc ends her account of Willibald by praising his exemplary life in Bavaria, where he laboured as a missionary and teacher. Hugeburc elaborates on his activities by drawing on the metaphors of Willibald as the (female) worker bee, carrying honey back to the hive, and Willibald as the hen, protecting her chicks (*Hodoeporicon*, 176). Thus Willibald does not decline into infirmity and weakness but remains vigorous and full of life. Again, as with his identification with female saints, gender lines are crossed but, ultimately upheld: Willibald is also a spiritual athlete (gendered male) (*Hodoeporicon*, 174) and a ploughman (*Hodoeporicon*, 176).

The heart of Hugeburc's narrative is not, however, Willibald's life as a missionary, but his life as a pilgrim, and it is this that makes Hugeburc's text so very remarkable. Her subject is less Willibald than his travels. Indeed another text with which Hugeburc's *Hodoeporicon* resonates is the late fourth-century, fragmentary *Pilgrimage of Egeria*, written in epistolary form by an early European woman, and addressed to a community of women, in which Egeria gives a detailed account of her own travels in the Holy Land.[22] It is tempting to speculate that Hugeburc may have been frustrated in her desire to go on such a pilgrimage herself, and set herself the task of writing her relative's life in order to share his experiences vicariously.[23] Hugeburc emphasizes from the very beginning of her account of Willibald's extended wanderings that she is basing her account on that given by Willibald himself, stating: 'We heard them from his own lips in the presence of two deacons who will vouch for their truth' (*Hodoeporicon*, 153). Here the deference to male authority serves to deflect attention away from what might otherwise be seen as Hugeburc's defiance of gender norms and literary convention. For what is most striking in this life of the still-living Willibald, and what sets it apart from other hagiographies, is its emphasis on places and scenes rather than miracles and on *travel* rather than acts, and its extended and detailed accounts, not of the pious individual himself, but of his journeys and locations. And at the same time as Hugeburc chooses to make the sites a major focus of her text, mapping in some considerable detail the routes taken, and the geographies traversed, she also locates the pilgrimage in time.

However this is not calendar time, in the sense of recording the actual years in which the events of the pilgrimage took place, but a combination of cyclic, seasonal or liturgical time, starting with the day, month and season (but not the year) when Willibald recounted his travels to his kinswoman and her companions: 'it was on the 20th of June, the day before the summer solstice' (*Hodoeporicon*, 153).[24] This date has a clear significance. It occurs only four days before the feast of the Nativity of St John the Baptist, and the two dates were often associated in medieval celebrations. Another missionary, St Eligius, bishop of Noyon-Tournai in North-East France, in the seventh century, was said to have denounced the continuity of pagan customs and festivals, and specifically prohibited marking this astronomical event with the following injunction: 'No Christian on the feast of Saint John or the solemnity of any other saint performs solestitia [solstice rites?] or dancing or leaping or diabolical chants.'[25] As Hugeburc's narrative reveals, John the Baptist as the precursor of Christ and as an itinerant ascetic is yet another important model for Willibald, although Willibald of course is figured as the one who follows rather than anticipates the Messiah. Immediately before their arrest in Syria, Willibald and his fellow pilgrims visited what is now the city of Homs, and a church dedicated to St John the Baptist by St Helena (*Hodoeporicon*, 161). In the Holy Land, they visit the monastery of St John the Baptist in Caesarea (*Hodoeporicon*, 164), and later the resting place of St John's body (*Hodoeporicon*, 169). More significantly, perhaps, the account of Willibald's extensive travels in the Holy Land is punctuated with an interlude describing his encounter in an olive plain with a ferocious lion, which did not attack him but rather let him pass with his companions (*Hodoeporicon*, 170). The lion is an attribute of St Mark, whose Gospel begins with the description of John the Baptist's 'voice ... crying in the desert' (Mark 1.3). Lions were also associated with the desert fathers and mothers, such as Paul of Thebes or Mary of Egypt, and the implication is that, inspired by John the Baptist, Willibald in his wanderings had become a desert father of his own time.[26] Willibald is described as accompanied by an Ethiopian and his camels, and a woman on a mule. This episode also resonates with Acts 8.26–39, in which Philip converts and baptizes the Ethiopian eunuch, but here Willibald is the one who is instructed: it is the Ethiopian who assures him that he need not fear the lion.

Time itself seems to be refracted in Hugeburc's account, as present and past seasons converge to provide a repetitive cycle. Following the reference to the summer solstice at the start of the text, the next season to be mentioned is the late summer, when Willibald and his father and brother set off on their first sea voyage from Hamblemouth, near modern Southampton (*Hodoeporicon*, 157).

The arrival of Willibald and Wynnebald in Rome occurs at the time of the Feast of Martin of Tours (11 November), which marks the beginning of winter. The brothers remained there, we are told, throughout the following Easter (*Hodoeporicon*, 158). A year later, Willibald, travelling without his brother, arrives in Cyprus, and remains there until the Feast of John the Baptist (*Hodoeporicon*, 161). He first arrives at the Church of the Holy Sepulchre in Jerusalem on the Feast of St Martin (*Hodoeporicon*, 166). His illness in Syria lasts for the season of Lent (*Hodoeporicon*, 169). His journey from Tyre to Constantinople in turn lasts from the Feast of St Andrew until shortly before Easter (*Hodoeporicon*, 170). Willibald's arrival in Monte Cassino, where he joins the monastic community at St Benedict's, is in autumn, marking his return to Europe, and also his greater maturity (*Hodoeporicon*, 172).

Willibald's life is also measured in reference to Christian numerology, in which the numbers seven and ten both represent perfection. Willibald's ten years of pilgrimage (seven since he left Rome) are mirrored in the ten years spent in St Benedict's monastery (*Hodoeporicon*, 172–3). The climax of the narrative is Willibald's final pilgrimage, as it were, which takes place when Willibald is directed by the Pope to go to Francia to join St Boniface in his mission, a journey that lasts from Easter to the Feast of St Andrew (*Hodoeporicon*, 174). Willibald travels via his father's grave in Lucca, and is sent by Boniface on to Eichstätt. Subsequently he visits his brother Wynnebald, meeting him again for the first time since his original pilgrimage to Rome; this reunion occurs, we are told, in the autumn (*Hodoeporicon*, 175). Thus his journey circles around and takes him, if not back to his geographical point of origin (he does not return to England), then back to the father and brother with whom he set off on his expedition. Again we are told that these travels (culminating in his consecration as bishop and the building of the monastery) last seven years in total (*Hodoeporicon*, 175).

Another remarkable feature of Hugeburc's text is the assiduous plotting of the journey, which enables the reader to construct a mental map from the mouth of the River Hamble across the channel to the coast of France, and from thence to Rouen and on to Lucca, where Willibald's father fell ill and died, and then by foot to Rome itself. From Rome, Willibald and his companions journeyed by land and sea down the coast of Italy to Sicily, across the Adriatic and on towards Asia, via Syria to the Holy Land. Strikingly, when Willibald and his men are finally released from their imprisonment, the men who vouch for them describe England as being on the very edge of the world: 'These men come from the West where the sun sets; we know nothing of their country except that beyond it lies nothing but water' (*Hodoeporicon*, 163). Willibald's travels around the Holy Land are viewed through the lens of the New Testament miracles: he comes from Damascus, and the site of the conversion of St Paul, arriving in Nazareth in Galilee, where the Annunciation took place, and so on (*Hodoeporicon*, 163). In this part of the narrative in particular the descriptions of the journey and the sights viewed far outweigh the details of the life of Willibald himself. Here, the voice of Hugeburc and the voice of Willibald momentarily converge when we are told 'There, between two fountains, they passed the night and the shepherd gave *us* [*nobis* rather than *illus*] sour milk to drink' (*Hodoeporicon*, 164).

If England stands at the edge of the Christian world, Jerúsalem of course is situated at its centre, and at the centre of Jerusalem lies the Church of the Holy Sepulchre, the site of Calvary, which is described in loving detail (*Hodoeporicon*, 165–6). Textually, Willibald's arrival in Jerusalem is marked by a reminder that Hugeburc's narrative is based on his eyewitness account: 'Willibald himself said that in front of the gate stood a tall pillar . . .' (*Hodoeporicon*, 166). But this cue is almost redundant because of the tremendous guidebook-like detail included in the descriptions of churches and sites in Jerusalem and its environs in particular. Here the architectural facets, furnishings and natural elements vie for dominance with the layering of Biblical context: in the Church of the Holy Sepulchre, the fifteen lamps on the rock where Christ's body was placed; the bronze candlestick on the spot of Christ's Ascension; the portable altar that can be carried into the grotto where Christ was born in the Church of the Nativity in Bethlehem. (*Hodoeporicon*, 166 and 167). The text is careful to distinguish replicas from original features, such as the replica crosses outside the Church of the Holy Sepulchre, or the replica rock in front of the entrance to the tomb (*Hodoeporicon*, 165 and 166). Jerusalem serves as Willibald's base for this period in his life and he returns there four times from his travels across the Holy Land.

To conclude, from a modern perspective, the life of Willibald can at times seem less like a hagiography than a naturalistic pilgrimage narrative. Hugeburc succeeds in describing her subject's journeys as if she had been there herself. The journey by boat to the continent is described as evocatively as any found in the Boniface correspondence, with 'the west wind blowing and a high sea running, amidst the shouting of sailors and the creaking of oars' (*Hodoeporicon*, 157). In recounting the journey by foot over the Apennines, Hugeburc assumes the perspective of her subject, admiring the 'peaks covered with snow and wreathed in banks of clouds' (*Hodoeporicon*, 158). The narrative has the authenticity of an eye-witness account. We are told that, on Willibald's arrival in Phygela after visiting the tomb of St John the Evangelist, he and his companions 'begged some bread and went to a fountain in the middle of the city, and, sitting on the edge of it, they dipped their bread in the water and so ate' (*Hodoeporicon*, 160). The details draw us into the story as if we, as readers, were present alongside Hugeburc when she listened to Willibald's recollections, as is illustrated by the visualization of the current position of the crosses exterior to the Church of the Holy Sepulchre, 'not inside the church, but outside beneath a pent roof' (*Hodoeporicon*, 165). Practical details of travel are also recounted, such as the difficulty of gaining a safe passage across Syria (*Hodoeporicon*, 169). The rather morally ambivalent account of Willibald's second visit to Tyre focuses on his arrest under suspicion of smuggling: it records that Willibald is indeed carrying balsam but has hidden it in a sealed gourd, and he is released (*Hodoeporicon*, 170).[27] Particularly fascinating is the account of the Hell of Theodric on the island of Vulcano. This description, with its focus on the natural rather than the supernatural world, is quite distinct from the visions of purgatory and hell found, for example, in the vision of the monk of Much Wenlock, discussed in Chapter 2: 'the black and terrible and fearful flame belching forth from the crater with a noise like rolling thunder . . . the enormous flames, and the mountainous clouds of smoke rising from below into the sky' (*Hodoeporicon*, 171–2). Hugeburc has little interest in the marvellous or the monstrous. This world – as experienced by and through her kinsman Willibald – is sufficient wonder in and of itself, and she does not need to look beyond.

The anxious hagiographer: Rudolf of Fulda's *Life of Leoba*

From the outset it is clear that Rudolf of Fulda's *Life of Leoba* is produced within a milieu of women's literary culture. Its subject is of course the saintly virgin Leoba, but in one manuscript witness, dating to the third quarter of the eleventh century, Munich, Bayerische Staatsbibliothek, Codex latinus monacensis (Clm) 11321, fols 101r–120r, the life is explicitly dedicated to another abbess, Hadamout, usually identified as Hathumod of Gandersheim (*c.* 840–874).[28] The dedicatee is instructed to read it for profit – she must seek to emulate Leoba in her own life – but also for her own pleasure (*Life of Leoba*, 205). As Hathumod was not born when Rudolf completed the *Life*, he must have added this dedication some years later. The audience is however extended in this dedication to include the entire community of nuns, not dissimilar to the wider readership intended by Rudolf from the start, which would clearly have also included the monastic community at Fulda itself.

From the start of the Prologue proper, Rudolf stresses that his *Life* depends heavily on the testimony of four female followers of Leoba: Agatha, Thecla, Nana and Eoloba (*Life of Leoba*, 205). Elizabeth Alvilda Petroff goes so far as to attribute two episodes in the *Life* to Agatha and Thecla, specifically.[29] But even as Rudolf acknowledges the importance of his four female witnesses, he locates their histories within the textual frame of clerical accounts, produced for the benefit of future generations, thus transforming the ephemeral memories of the nuns into the enduring memorials of the monks. According to Weston, 'Rudolf's textualization ... effectively writes the women he addresses out of the realm of textual and cultural production'.[30] While it is usually assumed that Rudolf states that the nuns' testimony was oral and only subsequently inscribed by male clerics ('each one copied them down according to *his* ability': *Life of Leoba*, 205; my italics), Clare A. Lees and Gillian R. Overing have pointed out that the Latin text is not clear on this point (*sui* might be read as 'their' rather than 'his'), and that the named nuns rather than the unnamed clerics may have produced these written accounts.[31] Whether or not we accept this reading, these women evidently collaborated in the writing of Leoba's hagiography.[32] Furthermore, according to a study by Virginia Blanton and Helene Scheck, the text itself gains much of its authority from Leoba herself, and, rather like Hugeburc's retelling of Willibald's travels, it must ultimately be based on its subject's own account of her experiences: as they put it, 'Leoba's *vita*, therefore, is as much a narrative of her own construction as it is one that Rudolf composes'.[33]

Despite, or perhaps *because* of this, from the outset, Rudolf comes across as a particularly anxious hagiographer. In terms of hagiographic models, Rudolf's *Life of Leoba* might be usefully contrasted with Venantius Fortunatus's sixth-century *Life of Radegund*.[34] It certainly begins very differently. While in his prologue Venantius Fortunatus alludes to his own 'homely style', he is a far more confident narrator.[35] Within both the dedication and also the Prologue to the *Life*, Rudolf, like Hugeburc, falls back on the humility topos in describing his own spiritual inadequacies, even using the same language of unworthiness (*Life of Leoba*, 205). However, while Rudolf prays for divine inspiration to provide him with sufficient rhetorical skill to be able to do justice to the virtues of his subject (skill in which, like Sulpicius Severus, he evidently feels he may otherwise prove to be inadequate), unlike Hugeburc, he does not apologize for his own lack of eloquence. And even though he does not enjoy the connection of kinship with Leoba that Hugeburc has with Willibald, and although, again unlike Hugeburc, he has never met his subject, far less heard her story directly from her own lips, this does not seem to matter to him. Rather, even in the opening lines, Rudolf expresses his concern about the incompleteness of his own narrative, which he blames on the inadequacy of his sources, because, as he explains, he has 'been unable to discover all the facts of her life' (*Life of Leoba*, 205). He goes further and blames one particular individual, a monk whom he identifies by name as Mago, who died a few years before Rudolf began writing (*Life of Leoba*, 205). Mago, we are told, often met with the four nuns, and recorded brief details of the conversations he had with them. However, Mago's scribbled jottings prove to be 'unintelligible' to Rudolf because they were written in shorthand on random scraps of parchment, and thus were undeveloped, disordered, and often ambiguous or unclear (*Life of Leoba*, 206). In Rudolf's opinion, Mago had planned to expand and reorganize his notes into a coherent narrative, but was prevented from doing so by his premature demise.

This relation of the practical difficulties that Rudolf encountered in writing this *Life* finds a somewhat unlikely but very well-known parallel in *The Book of Margery Kempe*, written some six centuries later in East Anglia, in commemoration of the life, pilgrimages and visionary experiences of a pious laywoman.[36] While the differences between the two texts are considerable (one a hagiography, the other straddling the boundary between autobiography and confessional text; one written posthumously, the other while its subject was still alive), both texts describe at length the difficulties that accompany working with inadequate, and impenetrable, source material. The final clerical scribe of *The Book of Margery Kempe*, like Rudolf, had to rework completely the material produced by his predecessor, an individual who has been convincingly identified as Kempe's own son.[37] Rudolf, who represents himself as Mago's successor, appointed to the role by the then abbot of Fulda, the great theologian Hrabanus Maurus, finds that he has to redo the work originally undertaken by Mago, but at a greater distance from the source. The history as recounted by the four nuns is only available via documents that may or may not have been produced by the nuns themselves via Mago's garbled work and via further oral accounts transmitted from one generation of monks to the next. Rudolf therefore makes it clear that his task is one of textual reconstruction, which involves structuring his source material into a coherent chronological narrative and filling in gaps as best he can.

This extended prefatory discussion of the challenges Rudolf faced in writing his *Life of Leoba*, while conventional in explaining the genesis of the work and establishing its authority and reliability, whether based on eyewitness accounts or written sources, or, not atypically, a combination of the two, seems somewhat excessively apologetic. Indeed the reader may wonder why Rudolf chose to mention Mago at all, since his work proved of so little use to him. The answer may be that Rudolf's intended immediate audience or his patron (Abbot Hrabanus) may have expected that Rudolf's *Life of Leoba* would be a straightforward transcription of Mago's earlier work, and indeed that Mago himself had been the chosen hagiographer and historiographer of Leoba's own community of nuns, just as several centuries later Margery Kempe first invited her son to record her life in her *Book*. If it were the case that Mago was the hagiographer elect of the sisters, it would explain why he was allowed such extensive access to the community and why he was allowed the opportunity to converse with the nuns at such length and with such frequency. In other words, Rudolf felt the need to justify and to explain his own overwriting, or perhaps, in this case, complete rewriting of Mago's account.

Rudolf's use of the humility topos differs, then, from that of Hugeburc, in so far as he expresses less concern about his lack of literary skill and about his presumption in writing and focuses more on justifying the authority of his sources, in particular the female witnesses to Leoba's sanctity. At the same time, implicit within the text is some disquiet about the double monastery of Wimborne, and also, as we will see, about Leoba's access to the inner sanctuaries of his own monastic house of Fulda. Indeed an exploration of the close spiritual relationships between men and women – and specifically between Boniface and Leoba – is at the heart of this narrative, although it is balanced by corresponding attention given to relationships between women, between Leoba and her spiritual mother, sisters and daughters, and other close associates. Rudolf appears to be a writer with two audiences in mind: on the one hand he is writing for other nuns, including Leoba's own community, but on the other, he recognizes the need to please his brethren at Fulda.

The ultimate authority of *The Life of Leoba* is, of course, not human (whether male or female), but divine, and as Rudolf explains, it is evidenced in the purity of life of the eyewitnesses and the monks who transmitted their stories, in the miracles that occur at the shrine of Leoba, and in the perfection of Leoba's spiritual mother, Abbess Tetta of Wimborne (*Life of Leoba*, 206–10).[38] Like Bede, writing over 100 years earlier about Ely and Whitby, Rudolf seems uncomfortable with the idea of a double monastery, and he evidently feels the need to defend Wimborne, emphasizing that although it was established as a single institution, governed by a woman, the communities of nuns and monks were kept strictly segregated, and the nuns entered with the expectation that they would only ever leave in very exceptional circumstances (*Life of Leoba*, 207).[39] Thus, having given a full and detailed account of his sources, Rudolf prefaces his life of Leoba proper with a short biography of Tetta herself, written with the clear aim of establishing the authority of the abbess, and the unimpeachable discipline with which she ruled her house. Tetta not only strictly policed the admittance of men, including high-ranking men of religion, into the community of women, but also conducted herself with discretion. As evidence of this, Rudolf (no doubt drawing on Leoba's memories) cites two miracles: the first illustrating her compassion in her intercession for the disturbed soul of an unpopular former prioress; the second demonstrating her discernment in identifying correctly the loss of the keys to the church as the work of the devil (*Life of Leoba*, 208–10). Furthermore, as Blanton and Scheck have argued, this 'mini biography' also incorporates Leoba's recollections of her own education.[40]

Leoba's piety, as celebrated by Rudolf, drawing on the reminiscences of Leoba and her followers, is clearly gendered feminine,[41] and this is all the more evident if it is contrasted to Hugeburc's portrayal of Willibald. Whereas Willibald's life is figured in terms of the ages of man, Leoba's is represented in terms of a spiritual life cycle, beginning with her miraculous conception (her mother was thought to be barren, and her parents feared they would never have children) and ending in her old age and death and the translation of her bones. Although both Willibald and Leoba are English religious in (chosen) exile, Willibald is from the start represented by Hugeburc as one who makes active choices about his own destiny, as manifested most clearly in his determination to set out on pilgrimage. Leoba, in contrast, is described in more passive terms, as one whose mother chose to dedicate her to God even *before* her conception, and as one summonsed by Boniface to leave Wimborne and travel to Francia to join his mission. Hollis is of the view that because Leoba's life 'could not be brought into entire conformity with the requirements of strict enclosure', Rudolf chose instead to emphasize other aspects of her piety: 'her virtues, not her actions, are offered as a model for imitation.'[42] There are certainly parallels to be drawn between Rudolf's representation of female sanctity and that of Bede.

As with Hugeburc's life of Willibald, bonds of kinship are celebrated even as they are transcended in *The Life of Leoba*.[43] Rudolf names Leoba's parents as Dynne and Æbbe, members of the English nobility (*Life of Leoba*, 210). Whereas Willibald's relationship with his father, and to some extent his brother, are central to Hugeburc's narrative, it is Æbbe who features prominently in Rudolf's, and thus Leoba's, own. Æbbe, conceiving in her old age, is a second Sarah (Genesis 21.2), and she is also explicitly identified in the text with Anna, mother of Samuel, who was also thought to be barren (1 Samuel/1 Kings) (*Life of Leoba*, 211). Æbbe is blessed with a dream or vision in which she finds she is carrying a church bell in her chest, which rings out joyfully (*Life of Leoba*, 210). This dream is strikingly reminiscent, of course, of the dream of Hild's mother discussed in Chapter 1, and shares its allusions to the Annunciation. Leoba will surely, like Hild, become a beacon of faith across not only England, but Germany too. Rudolf however does not fully draw out this meaning at this point. The role of interpreting the dream does not fall to Leoba's mother, as it does to Hild's, but to an anonymous nurse, who Gabriel-like announces the conception of Leoba, and then advises Æbbe to dedicate the child to divine service. Æbbe follows this path, and indeed Dynne is not even mentioned in relation to the decision concerning Leoba's consecration. Rather the infant Leoba is passed directly from Æbbe's care into the spiritual custody of Tetta. From this point on, Rudolf makes it clear that bonds of kinship have little significance to Leoba. When she becomes abbess in Germany, Leoba has no sense of exile or isolation. Rather, 'she never gave thought to her native country or her relatives' (*Life of Leoba*, 214). Nevertheless, as we will see, she did in fact travel to Germany with at least one kinswoman, who remained her companion and ally.

One aspect of Rudolf of Fulda's *Life of Leoba* that has received recent critical attention is Leoba's vision of a purple thread (*Life of Leoba*, 212).[44] In this vision, Leoba finds herself pulling this seemingly never-ending string out of her mouth, and balling it up in her hands, until she is quite exhausted with the effort of her eternal task. There is, perhaps, a sense that this is a version of the myth of Sisyphus, with Leoba trapped forever in an activity that seems meaningless. However, on awakening, Leoba is fully aware that the dream has hidden within it a divine message, and through one of her sisters she indirectly approaches an old nun from Wimborne who is blessed with the spirit of prophecy. The old nun immediately recognizes that it is Leoba who has experienced this vision and interprets it to mean that Leoba has been chosen by God both to instruct others, and also to serve as an exemplary model for them. This vision therefore mirrors but also builds upon Æbbe's earlier annunciation dream, but whereas Æbbe's dream concerned itself with Leoba's conception and dedication, and with the importance of instructing Leoba in Scripture, Leoba's own dream addresses her subsequent career as a teacher and missionary overseas: the old nun (who takes on a role akin to that of the nurse in relation to Æbbe's dream) likens the rolled-up ball of thread to the 'mystery' of divine instruction 'which turns earthwards through active works and heavenwards through contemplation' (*Life of Leoba*, 212–13). The colour of the thread is not explained, but purple is associated with wealth, kingship and ecclesiastical authority. In Proverbs 31.22 the virtuous woman is described thus: 'she hath made for herself clothing of tapestry: fine linen and purple is her covering.' The colour of the thread is therefore a further indication, should one be needed, that Leoba has been chosen by God to act in ways that might otherwise seem in defiance of St Paul's prohibition of women's teaching (1 Timothy 2.2).

According to Lees and Overing, the dream of the purple thread, its meaning unlocked by a fellow nun, also bestows authority on Leoba's sisters:

The purple thread which comes from within Leoba is a powerful affective image of how the saint and her community are linked to the divine through the practice of communal exegesis, through reading and interpretation. In short, Leoba and her nuns take the ball and run with it.[45]

Leoba's dream is further contextualized within her *Life* in terms of her ascetic practices. The ball of thread, which we are told, is emitted involuntarily from her 'bowels' (*Life of Leoba*, 212) is associated, indirectly, with Leoba's strict control over her own consumption of food. The links between medieval female piety and fasting have been explored in some detail.[46] Leoba does not starve herself, but she is moderate, avoiding luxurious food and drink, and partaking of sustenance only when her spiritual work is done (*Life of Leoba*, 211). Rudolf emphasizes also that Leoba eats and sleeps just enough to enable her to focus on her studies of the Bible and 'the writings of the church Fathers, the decrees of the Councils and the whole of ecclesiastical law' (*Life of Leoba*, 215). At the same time, however, Leoba does not impose her asceticism on others, neither members of her own community nor guests: indeed her generosity as a host is given special mention (*Life of Leoba*, 216).

A further miracle described by Rudolf centres on the healing of a nun called Williswind. Here the text signals the connection with Leoba's dream through the description of Williswind's illness which, we are told, is manifested through rectal bleeding and extreme stomach pain (*Life of Leoba*, 220). Leoba approached Williswind as she lay on her deathbed, and, announcing that her soul had not yet departed, fed her drops of milk which she herself blessed from her own small spoon, and thus Williswind was miraculously healed. (*Life of Leoba*, 221). The imagery here is clear: Leoba feeds Williswind as a mother feeds her child. Implicitly she is likened to the Virgin Mary feeding the Christ child, anticipating later representations of the Virgin Mary as physician found, for example, in the twelfth-century *Life of Christina of Markyate*, and also, as we will see in the next chapter, in the *Legend of Edith*.[47] But the use of her own spoon – the small size of which reflects Leoba's own self-restraint – indicates that Leoba's self-sacrifice supports the wider community. Leoba's teaching and exemplary life are counterbalanced by exercising a strict control over her own bodily functions which enables her to focus on study and contemplation. Her sanctity is further confirmed by her ability to heal others whose bodily functions fail.

Leoba's healing of the diseased nun Williswind illustrates a further aspect of her feminine sanctity, as described by Rudolf: the importance of friendships between women that extend the biological relationship between mother and daughter into the spiritual sphere. As mentioned above, the infant Leoba is passed from the care of her biological mother Æbbe into the protection of the Abbess Tetta, whose own miracles are narrated as a preface to the *Life of Leoba* proper. Tetta, as Leoba's first teacher, is angered when Leoba is summoned by Boniface to join his mission, but unable to oppose the instruction (*Life of Leoba*, 214). As one would expect, Rudolf pays particular attention to Leoba's career as abbess of Tauberbischofsheim: to the way she conducts herself, and to the ways in which she miraculously protects the house, metaphorically, from scandal, and literally, from destruction by fire and storm (*Life of Leoba*, 214–20). It is in the midst of these accounts that Rudolf mentions, almost in passing, Leoba's kinswoman Thecla, a fellow nun, who speaks out and urges Leoba to intervene on behalf of the community and the people from the locality (*Life of Leoba*, 219–20). Thecla is, of course, one of Rudolf's named sources. She had travelled with Leoba from Wimborne to Tauberbischofsheim, and went on to become abbess of Kitzingen.[48] Leoba may well have been Thecla's teacher. As we saw in Chapter 3, Boniface addressed at least one letter jointly to Leoba, Thecla and Cynehild. Marion Grau describes Leoba, Thecla and the other women who joined Boniface's mission as forming 'a literate diasporic elite'.[49] Raymond's passing reference to Thecla disguises how important the relationship between the two women was, with Thecla taking on the role of trusted councillor and advisor within the abbey. Thecla, according to Blanton and Scheck, could well have been 'partially responsible for passing on Leoba's story'.[50]

Rudolf pays even more attention to Leoba's relationship with her politically powerful patron Hildegard of Vinzgau (758–83), second wife of Charlemagne.[51] Rudolf recounts that Hildegard 'revered her with a chaste affection and loved her as her own soul' (*Life of Leoba*, 222–3). Weston draws our attention to just how remarkable, or indeed exceptional, this relationship is, describing it as a 'most particularized, most explicitly physicalized (not to say eroticized) example of female friendship'.[52] Leoba, we are told, instructed the queen, and served as her spiritual advisor, but shunned life at court. Rudolf recounts how, as she approached her death, the queen requested that Leoba come to her. Initially agreeing, with some reluctance, to visit Hildegard, Leoba insisted on leaving again immediately. Rudolf's account of their impassioned final farewell is particularly striking:

> abnuit ac solito affectuosius in amicam irruit, os, frontem, oculos deosculans et inherens amplexibus
>
> *Vita Leobae*, 130

[embracing her friend rather more affectionately than usual, she kissed her on the mouth, the forehead and the eyes]

Life of Leoba, 224

Leoba's deathbed adieu to the woman she refers to as the *animae meae portio pretiosa* [most precious half of my soul] (*Vita Leobae*, 130; *Life of Leoba*, 224) anticipates her own demise, which occurs shortly after her arrival back in Tauberbischofsheim. The inevitability of Leoba's death following Hildegard's seems to indicate that the former cannot live without the latter. Within the hagiographical tradition, and medieval writing more generally, the celebration of a relationship between two women is relatively rare. The closeness of the bond between Leoba and Hildegard seems the more surprising given the emphasis in Rudolf's text on the soul-friendship between Leoba and Boniface, which is, perhaps inevitably, Rudolf's principal focus. In describing this bond, there is no description of a poignant deathbed parting. Here, instead the focus is on the posthumous continuity of their relationship.

The evidence of the surviving letters in the Boniface correspondence, as discussed in Chapter 3, indicates that Leoba was proactive in courting Boniface's attention. Appealing to him as a kinsman whose duty it is to offer protection to her after the death of her parents, Leoba entreats him to give her instruction in writing and sends him an example of her verse.[53] Rudolf's version of events is somewhat different, and conforms more to expected patterns of gendered behaviour. Rudolf places Boniface in the active role, recruiting potential leaders for the monastic houses he is establishing in Germany. Rudolf gives the example of Sturm (later abbot of Fulda), sent to Monte Cassino (like Willibald) to learn monastic discipline and observance (*Life of Leoba*, 213). According to Rudolf, Boniface wrote to Tetta, asking that Leoba be sent to join his mission (*Life of Leoba*, 213–14). No mention is made of Leoba's initial approach or of any previous correspondence between the two. Rudolf does mention that Boniface and Leoba are kin (connected through Boniface's mother), but stresses that this is not a factor: it is Leoba's reputation that initially draws him to her (*Life of Leoba*, 214). Boniface's choice of Leoba to head one of the new religious houses is now represented as the ultimate fulfilment of Leoba's dream of the purple thread.

If Rudolf makes no reference to Leoba's initial letter to Boniface, or indeed to her short poem, he does nonetheless, throughout the *Life*, acknowledge her extraordinary erudition. Leoba's education, which began in her earliest years under the tuition of her mother Æbbe, and which was continued at Wimborne by Tetta and her sisters, bears immediate fruit. Leoba is devoted to studying, listening, reading and committing to memory all she has learnt (*Life of Leoba*, 211). Rudolf remarks that she 'wasted no time on girlish romances' (*Life of Leoba*, 211). Even when she rested, she employed a fellow nun to read to her from the Bible (*Life of Leoba*, 215). The centrality of learning to Leoba in Rudolf's *Life* is, then, entirely consistent with Leoba's letter, discussed in Chapter 3, in which she makes it clear that she hopes an association with Boniface will result in further opportunities for education and intellectual advancement.

Yet despite the importance of the bond between Boniface and Leoba to his narrative, Rudolf only returns to this topic in the final quarter of his *Life of Leoba*. He picks up on their relationship at the point when Boniface prepares to set off on his mission to Frisia, where he will meet his death. Having passed on his mantle to Lul, entrusting him especially with the completion of the monastery at Fulda (a matter that is of course of particular significance to Rudolf), and also with the arrangements for his burial, Boniface requests Leoba to come to him (*Life of Leoba*, 221). Mirroring his instructions to Lul, and gifting her his cowl, Boniface urges Leoba not to return to England (a point that is reiterated shortly after), but to continue their joint works. Placing her in the protection of the monks of Fulda, he requests that after her death she be buried alongside him (*Life of Leoba*, 222).[54] Rudolf subsequently reveals that Boniface's wishes were not in fact carried out to the letter, as Leoba was not placed in Boniface's tomb but buried next to the altar (*Life of Leoba*, 224). Later, we are told, Leoba's remains were moved to the west porch. While Rudolf explains these decisions in terms of concerns about disturbing Boniface's grave and the limitations of space, his *Life* provides a more nuanced understanding of why this was the case.[55] Again Rudolf betrays anxiety about the proximity of male and female religious when he explains that, after Boniface's martyrdom, Leoba was allowed to visit Fulda, even though women were excluded from the monastery, and he outlines the rules that were imposed to ensure that propriety was observed (*Life of Leoba*, 223). The kind of double burial that Boniface envisaged, in which their corpses lay side-by-side in anticipation of the resurrection (*Life of Leoba*, 222), may well have seemed potentially scandalous to the monks of Fulda.[56] Indeed, earlier in the narrative, Rudolf describes an occasion in which Leoba and her nuns were wrongly caught up in a scandal involving the murder of an illegitimate newborn infant (*Life of Leoba*, 216–18). For both nuns and monks, the importance of maintaining their reputations for perfect chastity was crucial, but nuns were disproportionately more vulnerable to threats to their reputations.[57]

Rudolf structures his text so that Boniface's instructions about their joint burial and his valediction to Leoba is followed by Queen Hildegard's deathbed leave-taking, and thus the soul friendship of Boniface and Leoba is counterbalanced by that between Hildegard and Leoba, with the effect of undermining its exclusivity, and thus its potentially dangerous intensity, while at the same time allowing a friendship between women to take a central position. The posthumous miracles that complete the *Life of Leoba*, conventional as they are, serve not only as final confirmation of Leoba's own sanctity, but also as reassurance that the decision of the monks of Fulda not to bury Boniface and Leoba in one tomb has divine authorization: 'these two, though they do not share a tomb, yet lie in one place and never fail to look on those who seek their intercession' (*Life of Leoba*, 226). And in order to reinforce the truth value still further, Rudolf includes the details that the two particular posthumous miracles that he describes can be testified to by monks of Fulda who are still alive and that he himself 'was present when they occurred' (*Life of Leoba*, 226).

Conclusion

Hugeburc is undoubtedly concerned that, as a text composed by a woman writer, her *Life* will not be judged to be authoritative. She is defensive about being seen as a teacher, and attempts to defuse potential criticism by alluding to her own 'weakness' and by emphasizing that she has relied on clerical testimony, and she makes it absolutely clear that she draws on Willibald's own first person account. Rudolf, on the other hand, struggles to justify his reliance on the eyewitness narratives of the four named nuns, even as, paradoxically, in naming the nuns alongside Leoba's first biographer, he does effectively attribute to them the status of author. But Rudolf too finds himself explaining at some length why he has taken on the role of hagiographer, perhaps because he was not the writer of choice of Leoba's community, and perhaps because of the distance in time that has passed since Leoba's death. Yet within his text, the word 'weak' is applied not to Rudolf, but to Leoba herself (when Boniface urges her to continue his mission beyond his death: *Life of Leoba*, 222).

Unlike Hugeburc, Rudolf cannot claim a direct acquaintance – far less a kinship bond – with Leoba, even if his writing derives in part, and indirectly, from her reminiscences. Indeed, for Hugeburc, the bond of kinship to her subject is crucial, and this is reflected in her narrative, which makes much of Willibald's biological relationships with his father and brother. For Rudolf, on the other hand, the connection of kinship between Boniface and Leoba, while still important, is somewhat underplayed (in comparison with the use made of it in

Leoba's first letter to Boniface).Although Leoba's parents, and in particular her mother, do figure in the early history of her life, Rudolf insists throughout that after she has travelled to Germany Leoba soon forgets her family and friends in England. Indeed unlike Hugeburc, who portrays Willibald's pilgrimage as a form of exile, Rudolf does not use this imagery to describe Leoba's journey overseas. Despite citing Boniface's concerns that Leoba might decide to return to England, Rudolf does not portray her as experiencing the pull of home.

While Hugeburc structures her biography of Willibald loosely in terms of the ages of man, culminating in his perfect mature manhood, Rudolf organizes Leoba's *Life* in terms of cyclic reproductive and spiritual time, from conception through to death and the promise of her final rebirth into eternal life. Having said this, spiritual time inevitably also frames Willibald's experiences. Willibald's life is marked by illness, a form of involuntary asceticism; Leoba's by a focus on her education and extraordinary learning and by the control she displayed towards the consumption of food in particular. Willibald is likened to the many saints whose shrines he visits – in particular John the Baptist and St Martin of Tours. Leoba's miraculous birth is framed in Biblical terms, but she directly compares herself to only one saint, the wrongfully accused Susanna (*Life of Leoba*, 217). More attention is paid by Hugeburc to Willibald's monastic career *as a career* than by Rudolf to that of Leoba beyond her earliest years.

Most remarkably of all, Hugeburc immerses herself in her vivid account of Willibald's travels, even merging her own voice with his as if she had been present, and it is clear that for Hugeburc it is the pilgrimage itself that fully captures her imagination. Her text is a naturalistic rather than marvellous life of a living saint, whereas Rudolf shores up the divine authority of his hagiography of the dead Leoba with supernatural miracles. Aware of the criticisms levelled both at double houses and at women's convents, Rudolf generally devotes considerable attention to deflecting criticism from the houses at Wimborne and Tauberbischofsheim. In more positive terms, Rudolf pays considerable attention to Leoba's relationship with Boniface (and the miracles that surround them), and also with her spiritual mother Tetta, with her own community, and with Queen Hildegard. And while Hugeburc's account ends while Willibald is still alive, Rudolf's moves inexorably not simply towards Leoba's death, but more significantly towards the details of her interment and translation, and the posthumous miracles that not only confirm Leoba's sanctity, but that justify the decisions concerning her burial made by his own monastery of Fulda.

Ultimately, a comparison of these two texts suggests that gender could be an important factor in the writers' strategies of self-authorization, as well as a factor in the representation of sanctity. But this comparison also illustrates the remarkable originality of a writer like Hugeburc, who as a woman composing the life of her saintly relative engaged with her subject matter – Willibald's travels – with an energy and enthusiasm seldom witnessed in a conventional hagiography. And for Hugeburc, and indeed for (Rudolf's) Leoba, if travel is exile, then exile is not to be feared but to be desired, embraced and celebrated.

(Re)writing Women's History at Wilton Abbey

Introduction

Goscelin of St Bertin (*c.* 1035–after 1107) is a significant figure in women's literary history at the very end of the early medieval period. A Flemish-born monk, he probably arrived in England in the years leading up to the Norman invasion. He wrote lives of many English saints, male and female, and following the death of his patron, Herman, bishop of Ramsbury and Sherborne (*d.* 1078) he seems effectively to have supported himself by working as an itinerant hagiographer. As a highly skilled writer, he was in great demand amongst the religious communities of the South of England, including the important houses of women at Wilton and Barking.

Goscelin enjoyed a close relationship with Wilton Abbey, and in the late 1070s he wrote the *Legend of Edith* (Eadgyth) of Wilton (961–984), daughter of Abbess Wulfthryth (*d. c.* 1000) and King Edgar (959–975). Edgar effectively abducted Wulfthryth from Wilton Abbey when she was a young woman and she returned there as soon as possible, bringing her daughter with her, and subsequently became abbess. Originally established in the early ninth century, Wilton was refounded during the Benedictine Reform, which was orchestrated in England for Edgar by Dunstan, archbishop of Canterbury, and Æthelwold, bishop of Winchester. Wulfthryth proved a powerful leader of the convent under the new regime. The reform movement provides an important context for understanding the *Legend*, and both Dunstan and Æthelwold figure in it. A few years later Goscelin also composed the *Liber confortatorius*, addressed to Eve, a young nun formerly of Wilton (*c.* 1058–*c.* 1125), which is the focus of Chapter 6. In the *Liber confortatorius*, Goscelin reflects in part on the time he spent with Eve in Wilton and makes explicit reference to St Edith, who, as we will see in this chapter, he represents at times as a recluse, albeit one living within a monastic community. In the following decades, Goscelin contributed to the collection of lives of the early medieval female saints at Ely (no longer a double monastery, as it had been refounded as an exclusively male Benedictine institution in the late tenth century) including material relating to Æthelthryth and Seaxburh,[1] and he went on to produce lives and/or translation narratives of Æthelburh, Hildelith and Wulfhild of Barking,[2] and a life of Mildrith of Minster-in-Thanet written for the male house at St Augustine's Abbey, Canterbury, where Mildrith's relics were located (see the discussion of the lives of Mildrith in Chapter 2).[3]

The Wilton and Barking commissions beg the question why the women's houses did not employ their own nuns to compose and update the lives of their saintly predecessors. Did they feel the sisters lacked the necessary talent or levels of literacy to do credit to such a task, or did it seem more appropriate or even more prestigious to employ a well-known and celebrated hagiographer to undertake this sort of work? Examining the former proposition first, the paucity of surviving evidence certainly suggests that, after the eighth century, women in England were far less engaged with literary culture. This may well have been connected to the Viking attacks of the ninth century, which had a disproportionately heavy impact on the women's religious houses (Goscelin includes accounts of the Viking invasions in his Barking *Lives*) and, of course, on their libraries. The Benedictine Reform, which imposed stricter rules of enclosure on women, and arguably restricted their immediate access to wider scholarly communities, was another factor.[4] Stephanie Hollis goes so far as to claim that, Goscelin's writing aside, 'there are no known Latin works written either for or by monastic women in the late Anglo-Saxon period *as it is usually defined*' (Hollis's emphasis).[5] From this, we might conclude that the matriarchs at Wilton Abbey had no choice but to look to someone outside their community to produce an account of their history.

Hollis is, however, overstating the case. As she acknowledges, Latin works *were* produced under the patronage of elite secular women, such as the pre-Conquest queens Emma of Normandy (*d.* 1052) and Edith of Wessex (*c.* 1025–1075), and also Matilda (1080–1118), wife of Henry I, who commissioned a life of her mother St Margaret of Scotland (*d.* 1093).[6] Furthermore Ælfric's famous homily on Judith (*c.* 1000) is just one example of a vernacular religious text written for women. There is also, albeit limited, evidence of book ownership in ninth- and tenth-century women's houses.[7] Goscelin's writing career should be located within this broader context of women's engagement with literary culture as patrons and readers.

In this context it is also worth noting the traces that exist of the lost work of the eleventh or early-twelfth-century '*inclyta versificatrix*' [celebrated woman poet], Muriel of Wilton,[8] and of the evidence of scribal and literary activity of women religious in the first half of the twelfth century in Barking and elsewhere.[9] There can be little doubt that the Wilton and Barking nuns were more than capable of writing their own histories, and it is likely that they were in fact engaged in this activity both before and after Goscelin's time. As Katie Ann-Marie Bugyis observes, 'the very communities that outsourced their hagiographical compositions did have members who possessed the requisite skills, but opted not to engage them for strategic reasons', reasons that include the need to promote the insular saints to the Norman administration.[10] The production of Goscelin's works for Barking and Wilton indicates the levels of engagement with literary culture these houses enjoyed.

What is more, Goscelin's writing may have encouraged more religious women to write, to record their own histories and those of saints of especial significance to them. One work that shows the influence of Goscelin is the late eleventh-century *Passio Sancti Eadwardi* or *Passion of St Edward*, which may well have been written by a nun of Shaftesbury for her own convent.[11] This text in some ways anticipates the French hagiographies written by nuns in the twelfth and thirteenth centuries, such as the life of Edward the Confessor by an anonymous nun at Barking, *La vie de sainte Catherine d'Alexandrie* by Clemence of Barking and *La vie seinte Audrée* (Æthelthryth) by one Marie, possibly of Chatteris Abbey in Cambridgeshire.[12]

In producing his hagiographical works for Barking and Wilton, Goscelin tailored his narratives to meet the specific requirements of his audience. His lives of the saints of Barking, for example, were commissioned in part to justify the translation of their bodies by Abbess Alviva (Ælfgiva) (*d.* 1080).[13] Goscelin overwrote and updated his source material, which included Bede's own *Ecclesiastical History*, in ways that invite a comparison with Bede's reworking of pre-existing accounts of Whitby, Ely and Barking in his 'Book of Abbesses' (discussed in Chapters 1 and 2). Indeed, just as Bede drew on the lost *liber* of Barking Abbey, so Goscelin, in his *Legend of Edith*, turned to written sources (no longer extant) which he found in the Wilton Library, including it would appear, lives of both Edith and her mother Wulfthryth that would almost certainly have been authored by members of the community. However, unlike Bede, Goscelin was more directly answerable to the women's houses, and partly as a consequence of this patronage and partly because of the very different purposes for which his histories were designed, Goscelin is more careful to credit at least some of his female authorities. Thus Goscelin famously cites by name the nun Judith (formerly Wulfruna) whose memories inform his narrative of Æthelburh's posthumous protection of Barking, and who was the chief source for his life of

Wulfhild.[14] As Bugyis notes, Goscelin 'unreservedly acknowledged the many women who offered essential testimonies'.[15] Responding to and developing my own arguments about Goscelin as an author who overwrote his female sources, Bugyis goes on to conclude that 'his admission of these female history-makers into his texts was more than just a rhetorical ploy aimed at self-legitimation; it was an act of genuine respect for the female authors, scribes and witnesses on whose knowledge he depended'.[16] Whereas Bede incorporated and freely adapted a variety of sources into his early history of the English church, Goscelin was more careful to record and preserve the traditions, memories and perspectives of his subjects.

This chapter, which focuses on one of Goscelin's hagiographies, the *Legend of Edith*, will examine in detail the representation of female authority within that text, with its emphasis on spiritual matrilineage and on a sanctity that is rooted in education and learning. The title of the chapter alludes to Cynthia Turner Camp's book, *Anglo-Saxon Saints' Lives as History Writing in Late Medieval England* (2015), in which she argues that hagiography can be understood in terms of historiography because 'saints' lives reconstruct the past', and further that they do so in ways that can be literary or poetic.[17] I am particularly interested here in the ways that Goscelin (re)produces a women's history of and for Wilton. I have chosen Goscelin's *Legend of Edith* because it appears to have been based on lost works by women, and because it was commissioned by the abbess of Wilton and her senior nuns and thus had a particularly close relationship to its intended female readers. Indeed, as we will see, it is likely that one version of the text was produced and adapted specifically for the Wilton house.

Goscelin of St Bertin, the Wilton community, and the production of Edith's *Legend*

Goscelin's *Legend of Edith* comprises two parts: the *Vita*, which focuses on her life and the miraculous events that immediately followed her death; and the *Translatio*, which focuses on posthumous events, including, self-evidently, the translation of Edith's body to its new burial place in the south porch of the church, a process that was instigated by her half-brother Æthelred.[18] The *Legend* is an elaborate work that comprises both narrative prose and poetry. The texts that comprise the *Legend* survive in three manuscripts. The earliest dates to the early twelfth century and is found in a collection of saints' lives in Cardiff, Central (formerly Public) Library, MS 1.381, fols 102v–120r. This manuscript includes the *Vita* but not the *Translatio* and is a revised version of the text. Oxford, Bodleian Library, MS Rawlinson C.938 dates to the thirteenth century and contains both the *Vita* (fols 1r–16r) and *Translatio* (fols 16r–29v). It probably represents the text in its original form and is the basis of the *Legend* as edited by André Wilmart in 1938.[19] However, although the Rawlinson manuscript is also the base text of the *Translatio* as it is translated into English by Michael Wright and Kathleen Loncar in *Writing the Wilton Women*, ed. Stephanie Hollis *et al*, in that edition the Cardiff manuscript is used as the base text for the *Vita*.[20] There is also a large collection of British saints' lives that includes both parts of the *Legend* in a fourteenth-century manuscript of English provenance: Gotha, Forschungsbibliothek, Codex Memb. I.81, fols 188v–203r. The text follows the version in Rawlinson, but with some additional changes and without the metrical sections.[21] The Cardiff manuscript is chosen as the base text for Wright and Loncar's translation because internal evidence suggests that it was adapted by Goscelin specifically for the Wilton community, a point I will return to later in this chapter.

Yet although the Cardiff manuscript was tailored specifically for the Wilton nuns, it is clear that, from its very inception, Edith's *Legend* was written for and with the assistance of Edith's own community. Goscelin was commissioned to write the text by Godgifu (Godiva), who served as abbess of Wilton between *c.* 1067 and 1090. In the Prologue to the *Vita*, he acknowledges that he was responding to the requests of the *matres* or 'senior nuns' of Wilton ('La légende de Ste Édith', ed. Wilmart, 38; *Vita*, 24) and he cites Godgifu and her fellow nuns as important sources of information about Edith. To address the issue of the commissioning first, Paul Antony Hayward argues that it was written for the house at Wilton 'to provide [Edith's cult] with archiepiscopal validation'.[22] Susan J. Ridyard suggests that Edith's mother Abbess Wulfthryth, who outlived her daughter, originally promoted the cult.[23] Certainly, according to Goscelin, Edith was sanctified in Wulfthryth's lifetime, a development encouraged by King Æthelred. It is possible that this cult only began to gain momentum around 1040, and that it was already in decline in the years after the Conquest, partly as a result of the abbey's ailing fortunes.[24] Consequently, perhaps following an example set by her immediate predecessor Abbess Ælfgifu, Godgifu hoped that reinvigorating it might generate a new wave of patronage and thus secure the abbey's long-term economic and political stability. Yet Wilton did already have a powerful patron: Edith of Wessex, whose decision to rebuild her namesake St Edith's wooden church at Wilton in stone is celebrated in the life of her husband, Edward the Confessor, which Queen Edith herself commissioned.[25] Goscelin makes no direct mention of this particular royal patronage, and his silence may be a reflection of the concerns of the nuns. It is possible that, as one consequence of the Benedictine Reform, which saw a shift in authority and power from abbesses to queens, the Wilton community had become increasing suspicious of royal interference.[26] Although Goscelin, on finding himself exiled following the death of his patron, Herman, bishop of Ramsbury and Sherborne, would also have been motivated by self-interest, and hoped to impress with his 'new histories, new written works' (*Vita*, 23), the fact that the Rawlinson MS includes a dedication to Lanfranc, archbishop of Canterbury, supports the interpretation that the *Legend* was written to build a wider support base for Wilton Abbey.

One feature that sets Edith's *Legend* immediately apart from the other hagiographies of female saints written by Goscelin is that, with the exception of his account of Edith's kinswoman, Wulfhild of Barking (*d.* after 996), there is far less distance in time between Edith's actual life and death and Goscelin's own lifetime. As already noted, Goscelin wrote, or overwrote, a whole series of hagiographical narratives, including those concerning the abbesses of Barking and Ely. His lives of the early abbesses are indebted to those found in Bede's *Ecclesiastical History*.[27] These are, then, overwritings of overwritings. Goscelin's *Legend* of Edith and the account of her mother's life that he embeds in the *Translatio* are in contrast closer to his own age, so it is worth paying particular attention to his probable sources. It is likely that Goscelin incorporated material from an extant earlier life of Wulfthryth into the *Legend*, and much of the information is likely to have been supplied by Brihtgifu, who had entered the convent as a child in Wulfthryth's lifetime, and who served as abbess of Wilton immediately before the Norman invasion (*c.* 1040–1065).[28] Goscelin integrates into the *Translatio* one narrative in support of Edith's sanctity which he implies was authored by Brihtgifu herself – or at least written down, in English, on her command: the story of the twelve dancing men from Colbeck, which he states was 'publicly described in the presence of Abbess Brihtgifu, who is well remembered, and committed to writing in the vernacular' (*Translatio*, 85).[29] There is then a distinctive immediacy to the *Legend*, with its emphasis on the recent past, and on the authoritative recollections of a recent head of the community.

Goscelin in fact appears to have had access to a range of written material. The phrase that Goscelin uses in relation to the Colbeck story, '*patriis literis*' [writing in the vernacular] ('La légende de Ste Édith', ed. Wilmart, 292), is anticipated much earlier in the *Legend*. In the Prologue to the *Vita*, Goscelin acknowledges that in compiling his work, he does not rely solely on oral testimony – 'testimony of faithful people' (presumably the Wilton nuns) – but also on written sources, and more specifically, '*patriis libris*' [local books], which might also be translated as 'native books' or 'books in the vernacular' ('La légende de Ste Édith', ed. Wilmart, 39; *Vita*, 25). While Michael Wright identifies these as works that Goscelin consulted in the library at Wilton,[30] this also raises the possibility (or probability) that, as with Bede's much earlier reference to a lost *liber* from Barking Abbey, these books were composed by women, and were written into, and thus overwritten, by Goscelin's own account. Bugyis makes a compelling case for these 'local books' including female-authored hagiographical and historical material by comparing Goscelin's *Legend of Edith* with the early fifteenth-century *Wilton Chronicle* (a text which may itself have been written by a nun[31]) and thus demonstrating that other accounts of the miracles of Edith and other Wilton saints existed alongside Goscelin's text in the late tenth and early eleventh centuries.[32]

In summary, in writing the *Legend of Edith*, Goscelin appears to have drawn on written material, possibly in the vernacular, which he found in the Wilton Library, and which in all likelihood had been composed by members of the Wilton community. Nevertheless, as we will see in the next section, in producing his history on the behest of the abbess and nuns of Wilton, and for their use, he implies that he relied more extensively on oral histories of Edith's life and miracles. In considering Goscelin's work in the context of an exploration of early women's writing, it is essential therefore to consider female authority as it is represented first in the *Vita* and subsequently in the *Translatio*, before going on to consider, briefly, its transmission to a readership of women religious.

Female authority in Edith's *Vita*

Goscelin's Prologue to his life of Edith, as it appears in the Rawlinson manuscript, immediately establishes the importance of women as authorities within his divinely inspired text. Anticipating the vision of Wilton as the New Jerusalem that concludes his *Liber confortatorius* (discussed in the next chapter), Goscelin weaves together Biblical verses to describe the plenitude of the feast of the bridegroom, Christ, to which he adds his own material: Edith, the former abbess of Wilton, is a 'precious jewel' and a 'gem' (*Vita*, 23), implicitly comparable to those encrusting the walls of the heavenly city. Edith's royal status is established at the start not by mentioning her father, King Edgar, but through references to her nephew, Edward the Confessor, and a reference to the current king,

William I. In this way, Goscelin connects to the present day the saint who had died almost a century earlier. Goscelin adopts two techniques to emphasize the immediacy and relevance of the narrative he is about to recount. First, he underlines Edith's continued posthumous presence in Wilton, and second, he stresses that his hagiography is based on eyewitness accounts. Goscelin announces that 'often in visions among the sisters she is seen as if still alive and embodied' (*Vita*, 24), and the places where Edith prayed and performed her devotions are remembered and venerated. Goscelin even reports the speech of sisters as they point out these sacred spots. Goscelin also names Godgifu, the current abbess of Wilton and an important instigator of the text's production, as one source, specifying that she is fifth in line from Edith's own mother, Wulfthryth. She and her sisters (whose rank as well as piety testifies to their reliability as witnesses),

> inter reliqua que ipse oculis conspexere, affirmant confidenter cum aliis idoneis testibus ea que ab his uenerabilibus matribus audiere, qui ipsam sanctam uirginem et uidere, et deuotissime sunt obsequute; quarum et parentele et religiose uite non minorem fidem quam libris noscuntur habere.
>
> 'La légende de Ste Édith', ed. Wilmart, 37

> [as well as the things which they saw with their own eyes, declare confidently, with other appropriate evidence, those things which they heard from the venerable senior nuns, who both saw the holy virgin herself and devotedly obeyed her; whose high birth and religious lives are recognized as being equal in credibility to books.]
>
> *Vita*, 24

Anticipating that his reliance on women as authorities will make him subject to criticism, Goscelin reminds potential detractors that it was Mary Magdalene who was entrusted to carry the message of the resurrection of Christ to the Apostles, and refers to Acts 2.17–18 to support the idea that women can speak divine truths, and that their words carry as much weight as any written authority. Nevertheless, Goscelin also recognizes the need to shore up his narrative with reference to a male authority, namely to his own patron Herman – who was himself blessed by a miracle performed by Edith, and who encouraged him to write this life (*Vita*, 24) – and also with reference to two archbishops, Lanfranc, to whom he dedicates his work, and Dunstan, who was tutor to Edith, and whose cult Lanfranc recognized.

Yet, even though women are acknowledged as reliable authorities within Goscelin's text and the testimonies of nuns are extensively drawn upon, there is something paradoxical about the centrality given to the bond between mother and daughter in the main text of the *Vita*. Goscelin is extremely guarded in his account in the *Vita* of the circumstances of Edith's conception. When Edgar took Wulfthryth away from Wilton in the first place, he may well have done so against her will, but he represents this abduction as the fulfilment of a divine plan. As Katherine O'Brien O'Keeffe states, Goscelin 'covers over the fact that Edgar's actions otherwise look very much like rape'.[33] Edith's birth itself is marked by a natal vision, which reveals that she is set apart by her sanctity from other infants: the room in which she is born is miraculously illuminated by light emanating from the crown of her head (*Vita*, 27). This event is reminiscent, of course, of the Gospel accounts of the nativity of Jesus, in which the Star of Bethlehem revealed the birth of the Messiah (Matthew 2.2). However it also resonates with other natal revelations concerning saintly abbesses, such as the account of the birth of Hild in Bede's *Ecclesiastical History* and the *Old English Martyrology*, or that of Leoba in Rudolf of Fulda's *vita*.

In the earlier narrative, Breguswith, Hild's mother, had a dream that she was searching for her husband (who had in fact been banished, and who was subsequently poisoned), 'When suddenly, in the midst of her search, she found a most precious necklace under her garment, and, as she gazed closely at it, it seemed to spread such a blaze of light that it filled all Britain with its gracious splendour'.[34] Given the shared imagery of the saint as a 'jewel' and the bright light that shines from the infant, found in Goscelin's text and in Bede, it is plausible that Goscelin may have had the passage from Bede in mind when he composed Edith's *Vita*. In their analysis of Breguswith's dream Clare A. Lees and Gillian R. Overing contend that 'this dream underscores the spiritual relation between Hild and Breguswith at the cost of obscuring any other relation between the two as mother and daughter'.[35] At the same time, Bede's narrative offers 'no evidence at all of Breguswith's own agency, her subjectivity or consciousness'.[36] In their opinion, Bede effectively marginalizes and silences Breguswith. These arguments, which prioritize the biological over the spiritual, can also be applied, at least in part to Goscelin's birth narrative. It cannot be denied that Wulfthryth has agency, because as Goscelin goes on to explain, she subsequently left her husband, taking her daughter with her, in order to devote herself to God, and thus shaped the future of Edith as her spiritual heir. According to O'Brien O'Keeffe, 'Goscelin's graceful rhetorical recasting of Wulfthryth's situation as cast-off narrates in a positive fashion as woman's (forced?) retirement from the world'.[37] Nevertheless, it is indeed striking that Wulfthryth herself has no voice. While we might expect her to have been the source of this story, it is ascribed only to hearsay, 'They say'. For Goscelin, as for Bede, the spiritual relationship between mother and daughter has greater significance than their biological connection, and the miracle of Edith's birth, even more perhaps than that of Hild's, has communal rather than personal import. Goscelin's failure to name Wulfthryth as the source of the natal vision is all the more surprising when we consider how central women's devotional life and women's visions are to the depiction of female sanctity in Edith's *Vita* and in the subsequent *Translatio*.

Within the *Vita*, Edith is represented not simply as an oblate, given by her mother to the monastic life, but as one who chose from infancy to become a nun.[38] Nor is she represented simply as a nun but also as one with 'the mind of a recluse' (*Vita*, 41). As Tom Licence explains, 'Goscelin thought fit to weave an anchoretic thread into his subject's spirituality'.[39] Edith's asceticism manifested itself through abstinence and self-mortification. Her private bodily penance was only made known by the testimony of 'senior nuns' (*Vita*, 38). Edith devoted herself to God in all things: in speaking and in writing and painting, in singing and in playing musical instruments, in weaving and in embroidering, in basket-making, and in nursing and in acts of charity (*Vita*, 38–40); activities fitting for a nun or a solitary.[40] Yet there are also implicit criticisms in Goscelin's account of Edith's life. She was fond of animals and kept pets, including exotic species (*Vita*, 41), and wore elaborate and luxurious outer garments; behaviour seemingly at odds with reclusive aspirations. But any reproaches are qualified by considering her innocence, humility and royal birth. Goscelin cites the example of the sumptuous purple outer layer which disguised her hair shirt (*Vita*, 38) and Edith's own riposte to the criticisms of Æthelwold, bishop of Winchester (*Vita*, 42–3). Indeed, the elaborate and expensive clothing in Edith's chest is even miraculously protected from a fire caused by a negligent servant, thus indicating divine approval of Edith's conduct (*Vita*, 43–4).

Exemplary models are crucial to Goscelin's narrative. Goscelin reports that Wulfthryth and Edith both sought and obtained, with the help of their supporter Benno of Trier, a relic of the True Cross: a fragment of an iron nail, which they preserved in a trout-shaped crystal reliquary (*Vita*, 44–5). Goscelin compares Wulfthryth to St Helena, the mother of Constantine (*Vita*, 44), who, according to legend, discovered the True Cross in the early fourth century and also the nails of the Cross, which she had transported to Constantinople. This comparison was evidently one that Wulfthryth and Edith wished to foster, and, given that Trier was a centre of the cult of Helena, it is likely that Benno encouraged this identification. Wulfthryth and Edith, while not able to make the journey to obtain their relic themselves, sent their messenger in their place to travel and purchase the precious object. When Æthelwold tried to persuade the women to present him with a piece of the nail fragment, and an attempt was made to split it, the nail miraculously reconstituted itself (*Vita*, 45–6). The significance of Helena as a role model for Wulfthryth and Edith extends further than Goscelin acknowledges directly, because of course Helena was inspired in her search by a vision of the Cross.

Visions and prophecies mark key moments of the *Vita*, and, as we will see in the next section of this chapter, are also central to the *Translatio* of Edith.[41] Such revelations, when experienced by women, uniquely bestow upon them the greatest authority, as they become conduits of the word of God. Early in the *Vita*, Edith's predictions concerning the death of her half-brother Edward, allegedly killed at the instigation of his stepmother, serve as further proof of her own sanctity (*Vita*, 50) and indeed Goscelin indirectly compares Edith to her blessed grandmother Ælfgifu (*Vita*, 51). He makes it clear that in subsequently choosing to reject the crown of England (*Vita*, 51–2), Edith is choosing to reject the patriarchal tradition of political power in favour of a matrilineal tradition, passed down via her grandmother and mother, of religious devotion.[42]

Prophetic visions also anticipate and follow Edith's death. During the celebration of the mass to celebrate the dedication of the new church that Edith had built at Wilton, Dunstan found himself overcome with a great grief, which, as he went on to explain, was caused by his realization that Edith – whom Dunstan describes, mirroring Goscelin's own metaphor, as 'this stellar jewel' – was soon to depart for heaven (*Vita*, 55–6). On her last night, Edith herself experienced a divine vision anticipating her imminent death (*Vita*, 56–7), but, in the tradition of the visions of death described by Bede in his accounts of the foundations of the early monastic houses in his 'Book of Abbesses' (discussed in Chapters 1 and 2), it is an anonymous nun who receives a revelation at the moment of Edith's death:

> Interim quedam soror, trepida currens in monasterium, audit tanquam in choro multitudinem psallencium; cui herenti occurrit quidam speciosi uultus et habitus gloriosi: «Ne appropies, inquit, huc, quia angeli sancti Godam puellam – sic enim graciosius appellabatur que patria uoce Bona cognominatur, conuenerunt ut ad eterna gaudia hinc secum auferant, quatinus cum isto concentu exercitus celestis aulam introeat perpetue iocunditatis.»
>
> 'La légende de Ste Édith', ed. Wilmart, 94–5

> [Meanwhile one sister, running in fear into the convent, heard what sounded like a great number of people singing psalms in the choir, and as she stood still someone with a splendid face and glorious clothing met her, and said: 'Do not come near to here, because the holy angels have met with the maiden Goda—this is what she was

called affectionately because in her native tongue it means "good" ... to carry her away with them from here to eternal joys, so that she may enter the court of everlasting bliss accompanied by that harmonious singing of the heavenly host.']

Vita, 58

Again, the importance of the matrilineal tradition is emphasized: Goscelin explains that Edith is known as 'Goda' [good], but the Cardiff manuscript also explains here that she took the name Edith from her aunt, Edith of Tamworth and in this context her grandmother, Ælgifu of Shaftesbury is mentioned again (*Vita*, 58). In the version of Edith's life found in the Rawlinson manuscript, it is recorded that Edith had in her possession written lives of her grandmother and aunt (quite possibly written by nuns from their own communities), which she 'read voraciously' alongside other books (*Vita*, 35 n.50), and which inspired her to even greater devotions.

The connections between the women are further reinforced by the appearance of Edith in a vision experienced by her grieving mother. Edith, who is dressed in bridal splendour, reassures her mother of her own salvation, and Wulfthryth, consoled by this promise, is able to renew her devotions on her daughter's behalf (*Vita*, 61). The matrilineal tradition celebrated in the *Vita* is not constrained by biological links. Edith's posthumous presence is also felt at the baptism of the child, Brihtgifu, the daughter of a noble family not connected by birth to Edith (*Vita*, 61). This is the same Brihtgifu who, as already noted, went on to be educated in Wilton and subsequently became abbess, and who also seems to have been responsible for the writing of an early life of Edith's mother Wulfthryth.

Goscelin's representation of Edith's sanctity does not depend entirely upon miracles and revelations, but also upon more practical, even mundane, matters, including her education and other day-to-day activities. Edith's education is in part ascribed to her mother, who is credited with teaching her the importance of appropriate female conduct (*Vita*, 32). Goscelin clearly sees Edith's learning as evidence of her piety. Throughout, he emphasizes the role of Edith's mother Wulfthryth as Edith's mentor and teacher:

> Ita colligitur in ecclesie gremium, in uirginale collegium, in diuinum gymnasium, in scolas uirtutum, in eiusdem et spiritualis et carnalis genitricis sinum.
>
> 'La légende de Ste Édith', ed. Wilmart, 47

> [So she was gathered into the bosom of the church, the college of virgins, the divine training school, the schools of virtue, into the bosom of her who was at the same time her spiritual and natural mother.]
>
> *Vita*, 30–1

However, while Edith's mother is credited with encouraging her daughter in her intellectual pursuits, this genealogy of female learning is qualified somewhat with an alternative narrative of paternal and clerical influence. Goscelin observes that her father, Edgar, offered his patronage to scholars and artists from home and abroad (*Vita*, 32) and specifies that Benno and another priest, Radbod of Rheims, took on the responsibility of teaching Edith, doing so from outside her window in deference to her sex (*Vita*, 32). Perhaps concerned that educating a young woman thus would seem inappropriate, Goscelin qualifies this account with the observation that Edith's true teacher was, of course, God (*Vita*, 33). The trope of sanctified feminine learning is familiar in medieval Christianity. St Katherine of Alexandria, for example, was famous for disputing with the pagan philosophers and orators, and for refuting their arguments. Despite this, Goscelin clearly continued to harbour reservations about enabling even the most exceptional of women to assert too much authority. Later in the *Vita* we are told that following Edith's consecration at Nunnaminster, and at her father's instigation, she was given responsibility for that house and two others, one of which was Barking, but that she refused to leave Wilton and remained under the rule and instruction of her own mother (*Vita*, 47–8). Goscelin's approving account of this decision – he describes Edith as one who has rejected 'the tabernacles of ambitious desire and rumour-bearing arrogance' (*Vita*, 48) – resonates with his earlier account of Edith's rejection of the crown and reveals that he continues to regard the idea of a woman exerting political and secular power with suspicion.

Edith's education was such that she was able to write as well as read. The Cardiff version of Edith's *Vita* (although not in Rawlinson)[43] records that:

> Colitur in monasterio orationalis eius pugil memorabili pignore, in quo apostolicae lucent formulae, uirginea eius manu cum subscriptis oratiunculis depictae. . . .
>
> 'La légende de Ste Édith', ed. Wilmart, 55

> [There is kept in her monastery a manual of her devotions as a token of her memory, in which the apostolic precepts shine out, written in her virginal hand with little prayers subjoined to them. . . .]
>
> *Vita*, 34

This book of devotional material, including chants and collects, written in Edith's own hand, was preserved in Wilton as an object of veneration. A prayer included by Goscelin in his *Liber confortatorius* may have been composed by Edith, and taken from this same volume, although it is not attributed to her.[44] Even as

Goscelin recognizes the need to preserve the memory of Edith's prayers and learning, he does not, in her *Vita* at least, see the need to preserve the contents of her book of devotions. Subsequently, Goscelin praises Edith for having 'hands as elegant as they were accomplished in painting and in writing as a scribe or as an author' (*Vita*, 38). Yet although Edith seems to have been a writer herself, and although she evidently produced her own collection of prayers and collects, the *Vita* pays more attention to her other pious activities, such as her embroidery and her building work.

While the hand-production of ecclesiastical vestments and an embroidered alb in which Edith depicted herself as Mary Magdalene kissing the feet of Christ, surrounded by the Apostles (*Vita*, 38–9 and 48), which Goscelin describes in some detail, conforms to the expectations of a devout young woman in this period, Edith's masterminding of the building and adornment of the chapel at Wilton is more unexpected. Goscelin makes it clear that she was fully engaged with the project from the inception of the idea, through to the planning, construction, and decoration by Benno (who was responsible for its wall paintings), and the dedication ceremony over which Dunstan presided. As Catherine E. Karkov puts it, 'As both patron and source for the subject if not the design of the paintings, Edith becomes the first member of the West Saxon royal family known to be the creator of a monumental work of art'.[45] Karkov also suggests that the cruciform design may have been inspired by the legend of St Helena, to whom, as we have seen, Edith and her mother were devoted.[46] Strikingly, Goscelin reports that Edith was actually present on the building site and not only provided sustenance and encouragement to the workmen, but actually engaged in physical labour (*Vita*, 53). Yet even as Goscelin alludes to the practical skills and efforts required in constructing the church, he simultaneously elides them in emphasizing the spiritual dimensions of the work.[47] Although not yet the New Jerusalem that it will become in Goscelin's account in the *Liber confortatorius*, this building is a 'divine bridal chamber' (*Vita*, 53) as well as a temple of Solomon (*Vita*, 54) and the dedication ceremony is described as a spiritual marriage, in which Edith is equated with Mary as the Queen of Heaven, and, like Margaret of Antioch, is married to the Lord.[48]

Women's testimony and Edith's *Translatio*

The *Translatio* of Edith, which, as noted above, is found in the Rawlinson manuscript, but not in Cardiff, develops many of the themes of the *Vita*, but it also departs from the *Vita* in significant ways. From the opening lines, emphasis is now placed on the most powerful and trustworthy of male testimonies rather than on members of Edith's own community: Edith's brother, King Æthelred, two of his most noble advisors, and Archbishop Dunstan are all recipients of visions of Edith. Indeed Edith's appearances before first the king, and then his advisors, seem to echo the resurrection of Christ, who according to Matthew 28.9–10, first appeared to Mary Magdalene and another Mary, but in referring to 'these three witnesses' (*Translatio*, 69) the text alludes to 1 John 5.7–8, likening the king and his two advisors to the Trinity.

Dunstan, who already figured in the *Vita*, is again present in the *Translatio*, even at the expense of historical accuracy as Goscelin wrongly represents Dunstan as responsible for translating Edith's remains.[49] In Goscelin's account, in giving her instructions to Dunstan that the time has come for the translation of her body, Edith's spirit cites as evidence that she has indeed been sent by God and that she is not some deceiving ghost the fact that when her corpse is exhumed it will be found to be complete and undecayed. As with the earlier English abbesses, such as Æthelthryth of Ely, the incorrupt body is evidence of the physical intactness and moral purity of the female saint. Yet, as also with Æthelthryth, whose perfection was marred by the faint scar which marked the location of the bubo that killed her, and which, according to Bede, she attributed to her former prideful habit of wearing necklaces (see Chapter 1), Edith's corpse bears the signs of feminine sin. Edith's spirit explains to Dunstan that the physical decay will be limited to 'the organs of the body, which I misused in girlish light-mindedness, that is my eyes, my hands, and my feet' (*Translatio*, 69). However, in accordance with a prediction made by Dunstan himself at the time of the consecration of the chapel at Wilton, Edith's thumb remains intact, because she used this thumb to cross herself. Dunstan's role as primary authority in the *Translatio* is further reinforced by the account of Dunstan's vision of St Denis, the patron saint of Edith's church at Wilton. Dunstan found himself transported in his sleep to the main altar in the Wilton church, where he saw Edith address St Denis, asking him to confirm the mission that was being entrusted to Dunstan (*Translatio*, 70). St Denis then turned to Dunstan, and, after assuring him of Edith's virginal purity, reiterated that the time for the exhumation of Edith's body had come. As Hollis observes: 'Goscelin's case for the acceptance of Edith as a *bona fide* saint does not rest on the oral traditions of the Wilton nuns. It rests above all on the claim that her remains were translated by Dunstan and that she was closely associated with him throughout her life.'[50]

Nevertheless, within Goscelin's narrative, relations between women do still remain at the foreground. Even though the translation of Edith's body is justified by the testimony of such eminent male authorities as Æthelred and Dunstan, Goscelin nevertheless goes on to figure the opening of Edith's crypt as a restoration of the daughter to her mother: 'She, who had been born in the womb, from the tomb was born again to the mother. She received back from the grave the daughter whom she had long ago buried' (*Translatio*, 71). Furthermore, having completed his account of exhumation and translation of Edith's body to the Chapel of the Archangel Gabriel in the church in Wilton (*Translatio*, 71), Goscelin only briefly describes the activities of some relic hunters which are foiled by Edith's corpse (*Translatio*, 72), before digressing onto the series of miracles performed not by Edith but by her mother Wulfthryth. For Goscelin, the sanctity of Edith is so closely entwined with that of her mother that the two have to be considered together. If Edith is likened to the Virgin Mary, then Wulfthryth is another St Anne (*Translatio*, 72–3). Wulfthryth is granted the ability to make the blind see, and to make those who can see blind; and she can call upon divine vengeance, and offer protection to those who seek it (*Translatio*, 73–4). Wulfthryth also emulated the building works of her daughter, and was responsible for the construction of a stone wall around Wilton (*Translatio*, 75). Goscelin reports that when she died, she was buried close to Edith, in front of the main altar, and although a wall divided the tombs of the mother and daughter, a passageway connected them (*Translatio*, 75), reminiscent, perhaps, of the canal through which Edith had travelled when her mother gave birth to her. The sacred bond between mother and daughter is figured as one that will continue beyond both their deaths.

Even if Dunstan plays a central role as authoritative male witness of Edith's sanctity, as is the case in Bede's accounts of women's visions in the early history of the abbeys at Whitby, Ely and Barking, the visions experienced by the community of nuns at Wilton are still given considerable weight by Goscelin. Goscelin records that following Wulfthryth's death, one elderly nun, Ælflaed, was particularly stricken by grief. Ælflaed was so overcome with her sense of loss that, when she had finished performing her duties, she insisted on staying in the choir of the church near her tomb, praying and singing the Psalms. Ælflaed was rewarded for her steadfast devotion with an Easter miracle: while the other nuns were in the refectory, Ælflaed remained alone in the church, where she witnessed the tomb shake and open, and a lamb emerge. After Ælflaed had summoned her sisters, the lamb then circled the tomb three times before vanishing back from where it had come (*Translatio*, 76). Goscelin draws an explicit comparison here between Ælflaed and Mary Magdalene, the first witness of the Resurrection, and interprets the miracle as clear evidence of the blessed state of grace enjoyed by Edith's mother.

Typically Ælflaed's vision is not an isolated one. Goscelin follows his account with a description of three miracles that took place at the tomb of Wulfthryth, in which a paralysed woman, a nun with dysentery and a disabled child were all cured from their afflictions (*Translatio*, 76–7). Later in the *Translatio*, Goscelin also describes the vision witnessed by Ælfgifu's kinswoman, Thola of Wilton, whom Ælfgifu had identified as a possible successor alongside Godgifu.[51] In this, Edith defends herself from the defamation of Ealdgyth, another Wilton nun, who during a visit to Salisbury, claimed that Edith had shown herself to be powerless to defend the abbey. To authenticate this vision, Goscelin stresses that it is recent: Thola is still alive at the time of writing, and the vision took place 'In the time of Bishop Herman, of pious memory' (*Translatio*, 90).

Goscelin ensures that, as evidence of Edith's sanctity, he cites miracles that occurred in relation to the most important men, and women, in the land. He records that King Cnut, who had a personal devotion to Edith, and was a generous benefactor of Wilton, was saved from drowning after he invoked her name during a fierce storm at sea (*Translatio*, 77–8).[52] Goscelin also reports that Ealred, archbishop of York, was saved in parallel circumstances on a voyage to Jerusalem (*Translatio*, 78). Cnut's and Ealred's visions of Edith calming the sea storms are both reminiscent of the Virgin Mary's role as protector of seafarers, and her title *Stella Maris*. Once again, although important – and thus implicitly reliable – high-status male witnesses are central to this text, they are carefully balanced by the testimony of other women. Goscelin describes Queen Emma's devotion to Edith, both as a patron and then as a sister-in-law (*Translatio*, 79). Indeed Queen Emma herself was witness to a miracle in which the corpse of a thegn, who had wrongly seized possession of land belonging to Edith, was miraculously if temporarily revived; the corpse then petitioned the queen to return the estate to its rightful owner (*Translatio*, 79–80).

While many of the miracles that Goscelin records seem entirely predictable, and even grotesque, they are nevertheless clearly heavily indebted to the testimony of the Wilton nuns, and their spoken and written accounts of the visionary experiences of the community as a whole. A significant number of the miracles happened to the nuns themselves. The miracles surrounding Ælfgifu, abbess of Wilton, serve the function of confirming the validity of her rule. Goscelin begins his narrative of Ælfgifu with a healing miracle. Ælfgifu is afflicted with scrofula, referred to in the text as 'the royal disease' (*Translatio*, 87). One of her eyes is badly swollen, and she seems near the point of death:

Assistit pia consolatrix dormienti et, corporeis luminibus sopitis, spiritualibus
melius uidenti. Signat benedicta medica assueto sibi signo Saluatoris oculum
naufragantem, pingit uirgineo pollice salutiferam crucem, permulcet celesti
suauitate tribulatam: «Et iam, inquid, ne timeas; ex hoc te conualescere scias.»

'La légende de Ste Édith', ed. Wilmart, 294–5

[The devoted giver of comfort came to her side as she slept, and while her corporeal
eyes were sunk in sleep, she was able to see all the better with her spiritual eyes. The
holy doctor [Edith] blessed the endangered eye with her customary sign of the
Saviour; with her virginal thumb she traced the health-bearing cross; she touched
the troubled one with heavenly gentleness. 'And now,' she said, 'do not be afraid:
from this time you will know that you are getting better.']

Translatio, 87

Edith, as the *benedicta medica* [holy doctor] falls within the tradition of Mary
the Physician or *maria medica*, in which women assume a responsibility for
medical care more generally ascribed to men.[53] Shortly afterwards, Goscelin also
recounts how Edith appeared in a vision offering consolation to the nuns when
they were afflicted by an epidemic (*Translatio*, 89–90). Equally striking, however,
is the fact that, from the perspective of hindsight, Goscelin aligns Edith's role as
healer with that of Edward the Confessor, whose act in curing a woman of
scrofula is recorded in his *Life*.[54]

After describing the healing miracle, Goscelin goes on to explain that Ælfgifu's
entire career was mapped out by revelations of Edith received a quarter of a
century before Ælfgifu was elevated to the position of abbess. He describes
variations of a vision shared by a certain woman called Ælfhild and by Ælfgifu,
in which Edith presented Ælfgifu with her veil and ring (*Translatio*, 88), signalling
that the mantle of Wilton would be passed on to her. Ælfhild's vision also
indicated that Ælfgifu would be buried next to Wulfthryth in the Wilton church.
This aspect of the revelation is echoed in another vision attributed to Ælfgifu, in
which she saw Wulfthryth lying in the Gabriel Chapel, and was invited to join
her; a vision that was fulfilled following her death, when she was buried on
Wulfthryth's right hand side (*Translatio*, 88–9). As might be expected, Ælfgifu's
moment of death is marked by blessings. At Ælfgifu's request, Edith's holy corpse
is brought to her bedside, so that she can seek her intercession. At that moment,
a sleeping nun hears divine words confirming that, at Édith's request, the Virgin
Mary is waiting in the church to welcome Ælfgifu to heaven (*Translatio*, 88–9).
These visions do not, however, stand alone in the text as confirmation of Ælfgifu's
authority. Goscelin is careful to note that she was made abbess by Edith's nephew,
King Edward (*Translatio*, 88).

The close relationship between the *Vita* and the *Translatio* is very clear. The *Translatio*, as might be expected, picks up and develops key themes in the *Vita*, such as women's authority, the close spiritual relationship between Edith and her mother, devout female friendships, and the significance of visions within the women's religious community at Wilton. At the same time, other aspects of the *Vita*, and especially the biographical elements – most notably Goscelin's ambivalent accounts of Edith's luxurious dress, or her menagerie – are omitted from the *Translatio*. Edith's role in the building of the chapel attached to the church at Wilton is, however, picked up on, albeit somewhat indirectly. Perhaps inevitably, the tombs of Edith and her mother are key loci in the spiritual drama surrounding Edith's translation and spiritual afterlife: their positioning and structure are of great significance, both in relation to the preservation of their own remains and in relation to Ælfgifu's burial, although it is striking that it is Wulfthryth's tomb that is given the more prominence. There is also an implicit opposition set up between the construction of the chapel by Edith, as it is described by Goscelin in the *Vita*, and activities of the craftsmen employed by Cnut to build a golden shrine or casket dedicated to Edith (*Translatio*, 78–9). These craftsmen were generously resourced and highly skilled but chose to line their own pockets and to hold back on the work for which they were employed. Goscelin figures their sinfulness as a desecration for which they are justly punished. Significantly, the casket that the craftsmen produced to house Edith's body depicted the events of Matthew 28.5–7, in which the angel appeared to Mary Magdalene and Mary, and announced the Resurrection of Christ. This casket, located at the heart of the church which Edith herself built, highlights the importance of women's visions, and women's relationships with one another. For Goscelin, then, as for the community at Wilton, such building work is an indicator of sanctity. That this view was shared more widely is evidenced by *The Life of King Edward*, which draws explicit parallels between Edward's construction of Westminster Abbey and Queen Edith's activities at Wilton in replacing St Edith's wooden church with a stone building. It is in this later church that Eve of Wilton was dedicated.[55]

Edith's legacy

Commissioned by Abbess Godgifu and based on the nuns' own oral recollections and written accounts, the composition of the *Legend of Edith* cannot be ascribed to Goscelin alone, any more than the construction of Edith's chapel at Wilton can be ascribed solely to the male artists, masons and labourers who also worked on it. As the *Legend*'s intended readers, the Wilton community further shaped the text that was produced for them and the surviving manuscript witnesses provide unique insights into some of the finer points in this process. As noted earlier, the version of Goscelin's *Vita* of Edith found in the Cardiff manuscript seems to have been tailored by Goscelin specifically for the use of the nuns of Wilton.[56] Bugyis, in her study of Goscelin's lost sources, suggests that this Wilton version does not include the *Translatio* as it would have been otiose, 'because the community already possessed their own collection of Edith's *miracula*'.[57] The Cardiff text excludes the prologue with its dedication to Lanfranc but expands other aspects of the *Vita*, and includes additional metrical compositions.[58] The strongest argument *against* the suggestion that the text has been produced specifically for the Wilton women is that the Cardiff manuscript excludes the passage found in Rawlinson in which it is recorded that Edith read saints' lives intensively, and was inspired by those concerning her grandmother, Ælfgifu of Shaftesbury and her aunt and namesake, Edith of Tamworth (*Vita*, 35 n.50), which the Cardiff manuscript replaces with an account of her devotion to St Denis, to whom Edith's chapel at Wilton was initially dedicated. However, references to both Ælfgifu of Shaftesbury and Edith of Tamworth are inserted elsewhere in the Cardiff text, which very much stresses Edith's position within an elite female genealogy. Furthermore the Cardiff manuscript also expands on the significance of Wulfthryth, who was clearly greatly revered by the Wilton community, as an exemplar for Edith. Hollis points out that the Cardiff manuscript also has a specificity that may be derived from local knowledge: 'the most substantial additions in Cardiff are concrete and specific accounts of the details of Edith's life (very plausibly derived from traditions current at Wilton)'.[59] The Cardiff manuscript is very careful to locate Edith's *Vita* in relation to the physical space of Wilton in its description of her menagerie, enclosed in a courtyard built along the southern wall of the abbey (*Vita*, 41), and it emphasizes that her book of devotions is preserved by the Wilton nuns 'as a token of her memory' (*Vita*, 34), in other words as a relic of great local significance.

Equally significantly in terms of making a convincing case for a Wilton provenance of the version found in the Cardiff manuscript, there is a clear connection between the Cardiff manuscript and Goscelin's subsequent work, the *Liber confortatorius*, which is addressed to Eve, a nun of Wilton. A series of additions to the Cardiff text anticipate the apocalyptic representation in that text of Edith as the mystical bride of Christ in a New Jerusalem that is equated with a heavenly Wilton. Hollis even goes so far as to suggest that the Cardiff manuscript 'was a version intended for Eve at Angers as well as for the Wilton community'.[60] Certainly the Cardiff text, and Edith's *Legend* more generally, might well have appealed to anchoritic women as well as to other women religious. Parallels can be found between Goscelin's representation of Edith's piety, and the representation of Christina of Markyate (*c.* 1096–after 1155) in her anonymous twelfth-century *Life* (which is discussed in more detail in the Coda). Hollis and Jocelyn Wogan-Browne, note, for example, that Goscelin's representation of the spiritual friendship of Edith and Bishop Dunstan, which is likened to that between the Virgin Mary and John the Apostle, is mirrored in Christina's vision of the Crucifixion, in which Christina is Mary and her supporter, Geoffrey, abbot of St Albans, is John.[61]

In addition to comparing the Cardiff *Vita* with that found in Rawlinson and to elucidating connections with later texts such as the *Liber confortatorius* and the *Life of Christina of Markyate*, it is fruitful to examine the Cardiff manuscript, as an entity in its own right, for what it reveals about the reception of the text. In this manuscript, a life of the fifth/sixth-century Breton saint Winwaloe, abbot of Landévennec (fols 1r–80v) is bound together with a collection of lives of the saints (fols 81r–146r), containing seven items: Goscelin's *Life of Æthelburh* (fols. 84r–94r), lections for St Hildelith (fols 94r–96v), the *Life of Edward, King and Martyr* (fols. 97r–102v), Goscelin's life of Edith (fols 102v–120r), a *Life of St David* (fols. 121r–129v), a metrical *Life of Mary of Egypt* (fols 130r–135v), and a hagiography of the Frankish hermit saint Ebrulf (fols 136r–146r).[62] Most of the items found in this manuscript speak to the interests of a house of women religious. While the assorted lives are fairly eclectic, one immediately striking inclusion is the *Life of Edward, King and Martyr*, a version of a text that, as has been mentioned already, may have been authored by a nun of Shaftesbury, or at any rate was produced for the convent.[63] This life of Edith's half-brother is in the same hand as that of the *Vita* of Edith.[64] The narrative of Mary of Egypt, with its account of the desert mother's devotion to the Virgin Mary, is one that would also have appealed particularly to women.[65] N. R. Ker contends that the first two items (the *Life of Æthelburh* and lections for St Hildelith) may have been copied for or at Barking Abbey and that all the items, including the life of Edith, were foliated at Barking Abbey around the end of the fifteenth century or beginning of the sixteenth.[66] The annotations found in Edith's *Vita*, which Ker also ascribes to the Barking nuns, certainly highlight female figures, such as a comparison of the nuns of Wilton to Christian Amazons on fol. 107r, or a comparison between Edith and both Martha and Mary on fol. 107v. Another annotation and a manicule direct the reader to Edith's prayer in the added passage about her book of devotions on fol. 106v (see Figure 5.1).

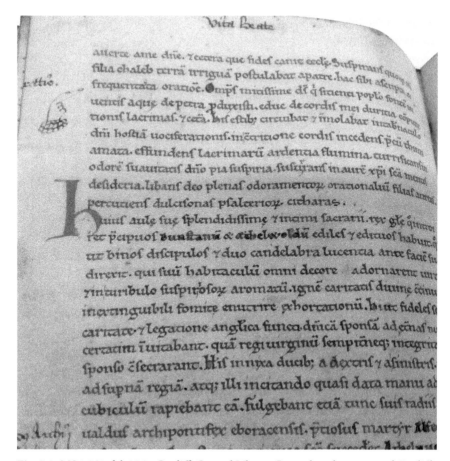

Fig. 5.1   MS 1.381, fol. 106v. Cardiff, Central Library. Reproduced courtesy of Cardiff Libraries.

In summary, the life of Edith that appears in the Cardiff manuscript is significant for a number of reasons. First, when read alongside the Rawlinson version, it reveals the sort of fine-tuning that a professional writer like Goscelin would make to a text when adapting it for a specific audience. Second, and more importantly in terms of my argument, it illustrates some of the ways that a community of readers, as the patrons and intended audience of the text, might indirectly or even directly shape the work being written for them. Third, when considered in terms of its surviving manuscript context, it is revealing about how the texts may have been appreciated by subsequent generations of monastic women.

Conclusion

A saint who appreciated her own regal dress, who kept animals for her own enjoyment and who did not do enough, posthumously, to defend the wealth of her abbey, Edith was no doubt a sometimes controversial figure. Yet her legacy was not insignificant. The chapel she had built was remembered long after it had been replaced, her prayer book was preserved amongst other relics, and the memory of her was revived – if overwritten – by one of the most important monastic hagiographers of the age. Edith's *Legend* was commissioned by Edith's own religious house, and it draws heavily on the testimony of the nuns, and on the narratives passed down through the generations in the community, including, crucially, some now-lost written sources authored by the nuns of Wilton. In his *Legend*, Goscelin records the history of the community even as he rewrites it, presenting Edith as an idealized example of female monastic spirituality inspired in turn by her familial predecessors (her mother, aunt, and grandmother). The Cardiff manuscript is testimony to the subsequent value of this text for women monastic readers. Goscelin clearly recognized the potential of Edith's life, or of his account of it, for a female audience, and as we will see in the next chapter, he exploited this when he came to write the *Liber confortatorius*, which he addressed to his beloved protégée, the recluse Eve of Wilton. Indeed the parallels between the two texts seem to indicate that Goscelin assumed Eve was already very familiar with his version of Edith's *Legend*. Yet perhaps Edith's most important legacy is one not fully acknowledged by Goscelin: that she provided inspiration for another young woman, who, in the face of limited options, nevertheless somehow felt empowered to forge her own path.

Textual Intimacies in and beyond Wilton

Introduction

Closely connected to Goscelin of St Bertin's *Legend* of Edith is another text written for, or in this case, *to* a Wilton religious. This is the *Liber confortatorius* [*Book of Consolation*].[1] The text survives in one twelfth-century manuscript, which has a North-West French provenance: London, British Library, MS Sloane 3103, fols 1r–114v. Goscelin wrote the *Liber* shortly after 1080, and addressed it to a young nun, Eve (*c.* 1058–*c.* 1125), who had recently left Wilton to become a recluse at Saint-Laurent du Tetre in Angers, France. Wilton functioned as a school for the elite and amongst those educated there alongside Eve were Gunhild of Wessex, daughter of King Harold Godwinson, and possibly also Margaret of Scotland (whose life was subsequently commissioned by her daughter Matilda).[2] During his time in Wilton, Goscelin appears to have assumed the role of tutor. The *Liber confortatorius* describes the close spiritual relationship that developed during that period between Goscelin and Eve, and Goscelin's subsequent anguish on discovering that after he had left the abbey, Eve too had departed in order to embark on a new devotional career that would exclude him completely from her life. Ostensibly the *Liber confortatorius* is a book of consolation in the tradition of Boethius's sixth-century *Consolatio Philosophiae* (*The Consolation of Philosophy*), in which Goscelin reflects on the meaning of his loss. Nevertheless it is framed as a letter to Eve, and also serves as a book of guidance for the recluse, apparently anticipating such works as the twelfth-century *De institutione inclusarum* or *The Formation of Anchoresses* by Ælred, abbot of Rievaulx, and the early thirteenth-century Middle-English *Ancrene Wisse* or *Guide for Anchoresses*. What Goscelin's text shares with the last two texts is that it is written for someone known to the author: Ælred wrote for his own sister and the author of *Ancrene Wisse* for three sisters whom he depicts as being in his spiritual care.

In writing the *Liber confortatorius*, then, Goscelin moves away from hagiography to a very different genre, which enables him to address Eve (who is both his audience and his subject) in a more intimate fashion, and also to explore the often negative emotions that he is experiencing as a consequence of her abrupt departure. At the same time, however, as we will see in the concluding section in this chapter, Goscelin seeks to establish connections between Eve and her Wilton predecessor, St Edith, connections which reveal something, perhaps, of his frustrated aspirations for his protégée. Goscelin, as a skilled writer of hagiographies, employed by a number of religious houses to chronicle their early histories, may have aspired to author a life of a contemporary saint. In Eve, he hoped he had found his subject. As I will outline in the sections that follow, Goscelin structures his *Liber* so that it moves from an account of his friendship with Eve and his subsequent tremendous sense of loss and anger that this has ended, through a discussion of spiritual warfare and advice on how to live as a recluse, to a climactic invocation of the Heavenly Jerusalem in which Goscelin imagines Eve joining St Edith in Paradise. In so doing, Goscelin continually insists not only on Eve's isolation but also on Eve's relationships with others: himself, her family, fellow nuns, friends and other recluses, living and dead, and the Virgin Mary and Christ.

The *Liber confortatorius*, unlike many of the other texts considered in this study – with some notable exceptions, such as Rudolf of Fulda's *Life of Leoba* – may seem to sit uneasily within a study of women's literary culture: it was not written by a woman, nor based on works potentially authored by women, nor in response to female patronage, although Goscelin does invite Eve to become his patron (*Book of Encouragement*, trans. Otter, 33). The *Liber* is very different from the hagiographies that are more typical of Goscelin's literary output, and it was not written for a specific religious community. There is certainly no reason to think that the Wilton community requested its production, although that community is represented overall in very positive terms in the text. In some respects the *Liber* is closer to Aldhelm's *De Virginitate* (discussed in Chapter 2) in that it provides guidance about how to live a devout life as a female religious, but it is far more personal in its address and far more tailored to an individual. Eve, as the intended recipient of this work, is also the implied reader. Having achieved a state of spiritual transcendence, only she can fully understand his meaning. This is a book about Eve, and a book for her. In the *Liber*, the female subject is also the intended audience. For this reason, it is an appropriate text to consider in detail in this study of early medieval women's literary culture.

From shared reading to solitary study

At the heart of the *Liber* is the soul friendship ('*unanimis tuus*' [your soul-friend]) between Goscelin and Eve,[3] which in the writing of the text is transformed into a relationship between author and subject, and author and inscribed and intended reader. This is a far more intimate and immediate relationship than that between author and subject in *The Legend of Edith*, for example, because Eve is a living woman who is directly addressed, although there is no evidence that she ever even received the *Liber*, far less read and responded to it.[4] MS Sloane 3103 is a twelfth-century manuscript produced several decades after Eve's death, which occurred in around 1125. It is not clear whether it is copied from Goscelin's holograph or a later version. It may well have been produced in the Abbey of Saint-Sauveur-le-Vicomte in Normandy, where Sloane 3013, which was initially bound in two parts (fols 1r–115v and 116r–122v), was subsequently housed.[5] There appear to be a number of scribal hands at work in the manuscript. The *Liber* is the first item and it is followed by a variety of textual and musical material relating to St Thomas Becket (fol. 114v), St Katherine of Alexandria (fols 115r and 116r) and St Bartholomew (fol. 115v), a brief history of William of Normandy, the *Brevis relatio* (fols 116v–121v)), a genealogy of English kings (fol. 121v), a letter from Bernard of Clairvaux to Pope Eugene III (fols 121v–122r), an excerpt from the treatise 'On the Triple Abode' once attributed to St Augustine of Hippo (fol. 122r) and, finally, an antiphon (fol. 122v). Clearly the *Liber* was of sufficient spiritual importance to be preserved in a monastic library alongside other devotional and historical material, yet there is no direct connection to Eve or her immediate locality. The Abbey of Saint-Sauveur-le-Vicomte is located some 170 miles north of Angers; in other words, quite a distance away from where Eve settled and almost half-way between Wilton and Angers. We can only speculate about how a copy of the *Liber* turned up in Normandy, about how closely MS Sloane 3103 is related to the manuscript that Goscelin produced, and about who made the decision that it should be copied and preserved. It is, however, possible that a copy of the *Liber* was dispatched to Angers but did not reach its intended final destination. There is certainly no evidence to suggest that the text was ever widely disseminated.

Wide dissemination of the text was in fact something that Goscelin explicitly opposed. In the Prologue, Goscelin figures the *Liber confortatorius* as an intimate communication that is not intended for public consumption. He expresses his concern that someone other than the addressee might take possession of the text, and embeds within it the entreaty that, should the letter go astray, the finder

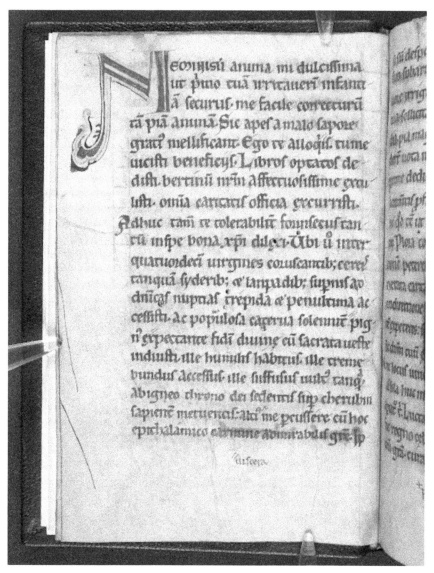

Fig. 6.1 Sloane MS 3103, f.3v. © The British Library Board.

is to return it directly to Eve, 'for whom alone it is manifestly intended' (*Book of Encouragement,* trans. Otter, 19). His impassioned claim that the letter is not aimed at a wider audience is of course rhetorical, at least in part. But the epistolary form of the *Liber confortatorius* is more than a literary commonplace. According to Goscelin, he and Eve had frequently corresponded (*Book of Encouragement,* trans. Otter, 25). The *Liber* is then represented as the continuation of this previous communication, and Goscelin suggests that a response will or at least should be forthcoming (*Book of Encouragement,* trans. Otter, 21). Nevertheless, despite its epistolary format, in other respects the *Liber,* which is subdivided into a Prologue and four books, has little in common with the correspondence with the missionary nuns in the Boniface collection discussed in Chapter 3, for example. And unlike later examples of anchoritic literature which offer guidance on living as a recluse, such as *Ancrene Wisse,* it does not set out to provide step-by-step instructions on living a contemplative life. The *Liber* is a work that encourages a reflective response.

In his reminiscences, in the first book, of the first flowering of love between himself and Eve, Goscelin places shared reading at its heart. As Rebecca Hayward and Stephanie Hollis note, 'from the beginning, Goscelin and Eve's friendship had a textual dimension':[6]

> Meministi, anima mi dulcissima, ut primo tuam irritauerim infantiam, securus me facile correcturum tam piam animam. . . . Libros optatos dedisti, Bertinum nostrum affectuosissime extulisti, omnia caritatis officia excurristi.
>
> > *Liber confortatorius,* ed. Talbot, 28

> [You remember, my sweetest soul, how I first vexed you when you were a child, quite certain I could easily correct such a pious soul. . . . You gave me books I very much wanted; you spoke affectionately of my Saint Bertin; you hastened to do all the offices of charity.]
>
> > *Book of Encouragement,* trans. Otter, 23

While this allusion to gift-giving might remind us of the importance of the exchange of books and letters between Boniface and his female followers some centuries earlier, the context here is quite different. Monika Otter, in the introduction to her translation of the *Liber,* points out the striking parallels between Goscelin and Eve and their more famous contemporaries, Abelard and Heloise.[7] Both couples are made up of a male teacher and female pupil brought together by a love of learning, although, according to Abelard's own account, shared reading proved a cover for his secret affair with Heloise:

> Primum doma una cuniungimur, postmodum amino. Sub occasione itaque discipline, amori penitus uaccabamus, et secretos recessus, quos amor optabat, studium lectionis offerebat. Apertis itaque libris, plura de amore quam de lectione uerba se ingerebant, plura erant oscula quam sententie; sepius ad sinus quam ad libros reducebantur manus, crebrius oculos amor in se reflectebat quam lectio in scripturam dirigebat.

[We were united, first under one roof, then in heart; and so with our lessons providing the opportunity we abandoned ourselves entirely to love. Her studies allowed us the private seclusion that love desired and then, with our books open before us, more words of love than of our reading passed between us, and more kissing than ideas. My hands strayed oftener to her bosom than to her books; love drew our eyes to look on each other more than reading kept them to our texts.][8]

There are parallels here too, with Dante's representation in the *Divina Commedia* [*Divine Comedy*] of Paulo and Francesca, the two lovers in the second circle of Hell, punished eternally for their lustful desires, which were kindled as together they read the story of Lancelot.[9] For Goscelin and Eve, in contrast to both these examples, the relationship is presented (albeit defensively) as chaste rather than sexual. Whereas Abelard in his *Historia Calamitatum* [*The Story of My Misfortunes*] confesses and laments the physical nature of his previous relationship with Heloise, Goscelin insists that his friendship with Eve was entirely spiritual. There are other important distinctions between Goscelin and Eve and Abelard and Heloise. As Otter explains, the intellectual environments in which the two couples flourished are quite distinct: Abelard and Heloise are situated firmly within a scholastic milieu of logic and debate, whereas Goscelin and Eve 'were both raised in a tradition of slow, meditative, reiterative reading'.[10] Whereas Heloise's and Abelard's correspondence has survived (even if the authenticity of Heloise's letters has been questioned), none of the letters exchanged by Goscelin and Eve when Eve was still at Wilton now exists.

In recognizing the importance of reading as the foundation of his relationship with Eve, Goscelin seeks to keep this activity alive, even though he is no longer present. Much later in the *Liber*, when he has moved on somewhat from lamenting what he has lost and begun to offer more constructive advice for the future, Goscelin exhorts Eve to live her life in her cell as one sealed up against worldly temptation and sinful gossip (*Book of Encouragement*, trans. Otter, 94–5). At the same time he urges her to remain open to all knowledge and learning: 'I would like the window of your cell to be wide enough to admit a library' (*Book of Encouragement*, trans Otter, 95–6). He goes on to recommend that Eve study Augustine's *Confessions* and *City of God*, Eusebius's *Ecclesiastical History* and its continuation, Orosius's *De Ormesta Mundi* [History of the World or History Against the Pagans] and Boethius's *Consolation of Philosophy* (*Book of Encouragement*, trans. Otter, 96).[11] As Mari Hughes-Edwards notes, Goscelin depicts Eve as intellectually independent, as one who is more than capable of self-education, and rightly observes that Goscelin grants Eve 'a degree of spiritual latitude not found in any other anchoritic guide'.[12] There is no sense here, as there is in the later *Ancrene Wisse*, that the woman recluse requires close supervision, or even scrutiny, by male clergy.

There can be no doubt then that Eve, the inscribed reader of the *Liber confortatorius* and its intended recipient, was an intelligent, highly educated and literate young woman. Nevertheless, at the same time as Goscelin celebrates Eve's Latinity and learning, and despite their earlier exchange of letters, writing is not an activity to which he ascribes any significance in relation to her new role.[13] Indeed, in one early passage, Goscelin imagines how *he* might benefit from a reclusive life similar to that which Eve has adopted – in his cell he would pray and read, and also compose and write (*Book of Encouragement*, trans. Otter, 32–3) – but he does not pause to consider that the opportunity to pursue the latter activities might now be available to Eve. This is in contrast to St Edith of Wilton, who, as we saw in the last chapter, according to Goscelin's own account produced a book of devotional material in her own hand, which included prayers that she may have composed herself.[14] Rather, Goscelin suggests that in her new-found solitude, Eve will devote her time to meditation and prayer and he instructs her to 'reweave the cloth of the psalms' (*Book of Encouragement*, trans. Otter, 98). The metaphor of weaving may also be intended to have literal connotations. Tom Licence suggests that spinning, weaving and embroidery were vital sources of income for the female recluse.[15] They may also have seemed more conducive to meditation than writing. Women recluses also often assumed an intercessory role,[16] and Goscelin asks Eve to intercede on his own behalf, likening himself to St Augustine of Hippo, saved by the tears of his mother (*Book of Encouragement*, trans. Otter, 31). Yet, even if, despite their common history of shared reading, and exchange of books and letters, Goscelin does not think of Eve as a writer, he does recognize that in choosing her own innovative religious path, against his wishes, she has become an independent woman, capable of independent thought. His assessment is well founded. Hollis is surely correct to suggest that in assuming the role of a recluse before the practice became widespread amongst devout women in England and continental Europe, Eve was 'at the forefront of cultural change'.[17]

From shared exile to solitary mourning

According to Goscelin's account, his soul friendship with Eve was not only based on their fervour for the love of God, expressed through their shared studying and conversations, but also rooted in their common experience as outsiders in English society. Exile is a recurring theme running through the *Liber confortatorius*. As Licence argues, and as we have seen in Boniface's self-representation, and in that of his female correspondents, 'the belief that exile, as a penitential or simply an ascetic exercise, could cleanse the soul from sin' had its origins in the earliest medieval Christianity.[18] In the case of Goscelin, of course, he is both the exile and the one who has been left behind. The *Liber* offers a nuanced exploration of the feelings of the immigrant. Goscelin's text is mired in nostalgia – according to Hughes-Edwards, it is 'steeped in the very past which he urges Eve to banish from her mind'.[19] He describes the suffering of the exile, and projects these feelings onto Eve. In the first book, Goscelin likens Eve's new circumstance, as a recluse in Angers, to the women of aristocratic or royal lineage whose betrothals serve to forge or to strengthen a political allegiance, and who have no choice but to leave the comfort and familiarity of their native lands, never to return (*Book of Encouragement*, trans. Otter, 41–2). The example he cites here is that of Adela, daughter of Count Robert I of Flanders, who was married to Canute IV of Denmark (*Book of Encouragement*, trans. Otter, 42). In contrast to the trials experienced by such women, Goscelin argues, the summons to leave one's home, family and friends to join Christ in order to enjoy everlasting happiness can be thought of as the opposite of the hardship, as something to embrace and to celebrate.

Goscelin also figures himself as an exile, claiming that he and Eve share a similar heritage. Goscelin contextualizes this in terms of the movement of peoples, starting with familiar examples from the Old Testament and from classical mythology, but then switching suddenly to their own recent shared history:

> hodieque Normanni in Angliam, Britanniam, in qua te quoque cum Anglica gente constat fuisse aduenam: sed in patre Dano et matre Lotaringa a claris natalibus filiam emersisse Anglicam.
>
> *Liber confortatorius*, ed. Talbot, 41

> [or nowadays the Normans to England or Britain, where the entire English people were once newcomers—including yourself, who, the well-born daughter of a Danish father and a Lotharingian mother, turned out English.]
>
> *Book of Encouragement*, trans. Otter, 42

Goscelin's list of exiles began with the exodus of the Israelites and the Babylonian and Assyrian captivities, and the transplantation of the Cuthites, but then slid somewhat uncomfortably into the legend of Aeneas's escape following the destruction of Troy which ultimately resulted in the founding of Rome and from this into the Norman colonization of England. Licence suggests that Troy here is both the '*locus classicus* of exiled homecoming' and also 'an antitype, in that their mission to found a city on earth was at odds with the objective of inheriting the heavenly city'.[20] Goscelin does not refer to himself in this discussion, but he is nevertheless implicated in this history. Originating from Flanders or the Duchy of Brabant, he was a monk at St Bertin in Saint-Omer in northern France before moving to England. Goscelin's reference to Eve's parentage, and more specifically to her father, draws an implicit parallel between the previously mentioned Adela and Eve's mother and Eve herself, whose identity – both foreign and English – is fundamentally divided.

The effect of the silent inclusion of Goscelin within this narrative frame is to lead the reader to assume that, at least to some extent, Goscelin is actually reflecting on his own traumatic experiences of exile, because, having lost contact with Eve, he can only speculate about her feelings. Goscelin vividly describes the pain endured by those Eve left behind in England, including the abbess of Wilton, her fellow nuns, her mother and father, and himself (*Book of Encouragement*, trans. Otter, 30). Later, he goes on to imagine that Eve struggles to reconcile herself with her separation from those she loves (*Book of Encouragement*, trans. Otter, 43). Again and again throughout the first book, Goscelin vacillates between thinking of himself as one whose intense suffering at the loss of Eve makes him unique and between reminding her, reproachfully, of the others who share his pain. Equally reproachfully Goscelin cites many examples of friends, both Christian and pagan, who did *not* have to endure separation from one another.

Most telling, perhaps, is the example taken from *The Life of St. Gertrude of Nivelles*, which describes her deep bond with Modesta, abbess of Trier, that developed despite the fact that the two women did not live close enough to one another to meet in person.[21] Goscelin reports the vision that Modesta experienced at the moment of Gertrude's death:

> Et de longinquo terrarum spatio ubi corporaliter obiit, presentialiter se ac si in corpore exhibuit, atque ita infit: «Ego sum Geretrudis quam multum dilexisti, quam magis affectu quam uultu nosti, quam scias hac hora ad Dominum de ergastulo migrasse corporali». Hec contemplatrix referendo audiuit ab his qui sanctam nouerant eamdem esse et faciem et staturam eius quam uiderat; inuentumque est eamdem horam obitus sui fuisse qua apperuerat.
>
> *Liber confortatorius*, trans. Talbot, 44

[Despite the great geographical distance of the place where she physically died, she herself showed present as if in the flesh; and she said, 'I am Gertrude, whom you loved very much, whom you knew better through your affection than you could have known her by sight; know that in this hour I have left the prison of my body and gone over to the Lord.' Later, the visionary heard from those who knew the saint that she was identical in appearance and stature with the figure that she had seen; and it was found that she had died in the same hour in which she had appeared to Modesta.]

Book of Encouragement, trans. Otter, 46

Jane Tibbetts Schulenburg notes the similarity between Modesta's vision and those experienced by nuns at the time of the death of Hild of Whitby, finding in them evidence of close same-sex female friendships.[22] To these examples we might also add those of the visions of Torhtgyth of Barking, which she experienced at the time of her beloved abbess's death, and, closer in time, the accounts of the death of Wulfthryth and Ælfgifu's vision, recorded by Goscelin himself in the *Legend of Edith*.[23]

In order to develop the parallel with Gertrude and Modesta still further, Goscelin cites the suffering of a female friend of Eve, evidently a nun at Wilton:

O quotiens Egidam tuam beatam pensabam, que te ut arctius diligebat, ita et loci et sexus unitate presentialiter sibi confouebat! Sed ecce sua sollemnia in merorem et solitudinem sunt conuersa....

Liber confortatorius, ed. Talbot, 45

[How often I have envied your friend Eadgyth, who not only loved you more intimately, but, since she shared your place and your sex, was able to warm herself in your presence! But now her rejoicing, too, has turned into mourning and solitude.]

Book of Encouragement, trans. Otter, 47

Goscelin's envy of Eadgyth is ill disguised. Not only did she formerly have the opportunity to live alongside Eve, but also, as he goes on to explain, she was able to say her farewells, something Goscelin repeatedly stresses he was denied. Goscelin thus takes the metaphors of the recluse as dead to the world and of her cell as grave (metaphors that become commonplace in later anchoritic literature) to considerable lengths, locating Eve simultaneously both within and without the tradition of seventh-century abbesses and their female soul friendships. Yet despite the force of Goscelin's extended lamentations, he never allows the reader to lose sight of the reality that Eve is not dead but merely absent, and that a mystical reunion between friends, similar to that between Gertrude and Modesta (or Hild and Torhtgyth, or Wulfthryth and Ælfgifu), if it is to happen at all, will take place only sometime in the distant future. Even as Goscelin labours to insist that his friendship with Eve was exceptional and exclusive, based on their shared love of God, their shared reading and their shared backgrounds, he finds himself forced to acknowledge that Eve had other relationships – including those with her fellow nuns – that were equally intense.

Social solitaries

How useful is it to think of Eve, in her reclusive life, in terms of exile? While, as Kathryn Maude argues, Goscelin is 'invested in her solitude as a rhetorical device, which calls attention to his own loneliness without her', the reality of her existence was rather different.[24] Licence sees Eve as part of much larger English and European anchoritic movement, [25] and Elizabeth M. Tyler has shown that as a recluse, Eve was far from isolated; rather she was part of a larger network of solitaries and male and female religious.[26] Indeed, at the same time as Goscelin 'imagines Eve in solitude',[27] he embeds the Eve of his *Liber confortatorius* within a textual community of anchorites. Hughes-Edwards states that in contrast to Ælred's *De institutione inclusarum* or the *Ancrene Wisse*, the *Liber* allows Eve 'a pronounced measure of acceptable reclusive sociability'.[28] Writing in praise of the anchoritic life in the second book of the *Liber*, Goscelin provides an English example of asceticism and martyrdom – that of Brihtric, who lived in a cell near Bury St Edmunds (*Book of Encouragement*, trans. Otter, 77–8).[29] Goscelin describes how the devil assailed Brihtric with his deceit, but was foiled following the intervention of Brihtric's friend Eilsius or Aelsi (possibly identifiable as the Abbot of Ramsey).[30] Goscelin then goes on to describe Brihtric's death at the hands of pirates, who burnt down the fortress to which his cell was attached. Brihtric refused to leave his cell and his corpse was found some days later, stretched out on the ground as if on the cross. Brihtric is such an important choice for Goscelin because he is much closer in time and space to Eve than many of the other exemplary saints that he lists (figures such as Blandina, one of the second-century martyrs of Lyon, whose suffering is recorded in Eusebius's *Ecclesiastical History*). Goscelin stresses that Brihtric's story has been widely circulated despite or rather because of its newness (*Book of Encouragement*, trans. Otter, 77). At the same time he emphasizes that his account is based on that of a trusted male eyewitness – Goscelin has heard it from Eilsius himself. Significantly he concludes the story with a rather cryptic reference to another recluse caught up in a conflagration, in this case a woman, who was miraculously saved from the flames, described as 'she who had been fighting the fight at your church before you' (*Book of Encouragement*, trans. Otter, 78). While there is some critical debate as to the identity of this woman, Barnes and Hayward suggest that Goscelin is referring to a recluse living near Eve in Angers.[31] The direct address to Eve that punctuates this abbreviated and allusive narrative makes stronger the connection between the woman and Eve. Taken together, the stories of Brihtric and of the anonymous female recluse seem designed not simply to encourage Eve in her resolute asceticism, but also to warn her of the very immediate dangers of her chosen existence, and to remind her of the vulnerability of seclusion.

At the same time that Goscelin reminds Eve of the risks of a life of isolation, he also acknowledges within the *Liber confortatorius* that, even having left Wilton, Eve may continue to enjoy close personal relationships with other religious. In the fourth book, Goscelin alludes to an anonymous anchoress who helped Eve become a recluse and whom Eve travelled to Angers to join (*Liber confortatorius*, trans Otter, 113). According to Otter, this is a reference to Eve's 'predecessor at Angers who recruited her and introduced her to the anchoritic life'.[32] When Eve arrived at Saint-Laurent du Tetre, which was attached to the Abbey of Le Ronceray (which already enjoyed a close cultural relationship with Wilton), she joined a ready-formed community of recluses of both sexes.[33] The idea that recluses were, to coin a phrase, social solitaries, embedded within the wider communities in which they lived, and benefitting from patronage, certainly seems to be confirmed by Goscelin's representation of Eve's new life:

> Quod autem te, o dulcissima, hic populus colligit, quod huius piissime matris cunctarumque sororum affectus in te redundat, quod te patrum et pontificum dignitas uisitat...
>
> *Liber confortatorius*, ed. Talbot, 92

> [But that you, my sweetest, are well received by the people there; that the venerable mother and all the sisters shower you with love; that dignified fathers and bishops visit you...]
>
> *Book of Encouragement*, trans. Otter, 113

This gives a very different impression of the anchoritic life than is the norm: Eve's arrival is publically celebrated, and rather than finding herself isolated, the recluse is at the centre of the community.

Eve at some point relocated to the church of Saint-Eutrope, also in Angers, where she may have lived with her niece.[34] Fascinatingly there is also evidence that Eve subsequently 'cohabited chastely' (as Barbara Newman puts it) with the recluse Hervé of Vendôme.[35] In a letter dated to *c.* 1102, Abbot Geoffrey of Vendôme wrote to Eve and Hervé, encouraging them to persevere in their life together.[36] This relationship was not without its critics. A poem in honour of Eve after her death, written by Hilary of Orléans, included the lines:

> Ibi uixit Eua diu cum Herueo socio.
> Qui hec audis, ad hanc uocem te turbari sencio.
> Fuge, frater, suspicari, non sit hic suspicio:
> Non in mundo sed in Christo fuit hec dilectio.[37]

> [There Eve lived for a long time with her companion Hervé.
> I sense that you are disturbed by this word, you who hear these things.
> Flee suspicion, brother, let there be no mistrust here.
> This love was not in the world but in Christ.][38]

Hilary is overtly concerned with deflecting criticism away from Eve. His account of Eve's life contradicts Goscelin's in a number of ways. For example, in addition to making no reference to Goscelin's role as her tutor, mentor and friend, he claims that Eve had already begun to live as a recluse while still residing in Wilton, and suggests that she moved away because even this life brought her too close to the company of her fellow nuns. As Maude suggests: 'Hilary's focus on Eve's move from community to solitude claims her for [a] narrative of monastic perfection, in which monks are trained within the monastery and then venture out into the metaphorical wilderness alone.'[39] Yet, despite or perhaps because of this, according to Hilary, Eve's funeral was a very public affair:

> Moniales adfuerunt, monachi, canonici.
> Spiritumque, sicut reor, conciues angelici

> [Nuns were present, monks and canons,
> and her spirit, as I believe, is a fellow citizen of the angels.][40]

Hughes-Edwards's analysis of these sometimes conflicting narratives is astute: 'Whatever the precise circumstances of Eve's later [or, we might add, earlier] experiences of solitude, in the *Liber* itself, Goscelin legislates for acceptable levels of interaction between recluses, communications between them and wider religious, and contact with the clergy (i.e. with male guests) – all of which implies the potential of this early medieval recluse to command a measure of post-enclosure public prominence.'[41] Whether or not Eve was contented in her life at Wilton, and whether or not she really did enjoy close friendships there, it is clear that even as a solitary, Eve was part of a dense religious network. From Goscelin's account, and from these later sources, it is apparent that Eve was an honoured figure, and one who was free to form intimate relationships of her own choice.

The recluse as spiritual warrior

The sorts of close friendships between Goscelin and Eve that Goscelin describes in his *Liber confortatorius* or that Eve subsequently formed with Hervé, are widespread throughout the Middle Ages. Goscelin himself cites many precedents from the Bible and from Christian history and legend. An influential model was the desert mother, Mary of Egypt, and although Goscelin does not specifically discuss Mary's friendship with the monk Zosimus, the legend was very well known and must have been familiar to Eve.[42] According to Goscelin's account, it seems that Eve was a visionary, and he gives the example of a specific revelation that Eve received concerning himself:

> Recolisne quod te a me cibatam pane candidissimo ante nostrum spiritum somniaueras, tibique inter edendum massas aureas in ore repertas, quas sensim in gremium colligebas? Respice panem uite et uerbum Domini super aurum desiderabile, ac de hoc auro eternum monile tibi labore confice...
>
> Liber conforatorius, ed. Talbot, 29

> [Do you remember when you told me your dream, in which I was feeding you with snow-white bread, and as you ate you found golden morsels in your mouth, which you collected in your lap? See, that is the bread of life and the word of God that is more to be desired than gold.]
>
> Book of Encouragement, trans. Otter, 25–6

Goscelin represents himself as both instigator of the vision and as interpreter, suggesting that the crumbs represent the Scriptures that Goscelin, as her former teacher, explicated for Eve. Goscelin attempts to control the meaning of his pupil's direct communication from God. However, he cannot and may not wish to deny the intimacy and eroticism inherent in this depiction of their relationship, an intimacy and eroticism that is far from unique to Eve's vision.

While for Goscelin, intense friendships between male and female religious are to be celebrated, his *Liber confortatorius* betrays some anxiety that others will be critical of such relationships, anticipating the condemnation of the later relationship between Eve and Hervé that Hilary seeks to dispel in his poem.[43] There is certainly evidence to suggest that some of their contemporaries viewed the relationship between Goscelin and Eve in a negative light. In the Prologue to the *Liber confortatorius*, Goscelin alludes to 'the whisperer of scandal, the lecherous eye, the pointing finger, the spewer of hot air and the dirty snickerer' (*Book of Encouragement*, trans. Otter, 19), and he goes on to assert that 'I would rather be ridiculed by the raised eyebrows of strangers than not do justice to love' (*Book of Encouragement*, trans. Otter, 20). It is, of course, possible to see this sort of self-vindication as a literary topos, a consolatory commonplace of the discourse of soul friendship. Certainly, I would argue, it is closely tied to the form of the *psychomachia* [conflict within the soul] that also influences the second book of the *Liber confortatorius*. The second book focuses on the metaphor of the soul as spiritual warrior responding to a divine call to arms and combating evil. Licence points out that Goscelin encourages Eve to read the *Life of St Antony* as a defence against Satan's ploys (*Book of Encouragement*, trans. Otter, 96),[44] but Goscelin's own treatise also serves a similar purpose. The first section of the second book draws on Virgil's *Aeneid*, Boethius's *Consolation of Philosophy*, Prudentius's *Cathemerinon* and Horace's *Satires*, alongside Scripture and other texts. Yet at the same time as Goscelin locates his account within a time frame that encompasses Classical myth, Biblical history and the writings of the Church Fathers and medieval theologians, he also stresses the immediacy of war, reminding Eve of the times when he found himself on a boat on the Thames that was at risk of sinking (*Book of Encouragement*, trans. Otter, 52), a memory that Goscelin translates into an allegory of the Christian's battle for salvation. In this book, Eve is a Perpetua in her courage and steadfastness, an Agnes in her resolution and self-sacrifice, a Genevieve in her fasting and asceticism, and a Blandina in her bravery in the face of agonizing torture.

Strikingly, in this context Goscelin represents himself as Eve's inferior, an 'unwarlike trumpeter' unable to match Eve's zeal for the divine (*Book of Encouragement*, trans. Otter, 72–3). Goscelin draws on, and reverses, traditional Aristotelian ideas of gender, presenting Eve as masculine in her mental acumen and spiritual might and militarism.[45] Somewhat surprisingly, Goscelin does not see himself as a fellow combatant. That is a role Eve alone is to assume; his own is more passive. Towards the end of the third book, he reminds Eve that in the past, when her faith had faltered, he had encouraged her with the words of Psalms 26.14 in the Vulgate: '"Expect the Lord, do manfully, and let your heart take courage, and wait you for the Lord"' (*Book of Encouragement*, trans. Otter, 109). But now, at the time of writing the *Liber*, it is Goscelin who is powerless, and who, driven by his emotional dependency upon Eve, writes for his own consolation rather than for that of his erstwhile protégée.

Emulating Edith

Within the *Liber confortatorius*, Goscelin makes explicit references to Edith of Wilton, although not to his own *Legend* of the saint (although he may assume

Eve's familiarity with that work). These references are significantly placed, occurring at the beginning and end of the *Liber*. At the start of the text, Goscelin tries to draw Eve back to Wilton in her imagination by asking herself to envisage herself conversing in the company of himself and a ghostly St Edith (*Book of Encouragement*, trans. Otter, 21). This description is in keeping with Goscelin's *Vita* of Edith, which, as we saw in the last chapter, stresses that Edith was remembered and venerated in Wilton long after her death and continued to appear to the nuns in visions. While they were both in Wilton Goscelin no doubt actively encouraged Eve to emulate this intelligent, learned and pious woman. He continues to do so now that Eve has relocated to Angers. Despite Eve's new vocation, Edith would have remained an important exemplar: within his *Vita*, Goscelin represented Edith as one who lived as a recluse within her community, devoting herself where possible to solitary devotional pursuits. Even in Eve's new life, Edith remains, for Goscelin at least, Eve's spiritual mother, showing her the path to saintliness.

The conclusion of the *Liber* is marked by its apocalypticism.[46] In the closing pages, Goscelin moves from advising Eve on how to conduct her life within her new cell to imagining events after her death. He describes the apotheosis of Eve as she enters paradise where she will meet the Wilton saint alongside her own former community: 'with your holy lady St. Edith and the whole chorus of sisters, all those her convent has educated for Christ, you will see from heaven your Wilton' (*Book of Encouragement*, trans. Otter, 147).[47] Strikingly Goscelin does not include himself in this vision, nor shortly after, when he goes on to describe the mystical marriage to Christ of 'your mighty queen Edith', witnessed by Christ's own mother Mary, within the New Jerusalem, which he now figures as a divinely rebuilt Wilton Abbey, ablaze with precious stones (*Book of Encouragement*, trans. Otter, 148).[48] This vision is reminiscent of Goscelin's treatment of Edith's mother Wulfthryth in Chapter 7 of his *Translatio* of Edith. Goscelin relates how, having continued her daughter's building work at Wilton by constructing a surrounding wall, Wulfthryth then died, or as he puts it, 'she passed to Jerusalem . . . to the eternal embraces of her beloved daughter in Christ, with whom she rejoices in the immortal spouse himself'.[49] Just as Wulfthryth found herself reunited with her daughter, so Eve will be reunited with her saintly foremother. By the conclusion of the *Liber*, Eve is no longer recognizable as the young girl with whom Goscelin exchanged books and letters, or the young woman who abruptly left Wilton without his knowledge and against his will. Nor is she simply the recipient of his book. She has achieved a state of spiritual transcendence that separates her from Goscelin far more than does physical distance. By bringing Edith of Wilton into the *Liber confortatorius*, Goscelin implies that Eve herself may also be sanctified in the future. But equally importantly, he establishes a close connection between the two women in order to remind Eve of her former role model, and to preserve a profound connection with the abbey that she has left, and thus, by extension a further connection with himself.

Conclusion

This chapter has examined Goscelin of St Bertin's exploration of a range of different forms of textual intimacy in the *Liber confortatorius*. From the outset, in the opening lines of the Prologue, Goscelin insists that the *Liber* itself is intended as a private communication, an extended letter directed solely at his former protégée. In the first book of the *Liber* in particular, Goscelin reflects upon a spiritual friendship that grew out of shared reading, study and exchange of letters and books, on an exclusive textual intimacy, which he fears is now lost to him, but which he desperately hopes to rekindle with the writing – and crucially the *reading* – of the *Liber* itself. Goscelin projects the continuation of this textual intimacy into the future. As he looks forward for Eve, he acknowledges his own physical absence from her devotional life, but offers her a road map of further reading and scholarship that she can undertake independently, although he does not anticipate her becoming a writer in her own right.

Goscelin also insists on other connections between himself and Eve, claiming that they have shared the experiences of exile, first in England, and now, for Eve, as a recluse in Angers. Yet at the same time, Goscelin acknowledges that while still in England Eve enjoyed other close companionships. In admitting the importance of these bonds, Goscelin undermines his own claims on the unique nature of his soul friendship with Eve. Likewise, in imaginatively reconstructing Eve's current life as a solitary, Goscelin locates Eve within a textual community of anchorites. Other later historical and literary sources confirm that Eve was not isolated as a recluse, but that she lived with other devout women, and at the end of her life with a male recluse, Hervé. Such co-habitation was potentially scandalous, and Eve's decisions had to be carefully justified and defended. While at the time of writing, Goscelin was not to know what the future held for Eve, there is reason to suspect, from allusions that Goscelin makes in the *Liber* to evil gossip and finger-pointing, that his own previous friendship with Eve had been subjected to hostile scrutiny. By the end of the *Liber*, Goscelin finally seems to admit to himself that his relationship with Eve is a thing of the past but, unwilling to let go completely, he offers Eve a replacement, St Edith, who will keep the ties with Wilton intact. In the closing sections of the *Liber*, the relationship between Edith and Eve comes to represent, for Goscelin (if not for the historical Eve), textual intimacy par excellence.

Coda

This study, which focuses on English literary and religious cultures between 650 and 1150 began with the question 'were there any women writers in the early Middle Ages?' Giving a simple answer proves unexpectedly difficult. The earliest surviving works definitively authored by named early medieval English women were produced by abbesses and nuns linked to Boniface's eighth-century mission to Germany: the letters and poems of Leoba of Tauberbischofsheim and her peers and successors, and the saints' lives written by Hugeburc of Heidenheim. Yet, undoubtedly, women were involved in the composition of texts from the time of the very foundation of the English church. The works of Bede and Aldhelm, for example, refer to abbesses and nuns documenting the history of their religious houses, recording visions and miracles, and writing letters and poems. Women must surely have been responsible for writing many of the anonymous texts that have in recent centuries been attributed to monks. There is a plethora of evidence to support the claim that women also engaged in literary culture in a variety of other ways, as patrons and commissioners of works, as scribes and archivists, and as recipients and readers. It is clear that male monastic writers at the beginning and also the end of this long period in history (as the example of Goscelin of St Bertin illustrates so vividly) drew upon or overwrote source material authored by women and women's oral testimonies. Only by unpacking the complex processes of the composition, circulation, reception and overwriting of early medieval texts can we begin to understand fully the importance of the contribution of women.

Textual production in the twelfth century: The St Albans Psalter and *The Life of Christina of Markyate*

To illustrate further the complexity of devout women's engagement with literary culture, I conclude with one final example, that of Christina of Markyate (*c.*

1096–after 1155). Christina illustrates very clearly the intricacy of women's engagements with literary culture at the end of the early medieval period, while also providing a fitting conclusion to this study because of what she contributes to the narrative of women's literary and spiritual history in the late eleventh and early twelfth century.[1] Two surviving twelfth-century texts are closely associated with Christina. The first is the beautifully and lavishly illustrated St Albans Psalter (Hildesheim, Dombibliothek, MS St Godehard 1).[2] This exquisite psalter appears to have been adapted for either Christina and/or her community at some point and it may even been produced specifically for Christina.[3] It could well have been presented to her at a significant moment, for example following her consecration in *c.* 1131. The second text is the unfinished *Life of Christina of Markyate*, which was written in the 1130s or 1140s by an anonymous monk of St Albans, identified by Katie Ann-Marie Bugyis as the sacristan and future abbot Robert de Gorron (*d.* 1166).[4] The *Life*, which is missing its ending, survives in its most complete form in only one fourteenth-century manuscript: London, British Library, MS Cotton Tiberius E.I, volume 2, fols 145r–167v. The Tiberius manuscript, which is of English provenance, dates to the second half of the fourteenth century, and was once owned by Thomas de la Mare, abbot of St Albans in the second half of the fourteenth century. The Tiberius manuscript almost certainly lost its final leaf in the fire that destroyed and damaged manuscripts in the Cotton collection in the eighteenth century. However, in the previous century, the antiquarian Nicholas Roscarrock (*c.* 1548–1633/4) had viewed the *Life* and produced a summary in his monumental 'Briefe Regester or Alphabeticall Catalogue of such Saincts and sainte like persons as have graced our Island of Great Brittaine, Ireland and other British Iselands' (*c.* 1644): Cambridge, Cambridge University Library, MS Add. 3041, fols 3r–402v (at fols 123v–125r). A comparison between Roscarrock's synopsis of Christina's *Life* and the version in the Tiberius manuscript reveals that the manuscript was already incomplete at the time Roscarrock viewed it and that only a small amount of text was subsequently lost.[5] Extracts of Christina's *Life* also appear in another St Albans production: a continuation of Matthew Paris's mid-thirteenth century *Gesta abbatum monasterii Sancti Albani* written by Thomas Walsingham in the late fourteenth century (London, British Library, MS Cotton Claudius E.IV, volumes 1–2, fols 97v–321r, at fols 111v–113r).[6] These extracts, which differ slightly but significantly from the surviving *Life*, attest to the existence of another copy, now lost.[7] They also refer directly to a copy of the *Life* (possibly their source) held at Markyate Priory.[8] It has been argued that Robert de Gorran's uncle, Geoffrey de Gorran, abbot of St Albans from 1119 to 1146, commissioned both the psalter and the *Life*, and it is possible that Geoffrey himself contributed the so-called Alexis quire (so-called because it contains a *Life of St Alexis*) to the St Albans Psalter.[9] This quire includes a Latin *psychomachia*, apparently addressed to Christina, which which bears some comparison with the elements of *psychomachia* in Goscelin of St Bertin's *Liber confortatorius* (discussed in Chapter 6).

The production of both the *Life of Christina of Markyate* and the St Albans Psalter reveals something of the possible extent of female involvement in the creation of what would conventionally be thought of as male-authored works.[10] Although the author of *The Life of Christina of Markyate* does not explicitly state at any point that Geoffrey of St Albans has commissioned the writing of this 'simple life of the virgin' (*Life of Christina of Markyate*, 157), the text is aligned with the interests of the abbot, and the author makes it clear that Geoffrey was a key source of material used in writing the hagiography by retelling episodes from Geoffrey's point of view and relaying his thoughts and concerns. On one occasion the text seems to address Geoffrey directly in his role as Christina's spiritual mentor: 'because, as you have learned by experience, she revered you more than all the pastors under Christ' (*Life of Christina of Markyate*, 127). The *Life* itself appears to have been written for the edification both of the monks at St Albans *and* of the nuns at Markyate and in support of the (potentially conflicting) interests of both houses. Clarissa Atkinson suggests that it would have been read out to the community of women.[11] Geoffrey was by no means the only or indeed the main source of information about Christina. While the hagiographer (whether Robert de Gorran or another monk of St Albans) may be thought of as overwriting Christina's experiences as Rudolf of Fulda overwrote those of Leoba some three centuries earlier, it is important once again not to oversimplify the process of composition. The writer describes how in compiling material he consulted a range of people, including Christina's family, friends and supporters, and even spoke to Christina herself (see, for example, *Life of Christina of Markyate*, 105). Douglas Gray went so far as to argue that this is an example of 'collaborative composition' and commented on the 'oscillation between the voice of the clerical narrator and what very much sounds like the voice of Christina herself'.[12] However, on other occasions the monk simply describes overhearing Christina relating events (*Life of Christina of Markyate*, 87) and acknowledges that she also withheld information from him (*Life of Christina of Markyate*, 151). It does not appear then that Christina was fully engaged in the process of composition (Bugyis calls her an 'incompliant source').[13] In contrast, Christina's sister Margaret, who shared Christina's vocation and joined her community at Markyate, may have actively encouraged its production. As someone 'who knew [Christina's] secrets' (*Life of Christina of Markyate*, 145), Margaret would have been an important source of information and the author records that Margaret had remarked that Christina's visions were 'worthy to be remembered by those who come after us' (*Life of Christina of Markyate*, 155). Bugyis describes Margaret as 'the resident expert on and likely first chronicler of Christina's holy deeds'.[14] In other words, Margaret may have been responsible for much of the narrative material (oral or written) that was subsequently overwritten by the monk of St Albans responsible for the *Life of Christina of Markyate* in its final form.

Like *The Life of Christina of Markyate,* the St Albans Psalter was produced at the abbey itself, but there is strong evidence to support the view that the psalter was tailored specifically for Christina and her nuns.[15] For example, great emphasis is placed in the illustrations on the roles of women, and Christina herself is depicted in two historiated initials (although one, the important initial illustrating Psalm 105, was pasted in later and was not part of the original fabric of the manuscript).[16] The canticles, collects and litany are appropriate for use in a women's community.[17] The Alexis quire was probably compiled independently and subsequently integrated into the psalter, but there is compelling evidence that it was directed specifically at Christina.[18] It includes a famous letter from St Gregory advocating the use of images to teach those who are unable to read, written in French and Latin, which could have been used to instruct Christina and her fellow nuns in both languages. The psalter also includes a calendar that makes reference to the dedication of Markyate Priory in 1145, and has annotations relating to the deaths of members of Christina's family, including her parents and brothers, to the death of Geoffrey of St Albans, and to the death of the hermit Roger with whom Christina had shared a cell.[19] They also include Christina's own obit so it is clear were added at the instigation of someone close to Christina and a possible candidate is, again, her sister Margaret.[20] Fascinatingly, Bugyis identifies the scribe of the obits of Geoffrey, Christina and her family members also as Robert de Gorran, the same monk who she believes wrote Christina's *Life*.[21] Christina herself may have made additions to the manuscript by sewing fabric curtains into it to protect some of the illustrations.[22] This sort of active engagement or interaction with these works indicates something of the complexity of textual production in this period, where works commissioned and created by men for a woman or community of women reveal something of the interests and concerns of the female audience or readership.

Christina of Markyate and her predecessors

Reading Goscelin's *Liber confortatorius* alongside the St Albans Psalter and the *Life of Christina of Markyate* enables us to understand the intricacies of the relationships between male writers and patrons and female subjects and readers and throws light on the lives of Eve of Wilton and Christina of Markyate themselves, two women religious living around the time of the so-called Conquest, neither of whom was of royal lineage, unlike many of the earlier women in this study. Eve, who was born less than a decade before the Conquest and is described by Goscelin as 'well-born', was the daughter of immigrants.[23] Christina (born Theodora), born almost forty years after Eve, is described in her hagiography as 'of a family of ancient and influential English nobles' (*Life of Christina of Markyate*, 83), although her father's name, Autti, is of Old Danish origin, and her mother's name, Beatrix, is Latin and may indicate French descent. From the evidence provided in her *Life*, we know that her parents were wealthy, and Autti at one point presided over the Gild Merchants of Huntingdon (*Life of Christina of Markyate*, 49). The backgrounds of Eve and Christina are however marked by significant differences. Eve's parents gave her to Wilton Abbey when she was still a young child and at an early age Goscelin of St Bertin took on the role of her instructor and mentor, but Christina's spiritual path was not so straightforward. From her earliest years, Christina aspired to dedicate her life to God and she formed a deeply felt attachment to St Albans Abbey. Her parents resisted her desire to become an oblate, and although they may even have been in a position to consider funding the establishment of a minor religious house for her to enter, the gains of an advantageous matrimonial alliance proved too tempting.[24] As it was, they strongly opposed Christina's ambitions and she was coerced into a marriage from which she was forced to flee in secrecy. For many years after, Christina lived a life of non-monastic female piety; in contemporary parlance, she was a *nunne* rather than a *mynecenu* [cloistered woman].[25] Initially Christina resided in hiding with a female recluse called Alfwen, then with Roger, a respected and greatly honoured hermit of St Albans (*d. c.* 1122), and eventually (not unlike Eve in France) with a small group of women, which in Christina's case included her sister Margaret. After being released from the bonds of matrimony and having gained the patronage of Geoffrey, abbot of St Albans, she took her vows in the early 1130s, becoming founding prioress of Markyate in 1145.

Whereas Eve began her life as a nun, but chose to become a recluse, Christina had become a recluse out of necessity but subsequently professed as a nun. Eve and Christina's backgrounds differ in other ways too. Eve was monastically educated, highly literate and presumably multilingual, able to communicate in English, French and Latin. Christina probably had limited literacy: it is likely that she was unable to write and her reading skills may have been limited to studying the Psalms, the recitation of which were central to her devotional life (*Life of Christina of Markyate*, 93 and 99). Christina's first language was English, as we are reminded by the *Life*, which records that her supporter, the hermit monk Roger, addressed her as '"*myn sunendaege dohter*"' ['my Sunday daughter'], (*Life of Christina of Markyate*, 106–7), but of course she lived in a similar linguistic context to Eve, in which French and Latin were in widespread use.[26] It seems likely that once Christina became a nun, if not before, she would have undertaken a structured programme of study, but, as noted in Chapter 6, much of her time would also have been devoted to weaving, sewing and embroidery (see, for example, *Life of Christina of Markyate*, 161–3). Indeed, when he was abbot of St Albans and as part of his campaign to secure papal privileges for his community, Robert de Gorran sent Urban IV gifts of mitres and sandals that Christina had produced, which the pope graciously received.[27] Textile work was a form of artistry favoured by devout women and shared across class lines. As we saw in the previous chapter, Eve also engaged in needlework, and we might recall that Goscelin's *Vita* of Edith of Wilton records the saint's skills in embroidery.[28] Despite the differences in their backgrounds, education and personal circumstances, both Eve and Christina came to be regarded as authoritative figures in their communities, and to be highly revered by their supporters, although their positions of power also inevitably made them vulnerable to criticism and detraction.

The *Life of Christina of Markyate* provides a particularly appropriate end point for this study because it is a work that also connects back to other texts considered in this book, including *The Legend of Edith* and the lives of the early medieval abbesses, in particular Æthelburh of Barking, Æthelthryth of Ely and Hild of Whitby. Indeed it is revealing that in Cotton Tiberius E.I Christina's *Life* appears, on a new folio and copied in a different hand, appended to the end of the *Sanctilogium Anglie*, the fourteenth-century encyclopaedic collection of British saints' lives from before and after the Conquest compiled by the chronicler John of Tynemouth.[29] Latin hagiographies of a number of saintly women appear in this collection, including (alongside an extensive list of male saints) Margaret of Scotland (volume 2, fols 11v–13v), Æthelthryth (volume 2, fols 19r–20v), Seaxburh (volume 2, fols 31v–32r), Mildrith (volume 2, fols 33r–35r), Edith of Wilton (not the version by Goscelin; volume 2, fols 66v–68r),[30] Æthelburh (volume 2, fols 79v–81r), Frithuswith (volume 2, fols 85v–87r), Ælfflaed (volume 2, fols 90r–91r), and Hild (volume 2, fols 113v–115r). Likewise, the summary of Christina's *Life* that Roscarrock includes within his exhaustive collection locates it within a firmly insular tradition that harks back to the earliest history of the church and its founding mothers as well as fathers.

The St Albans Psalter and *The Life of Christina of Markyate* both suggest that legendary and historical women provided important exemplary models for Christina, and that she (or those close to her) understood her to be emulating the lives of these exalted predecessors.[31] The St Albans Psalter calendar includes within it the feasts of three early medieval English women saints: Hild of Whitby, Æthelthryth of Ely and Frithuswith (Frideswide) of Oxford (*d.* 727). Tantalizingly, these saints' names are amongst those added in the hand that Bugyis argues is that of Robert de Gorran.[32] Such elite models of female sanctity are of a very different social standing to Christina of Markyate (or Eve of Wilton, for that matter), but if we accept that the calendar was produced with Christina in mind, they were presumably selected because they too had a particular significance to Christina and her fellow nuns. Jane Geddes observes that Hild would have been picked out because of her status as 'the earliest English abbess, a powerful leader of women',[33] and in fact all three were early founding abbesses and thus might be thought of as mothers of the English church. Furthermore, Whitby and Ely were double monasteries, where the communities of nuns and monks were governed by a single superior. Bugyis suggests that Geoffrey of St Albans and the writer of Christina's *Life* 'were familiar with various Continental models of "double" monastic organization, and possibly even interested in replicating such a model by joining Markyate to St Albans'.[34] However, it is equally plausible that Christina and her circle themselves looked back to the early English foundations and their founding mothers to support such ambitions. They would also have seen parallels between the lived experiences of these founding mothers and that of Christina because, for example, Æthelthryth and Frithuswith initiated a strong insular tradition of married women saints who sought to preserve their chastity.

Elements of Christina's *Life* resonate too with Goscelin's *Legend of Edith*. Christina's precocious piety as an infant and her decision, made while she was still a girl, to dedicate herself to God mirrors Edith's self-consecration aged only two.[35] What is more, Christina's *Life* opens with a natal vision that echoes those experienced both by Hild's mother Breguswith (discussed in Chapter 1 and Chapter 5) and by Edith's mother Wulfthryth (discussed in Chapter 5). Breguswith, while pregnant with Hild, dreamt of a necklace that shone its light across all of Britain.[36] A beam of light emanating from her newly born daughter's crown illuminated the bedchamber of Wulfthryth.[37] The pregnant Beatrix in turn saw a white dove fly to her from the monastery and it remained with her for seven days (*Life of Christina of Markyate*, 35). There are further parallels too between Edith and Christina. As also noted in Chapter 5, Hollis and Wogan-Browne suggest that Goscelin's account of the consecration of Edith's church, which describes the friendship between Dunstan and Edith in Trinitarian Terms (Dunstan leads Edith to Christ and 'a John was seen to pay reverence to a Mary')[38] is reflected in a striking vision that Christina receives of the Crucifixion, in which 'she saw Jesus standing at the altar. .. And turning her eyes she saw her close friend [Geoffrey] for whom she was anxious standing at her right side, which was the Lord's left side' (*Life*, 181–3).[39] Christina assumes the position of Mary and Geoffrey appears in the place of John as commonly represented in medieval depictions of the Crucifixion, such as the illumination of the 'Descent from the Cross' in the St Albans Psalter itself.[40] Taken together, these examples are suggestive of shared traditions of early medieval English sanctity that helped shape Christina of Markyate's religious life and patterns of female devotion more generally both before and after the Conquest.

Looking forward

At the same time, as it looks back, however, *The Life of Christina of Markyate* also looks forward to devotional, visionary and hagiographical writings of the later Middle Ages such as Ælred of Rievaulx's *De Institutione inclusarum* [*The Formation of Anchoresses*], written for his sister between 1160 and 1162; the early thirteenth-century *Ancrene Wisse* and related anchoritic texts; Marie de France's late twelfth-century version of *St Patrick's Purgatory*; the mystical treatises of Julian of Norwich; *The Book of Margery Kempe*; the early fifteenth-century anonymous Winchester anchoress's epistolary text, *A Revelation of Purgatory*; the *Life of St Catherine* by Clemence of Barking (*fl.* 1163–*c.* 1200) and other French saints' lives authored by English women; the lives of the women saints in the Katherine Group; and the legends of women saints translated by Osbern Bokenham (1393–*c.* 1464) for women patrons. *The Life of Christina of Markyate* thus provides a hinge, as it were, between women's literary and religious cultures in the early and later Middle Ages.

In my previous study, *Medieval Women's Writing* (2016), I looked at some of the ways *The Life of Christina of Markyate* anticipates these later texts, and it is important to reiterate here the necessity of thinking across conventional period boundaries. In *Living Through Conquest*, Elaine Treharne attacks the traditional chronologies and hierarchies of linguistic and literary study:

> The division of literary history into ever more precise and specific periods and interests is a familiar, and perhaps inevitable consequence of the politicization of university curricula, professional associations and academic subject areas. Our need to mark out and 'defend' our teaching and research specialisms, coupled with the modern obsession with labelling and categorizing, makes it unsurprising that literary-historical eras such as 'the medieval' are broken down yet further into 'Anglo-Saxon', 'Old' or 'Middle' English.[41]

Treharne's primary concern here is with the resultant marginalization of those texts that are seen to fall between literary periods, specifically vernacular texts produced in the second half of the eleventh and in the twelfth centuries. My concern with the limits of chronology and periodization is different – it is with examining the continuities, and indeed the discontinuities, in women's literary culture. In the later Middle Ages, more works by named women are known and studied. This is in part because more of these works are written in the vernacular (or vernaculars, as some are written in French rather than English) rather than in Latin, and are therefore more accessible to a twenty-first-century readership. It may also be because more of these works are written by laywomen (some of less exalted rank, socially), in contrast to those by abbesses and nuns discussed in this study, although they are still predominantly religious or devotional in content. However, broadly speaking the forms and genres remain very similar: poems, letters, saints' lives and visionary texts, although inevitably there is less concern with the foundation and establishment of women's religious communities. As Bugyis so pertinently observes, 'though there may not be a "continuous" tradition of literary culture in communities of women religious from the early Anglo-Saxon period to the dissolution of the monasteries in the late 1530s, it was recurrently "renewed and reinvented" throughout the Middle Ages'.[42] For the later period, as for the earlier, texts by women have certainly been lost, although traces of some (but not all) remain. For the later period, as for the earlier, the case can be (and often is) made for women's authorship of anonymous texts. And for the later period, as for the earlier, women's testimonies and narratives may also have been overwritten by male authors whose intention was to preserve rather than to obliterate, to modernize rather than to silence. The nature of women's broader engagement with literary culture does not fundamentally change: from the early Middle Ages right through to the later

Middle Ages and beyond, women continue to compose texts themselves and to commission them, women have texts addressed to them, and women read, copy, archive, exchange and circulate manuscripts. The legacy of the vibrant literary culture of women in the early Middle Ages continued through and after the Conquest.

Notes

Introduction

1 Jane Stevenson, *Women Latin Poets: Language, Gender, & Authority from Antiquity to the Eighteenth Century* (Oxford: Oxford University Press, 2005), 93. See also Emily V. Thornbury, *Becoming a Poet in Anglo-Saxon England* (Cambridge: Cambridge University Press, 2014), 64.

2 Aidan Conti, 'The Literate Memory of Hugeburc of Heidenheim', in *Feminist Approaches to Anglo-Saxon Studies*, ed. Robin Norris, Rebecca Stephenson and Renée Trilling (Tempe, AZ: Arizona Center for Medieval Studies, forthcoming). See, for example, Felice Lifshitz, *Women in Early Carolingian Francia: A Study of Manuscript Transmission and Monastic Culture* (New York: Fordham University Press, 2014).

3 Jennifer Summit, *Lost Property: The Woman Writer and English Literary History, 1380–1589* (Chicago: University of Chicago Press, 2000), 5.

4 Christine E. Fell, 'Some Implications of the Boniface Correspondence', in *New Readings on Women in Old English Literature*, ed. Helen Damico and Alexandra Hennessey Olsen (Bloomington, IN: Indiana University Press, 1990), 29.

5 Fell, 'Some Implications of the Boniface Correspondence', 29.

6 See Clare A. Lees and Gillian R. Overing, 'Women and the Origins of English Literature', in *The History of British Women's Writing, 700–1500*, ed. Liz Herbert McAvoy and Diane Watt (Basingstoke: Palgrave Macmillan, 2012), 31. See also A. J. Minnis, *Medieval Theory of Authorship: Scholastic Literary Attitudes in the Later Middle Ages* (Aldershot: Scholar Press, 2nd edn, 1988), 10–12; Alexandra Barratt, ed. *Women's Writing in Middle English* (London: Longman, 1992), 6; Jennifer Summit, 'Women and Authorship', in *The Cambridge Companion to Medieval Women's Writing*, ed. Carolyn Dinshaw and David Wallace (Cambridge: Cambridge University Press, 2003), 92–3.

7 See in particular D. H. Turner, 'Illuminated Manuscripts', in *The Golden Age of Anglo-Saxon Art and Culture, 966–1066*, ed. Janet Backhouse, D. H. Turner and Leslie Webster (Bloomington, IN: Indiana University Press, 1984), 46–87; Janet Backhouse, 'Literature, Learning and Documentary Sources' in *The Golden Age of Anglo-Saxon Art and Culture,* ed. Backhouse, Turner and Wesley, 143–71; Michelle P. Brown, *Anglo-Saxon Manuscripts* (London: The British Library, 1991), 25; Brown, 'Female-Book Ownership and Production in Anglo-Saxon England: The Evidence of

the Ninth-Century Prayerbooks', in *Lexis and Texts in Early English: Studies Presented to Jane Roberts*, ed. Christian J. Kay and Louise M. Sylvester (Amsterdam: Rodolpi, 2001), 45–67; Rosamond McKitterick, 'Nuns' Scriptoria in England and Francia in the Eighth Century', *Francia* 19 (1992): 1–35. See also Lifshitz, *Women in Early Carolingian Francia*; Alison I. Beach, *Women as Scribes: Book Production and Monastic Reform in Twelfth-Century Bavaria* (Cambridge: Cambridge University Press, 2004); and P. R. Robinson, 'A Twelfth-Century Scriptrix from Nunnaminster', in *Of the Making of Books: Medieval Manuscripts, Their Scribes and Readers: Essays Presented to M.B. Parkes*, ed. P. R. Robinson and Rivkah Zim (Aldershot: Ashgate, 1997), 77–93.

8   See Mechthild Gretsch, 'Æthelwold's Translation of the *Regula Sancti Benedicti* and Its Latin Exemplar', *Anglo-Saxon England* 3 (1974): 125–51, esp. 137–9; and Joyce Hill, 'Rending the Garment and Reading By the Rood: *Regularis Concordia* Rituals for Men and Women', in *The Liturgy of the Late Anglo-Saxon Church*, ed. Helen Gittos and M. Bradford Bedingfield (London: Henry Bradshaw Society, 2005), 53–64.

9   This argument, which I develop more fully here, was posited in my chapter in *The Cambridge History of Early Medieval Literature*: Diane Watt, 'Literature in Pieces: Female Sanctity and the Relics of Early Women's Writing', in *The Cambridge History of Early Medieval English Literature*, ed. Clare A. Lees (Cambridge: Cambridge University Press, 2012), 357–80.

10 Bernhard Bischoff, 'Wer ist die Nonne von Heidenheim?', *Studien und Mitteilungen zur Geschichte des Benediktinerordens und seiner Zweige* 49 (1931): 387–88.

11 Joan M. Ferrante, *To the Glory of Her Sex: Women's Roles in the Composition of Medieval Texts* (Bloomington, IN: Indiana University Press, 1997), 3.

12 James Simpson, *Reform and Cultural Revolution: 1350–1547*, The Oxford English Literary History Vol. 2 (Oxford: Oxford University Press, 2002). The main discussion of Margery Kempe and Julian Norwich is at 438–50. See also Laura Ashe, *Conquest and Transformation, 1000-1350*, The Oxford English Literary History Vol. 1 (Oxford: Oxford University Press, 2017).

13 David Wallace, ed., *The Cambridge History of Medieval English Literature* (Cambridge: Cambridge University Press, 1999), xx.

14 Virginia Woolf, *A Room of One's Own* (1929, reprinted Harmondsworth: Penguin, 1945); Kate Millett, *Sexual Politics* (Garden City, NY: Doubleday, 1970); Ellen Moers, *Literary Women: The Great Writers* (Garden City, NY: Doubleday, 1976); Elaine Showalter, *A Literature of their Own: From Charlotte Brontë to Doris Lessing* (Princeton, NJ: Princeton University Press, 1977); Sandra M. Gilbert and Susan Gubar, *The Madwoman in the Attic: The Woman Writer and the Nineteenth-Century Literary Imagination* (New Haven, CT: Yale University Press, 1979); and Janet Todd, *Feminist Literary History: A Defence* (Cambridge: Polity , 1988). For a critique, see

Margaret J. M. Ezell, *Writing Women's Literary History* (Baltimore, MD: Johns Hopkins University Press, 1993).

15 Sandra M. Gilbert and Susan Gubar, eds., *The Norton Anthology of Literature by Women: The Traditions in English* (New York: W.W. Norton, 1st edn, 1985), 15.

16 Carole M. Meale, ed., *Women and Literature in Britain, 1150–1500* (Cambridge: Cambridge University Press, 2nd ed., 1996); Summit, *Lost Property*; Jocelyn Wogan-Browne, *Saints' Lives and Women's Literary Culture c. 1150–1300: Virginity and its Authorizations* (Oxford: Oxford University Press, 2001); Dinshaw and Wallace, eds., *Cambridge Companion to Medieval Women's Writing*; and David Wallace, *Strong Women: Life, Text, and Territory 1347–1645* (Oxford: Oxford University Press, 2011).

17 Laurie A. Finke, *Women's Writing in English: Medieval England* (Harlow: Longman, 1999).

18 Sandra M. Gilbert and Susan Gubar, eds., *Norton Anthology of Literature by Women: The Traditions in English*, 2 vols. (New York: W.W. Norton, 3rd edn, 2007).

19 Gilbert and Gubar, ed., *Norton Anthology of Literature by Women* (3rd edn, 2007), vol.1, 1.

20 Elaine Treharne, *Living Through Conquest: The Politics of Early English, 1020–1220* (Oxford: Oxford University Press, 2012); Elizabeth M. Tyler, *England in Europe: Royal Women and Literary Patronage c. 1000–c. 1150* (Toronto: Toronto University Press, 2017).

21 Jane Chance, *Woman as Hero in Anglo-Saxon Literature* (Syracuse, NY: Syracuse University Press, 1986); Helen Damico and Alexandra Hennessey Olsen, eds., *New Readings on Women in Old English Literature* (Bloomington, IN: Indiana University Press, 1990); Shari Horner, *The Discourse of Enclosure: Representing Women in Old English Literature* (Albany, NY: SUNY Press, 2001); and Carol Braun Pasternack and Lisa M.C. Weston, eds., *Sex and Sexuality in Anglo-Saxon England: Essays in Memory of Daniel Gillmore Calder* (Tempe, AZ: Arizona Center for Medieval and Renaissance Studies, 2004).

22 See, for example, Marilynn Desmond, 'The Voice of Exile: Feminist Literary History and the Anonymous Anglo-Saxon Elegy', *Critical Inquiry* 16 (1990): 572–90.

23 Elaine Treharne and Greg Walker with William Green, eds., *The Oxford Handbook of Medieval Literature in English* (Oxford: Oxford University Press, 2010); Lees, ed., *Cambridge History of Early Medieval English Literature*.

24 Judith M. Bennett, *History Matters: Patriarchy and the Challenge of Feminism* (Manchester: Manchester University Press, 2006), 42.

25 See the critique of Bennett's book by Mary Dockray-Miller in her survey article, 'Old English Literature and Feminist Theory: A State of the Field', *Literature Compass* 5, no.6 (2008): 1049.

26 R.M. Liuzza, ed., *Old English Literature: Critical Essays* (New Haven, CT: Yale University Press, 2012), xi.

27 Diane Watt, *Medieval Women's Writing: Works by and for Women in England,*
    1100–1500 (Cambridge: Polity, 2007).

28 McAvoy and Watt, eds., *History of British Women's Writing.*

29 Lees and Overing, 'Women and the Origins of English Literature', 31–40; Catherine
    A. M. Clarke, 'Literary Production Before and After the Conquest', in *History of*
    British Women's Writing, ed. McAvoy and Watt, 40–50.

30 Lees and Overing, 'Women and the Origins of English Literature', 31.

31 Clarke, 'Literary Production Before and After the Conquest', 41.

32 Watt, 'Literature in Pieces', 357–80.

33 Peter Dronke, *Women Writers of the Middle Ages: A Critical Study of Texts from*
    Perpetua (†203) to Marguerite Porete (†1310) (Cambridge: Cambridge University
    Press, 1984).

34 Stephanie Hollis, *Anglo-Saxon Women and the Church: Sharing a Common Fate*
    (Woodbridge: Boydell Press, 1992); Clare A. Lees and Gillian R. Overing's *Double Agents:*
    Women and Clerical Culture in Anglo-Saxon England (2001, reprinted with a new
    preface, Cardiff: University of Wales Press, 2009); and Stephanie Hollis with W. R. Barnes,
    Rebecca Hayward, Kathleen Loncar and Michael Wright, eds., *Writing the Wilton*
    Women: Goscelin's Legend of Edith *and* Liber confortatorius (Turnhout: Brepols, 2004).

35 Stevenson, *Women Latin Poets* (the discussion of Anglo-Saxon women is at 92–6).

36 Catherine A. M. Clarke, *Writing Power in Anglo-Saxon England: Texts, Hierarchies,*
    Economies (Cambridge: D.S. Brewer, 2012); Tyler, *England in Europe.* Tyler also gives
    detailed consideration to Goscelin of St Bertin and Wilton.

37 Clare A. Lees and Gillian R. Overing, 'Birthing Bishops and Fathering Poets: Bede,
    Hild, and the Relations of Cultural Production', *Exemplaria* 6 (1994): 35–65;
    reprinted in slightly revised form as the first chapter of *Double Agents,* 19–55.

38 Lees and Overing, 'Women and the Origins of English Literature', 31.

39 See Dronke, *Women Writers of the Middle Ages*; Stevenson, *Women Latin Poets*; Jane
    Stevenson, 'Anglo-Latin Women Poets', in *Latin Learning and English Lore: Studies in*
    Anglo-Saxon Literature for Michael Lapidge, ed. Katherine O'Brien O'Keeffe and
    Andy Orchard, 2 vols. (Toronto: University of Toronto Press, 2005), vol.2, 86–107.

40 Tyler, *England in Europe,* 3.

41 D. Patricia Wallace, 'Feminine Rhetoric and the Epistolary Tradition: The Boniface
    Correspondence', *Women's Studies* 24 (1995): 230.

42 Roberta Gilchrist, *Gender and Material Culture: The Archaeology of Religious Women*
    (London: Routlege, 1994).

43 Stevenson, 'Anglo-Latin Women Poets', 95; J.S.P. Tatlock, 'Muriel: The Earliest English
    Poetess', *PMLA* 48 (1933): 317–21; Tyler, *England in Europe,* 318–24.

44 See Catherine Cubitt, 'Virginity and Misogyny in Tenth- and Eleventh-Century
    England', *Gender & History* 12, no.1 (2000): 1–32; Lees and Overing, *Double Agents,*
    165–7; Helene Scheck, *Reform and Resistance: Formations of Female Subjectivity in*
    Early Medieval Ecclesiastical Culture (Albany, NY: SUNY Press, 2008), 73–119.

45 See Elisabeth van Houts, 'Women and the Writing of History in the Early Middle Ages: The Case of Abbess Matilda of Essen and Aethelweard', *Early Medieval Europe* 1 (1992): 53–68.

46 *Encomium Emmae Reginae*, ed. Alistair Campbell, reprinted with a supplementary introduction by Simon Keynes (1949, Cambridge: Cambridge University Press, 1998); *The Life of King Edward Who Rests at Westminster Attributed to a Monk of Saint-Bertin*, ed. and trans. Frank Barlow (Oxford: Clarendon Press, 2nd edn, 1992).

47 See Mary Dockray-Miller, 'Judith of Flanders and Her Books: Patronage, Piety, and Politics in mid-eleventh century Europe', in *Telling Tales and Crafting Books, Essays in Honor of Thomas H. Ohlgren*, eds. Dorsey A. Armstrong, Shaun F. D. Hughes, and Alexander L. Kaufman (Kalamazoo, MI: Medieval Institute Publications, 2016), 267–322. Dockray-Miller also mentions evidence of similar commissions by Judith's female relatives by marriage, Gytha and Gunnhild, and Edward the Confessor's sister Goda (314).

48 Sarah McNamer, *Affective Meditation and the Invention of Medieval Compassion* (Philadelphia: University of Pennsylvania Press, 2010), 17.

49 Bede's prose *Life of Cuthbert*, in *Two Lives of St. Cuthbert: A Life by an Anonymous Monk of Lindisfarne and Bede's Prose Life*, ed. and trans. Bertram Colgrave (1940, Cambridge: Cambridge University Press, 1985), 142–307. See Catherine E. Karkov, 'Whitby, Jarrow, and the Commemoration of Death in Northumbria', in *Northumbria's Golden Age*, ed. Jane Hawkes and Susan Mills (Stroud: Sutton, 1999), 130–2.

50 Anonymous, *Life of Cuthbert*, in *Two Lives of Saint Cuthbert*, ed. and trans. Colgrave, 60–139. All in-text references are to this translation.

51 Stephen of Ripon, *The Life of Bishop Wilfrid by Eddius Stephanus*, ed. and trans. Bertram Colgrave (1927, Cambridge: Cambridge University Press, 1985). All in-text references are to this translation.

52 Hollis, *Anglo-Saxon Women and the Church*, 206.

53 Hollis, *Anglo-Saxon Women and the Church*, 179.

54 Hollis, *Anglo-Saxon Women and the Church*, 188.

55 *Bede's Ecclesiastical History of the English People*, ed. and trans. Bertram Colgrave and R. A. B. Mynors (Oxford: Clarendon Press, 1969), 4.27–32, pp. 430–49, and 5.19, pp. 516–31.

Chapter 1

1 *Bede's Ecclesiastical History of the English People*, ed. and trans. Bertram Colgrave and R. A. B. Mynors (Oxford: Clarendon Press, 1969). All in-text references to the *Ecclesiastical History* (hereafter *EH*) are to this edition.

2 See Diane Watt, *Secretaries of God: Women Prophets in Late Medieval and Early Modern England* (Cambridge: D.S.Brewer, 1997).

3 For a detailed discussion, see Virginia Blanton, *Signs of Devotion: The Cult of St. Æthelthryth in Medieval England, 695–1615* (University Park, PA: Penn State University Press, 2007), 19–63; for a wider context, see also Virginia Blanton, 'Presenting the Sister Saints of Ely, or Using Kinship to Increase a Monastery's Status as a Cult Center', *Literature Compass* 5.4 (2008): 755–71.

4 *Liber Eliensis: A History of the Isle of Ely from the Seventh Century to the Twelfth*, trans. Janet Fairweather (Woodbridge, Suffolk: Boydell Press, 2005), 1–83.

5 Blanton, *Signs of Devotion*, 63; see also John Black, '"*Nutrix* pia": The Flowering of the Cult of St Æthelthryth in Anglo-Saxon England', in *Writing Women Saints in Anglo-Saxon England*, ed. Paul E. Szarmach (Toronto: University of Toronto Press, 2013), 172–75.

6 Clare A. Lees and Gillian R. Overing, *Double Agents: Women and Clerical Culture in Anglo-Saxon England* (2001, reprinted with a new preface Cardiff: University of Wales Press, 2009), 171; see also Lees and Overing, 'Women and the Origins of English Literature', in *The History of British Women's Writing, 700–1500*, ed. Liz Herbert McAvoy and Diane Watt (Basingstoke: Palgrave Macmillan, 2012), 32-35.

7 For an excellent analysis of the implications of prosimetrical writing in early medieval texts, see Catherine A. M. Clarke, *Writing Power in Anglo-Saxon England: Texts, Hierarchies, Economies* (Cambridge: D.S. Brewer, 2012), 145–70.

8 Allen J. Frantzen, 'The Fragmentation of Cultural Studies and the Fragments of Anglo-Saxon England', *Anglia* 114 (1996): 323. The Old English Bede (ninth century) omits the *Hymn* with its elaborate Latinity: Black, 'The Cult of St Æthelthryth', 175–6.

9 Blanton, *Signs of Devotion*, 49.

10 Lees and Overing, *Double Agents*, 43.

11 Blanton, *Signs of Devotion*, 23.

12 Goscelin of Saint-Bertin, *The Hagiography of the Female Saints of Ely*, ed. and trans. Rosalind C. Love (Oxford: Clarendon Press, 2004), xiv. See also Mary Dockray-Miller, *Motherhood and Mothering in Anglo-Saxon England* (London: Macmillan, 2000), 10–15.

13 Blanton, *Signs of Devotion*, 62.

14 On Bede's account of Hild and the foundation of Whitby, see Catherine E. Karkov, 'Whitby, Jarrow, and the Commemoration of Death in Northumbria', in *Northumbria's Golden Age*, ed. Jane Hawkes and Susan Mills (Stroud: Sutton, 1999), 129–30.

15 Computer-assisted statistical analysis of parts of the *Ecclesiastical History* supports the argument that Bede drew heavily on a lost written source in writing his life of Hild, and fascinatingly indicates that Bede's immediate source also included the material about Barking that he drew upon in his account of Æthelburh (see

Chapter 2): Sarah Downey, Michael D. C. Drout, Veronica E. Kerekes and Douglas C. Raffle, 'Lexomic Analysis of Medieval Latin Texts', *The Journal of Medieval Latin* 24 (2014): 255–62.

16 J. E. Cross, 'A Lost life of Hilda of Whitby: the Evidence of the *Old English Martyrology*', *The Early Middle Ages, Acta* 6 (1979): 21–43.

17 Christine Rauer, 'Female Hagiography in the *Old English Martyrology*', in *Writing Women Saints*, ed. Szarmach, 15–17. Rauer is responding to Sarah Foot's arguments in her essay 'Anglo-Saxon Minsters: A Review of Terminology', in *Pastoral Care Before the Parish*, ed. John Blair and Richard Sharpe (Leicester: Leicester University Press, 1992), 222.

18 See Peter Hunter Blair, 'Whitby as a Centre of Learning in the Seventh Century', in *Learning and Literature in Anglo-Saxon England: Studies Presented to Peter Clemoes on the Occasion of his Sixty-fifth Birthday*, ed. Michael Lapidge and Helmut Gneuss (Cambridge: Cambridge University Press, 1985), 3–32; Stephanie Hollis, *Anglo-Saxon Women and the Church: Sharing a Common Fate* (Woodbridge: Boydell Press, 1992), 253–8 and 261–70.

19 Lees and Overing, *Double Agents*, 19–55.

20 Lees and Overing, *Double Agents*, 31. This may in part be explained by Bede's sources. Statistical analysis indicates that Bede's source for his account of the Synod of Whitby was authored by his former teacher, Ceolfrith, abbot of Monkwearmouth-Jarrow, and was quite distinct from his source for Hild's life: Downey, Drout, Kerekes and Raffle, 'Lexomic Analysis', 262–72.

21 On Bede's overwriting of Hild's 'maternal genealogy' that included Eanflæd and Ælfflæd, see Mary Dockray-Miller, *Motherhood and Mothering in Anglo-Saxon England* (London: Macmillan, 2000), 15–17.

22 Hollis, *Anglo-Saxon Women and the Church*, 248 and n.32. See also Christine E. Fell 'Hild, Abbess of Streonæshalch', in *Hagiography and Medieval Literature: a Symposium*, ed Hans Bekker-Nielsen, Peter Foote, Jørgen Højgaard Jørgensen and Tore Nyberg (Odense: Odense University Press, 1981), 76–99.

23 Helene Scheck and Virginia Blanton, 'Women', in *A Handbook of Anglo-Saxon Studies*, ed. Jacqueline Stodnick and Renée R. Trilling (Chichester: Blackwell, 2012), 272.

24 *The Old English Martyrology: Edition, Translation and Commentary*, ed. and trans. Christine Rauer (Cambridge: D.S. Brewer, 2013). All in-text references to the *Old English Martyrology* are to this text.

25 Cross 'A Lost Life', 24.

26 Lees and Overing, *Double Agents*, 31–2 and 68–71; Karkov, 'Whitby, Jarrow and the Commemoration of Death', 130–32.

27 Mechthild Gretsch, *Ælfric and the Cult of Saints in Late-Anglo-Saxon England* (Cambridge: Cambridge University Press, 2005), 63; Karkov, 'Whitby, Jarrow and the Commemoration of Death', 132–3.

28 Andrew Breeze, 'Did a Woman Write the Whitby Life of St Gregory?', *Northern History* 49 (2012): 345–50.

29 For the online catalogue entry for and facsimile of the manuscript, see http:// www.e-codices.unifr.ch/en/list/one/csg/0567. For an edition, see *The Earliest Life of Gregory the Great by an Anonymous Monk of Whitby*, ed. and trans. Bertram Colgrave (Lawrence, KS: University of Kansas Press, 1968). All in-text references to the *Life* are to this edition unless otherwise stated. According to Colgrave, MS Cod. Sang. 567, which he suggests may well have been copied in the scriptorium of the monastic library of St Gall, was not directly derived from the original Whitby manuscript, but from an intermediary (66 and 69).

30 Walter Goffart's reading of the Whitby *Life* is highly critical, but Goffart makes a convincing case that Bede did use it as a source, albeit to a limited extent: Walter Goffart, *The Narrators of Barbarian History (A.D. 550–800): Jordanes, Gregory of Tours, Bede, and Paul the Deacon* (Princeton: Princeton University Press, 1988), 235–328; esp. 263–7; see also Gretsch, *Ælfric and the Cult of Saints*, 50.

31 On the construction of ethnic and political identities within the *Life*, see Erin Thomas A. Dailey, 'The *Vita Gregorii* and Ethnogenesis in Anglo-Saxon Britain', *Northern History* 47 (2010), 195–207.

32 John Edward Damon, *Soldier Saints and Holy Warriors: Warfare and Sanctity in the Literature of Early England* (Aldershot: Ashgate, 2003), 32.

33 *Earliest Life of Gregory*, ed. and trans. Colgrave, 146 n.48.

34 Uppinder Mehan and David Townsend, '"Nation" and the Gaze of the Other in Eighth-Century Northumbria', *Comparative Literature* 53 (2001): 1–26.

35 For an analysis of Gregory's linguistic play, see Clare A. Lees, 'In Ælfric's Words: Conversion, Vigilance and the Nation', in Ælfric's *Life of Gregory the Great* in *A Companion to Ælfric*, ed. Hugh Magennis and Mary Swan (Leiden and Boston: Brill, 2009), 271–96.

36 Mehan and Townsend, '"Nation" and the Gaze', 17.

37 Lees, 'In Ælfric's Words', 276.

38 Breeze, 'Did a Woman Write?', 347.

39 On the sexuality of this scene in various retellings, see Allen J. Frantzen, 'Bede and Bawdy Bale: Gregory the Great, Angels, and the "Angli"', in *Anglo-Saxonism and the Construction of Social Identity*, ed. Allen J. Frantzen and John D. Niles (Gainesville: University Press of Florida, 1997), 17–39; Kathy Lavezzo, 'Gregory's Boys: The Homoerotic Production of English Whiteness', in *Sex and Sexuality in Anglo-Saxon England: Essays in Memory of Daniel Gillmore Calder*, ed. Carol Braun Pasternack and Lisa M. C. Weston (Tempe, AZ: Arizona Center for Medieval and Renaissance Studies, 2004), 63–90; and Kathy Lavezzo, *Angels on the Edge of the World: Geography, Literature, and English Community, 1000–1534* (Ithaca, NY: Cornell University Press, 2006), 27–45.

40 On the gendering of conversion, see Hollis, *Anglo-Saxon Women and the Church*, 15–45.

41 Gretsch, *Ælfric and the Cult of Saints*, 25–6.

42 Karkov, 'Whitby, Jarrow and the Commemoration of Death', 133.

43 *Earliest Life of Gregory*, ed. and trans. Colgrave, 154 n.77.

44 Breeze, 'Did a Woman Write?', 349.

Chapter 2

1 See Stephanie Hollis, 'Barking's Monastic School, Late Seventh to Twelfth Century: History, Saint-Making and Literary Culture', in *Barking Abbey and Medieval Literary Culture: Authorship and Authority in a Female Community*, ed. Jennifer N. Brown and Donna Alfano Bussell (York: York Medieval Press, 2012), 33–55.

2 *Bede's Ecclesiastical History of the English People*, ed. and trans. Bertram Colgrave and R. A. B. Mynors (Oxford: Clarendon Press, 1969). All in-text references to the *Ecclesiastical History* (hereafter *EH*) are to this edition.

3 Lisa M. C. Weston, '*Sanctimoniales cum sanctimoniale*: Particular Friendships and Female Community in Anglo-Saxon England', in *Sex and Sexuality in Anglo-Saxon England: Essays in memory of Daniel Gillmore Calder*, ed. Carol Braun Pasternack and Lisa M. C. Weston (Tempe, AZ: Arizona Center for Medieval and Renaissance Studies, 2004), 41.

4 Weston, '*Sanctimoniales cum sanctimoniale*', 41.

5 The recent lexomic analysis of the *Ecclesiastical History* that connects Bede's accounts of Whitby and Barking suggests, however, that the Barking *liber* might have been part of a longer single work about early medieval abbesses and their houses. Even if this were the case, it is likely that such a work would originate from a powerful community of women religious. See Sarah Downey, Michael D. C. Drout, Veronica E. Kerekes and Douglas C. Raffle, 'Lexomic Analysis of Medieval Latin Texts', *The Journal of Medieval Latin* 24 (2014): 255–62.

6 Mary Clayton, *The Cult of the Virgin Mary in Anglo-Saxon England* (Cambridge: Cambridge University Press, 1990). Stephanie Hollis points out that one model for such 'visions of ascending souls' is the life of Benedict in Gregory's *Dialogues*: *Anglo-Saxon Women and the Church: Sharing a Common Fate* (Woodbridge: Boydell Press, 1992), 260. See *The Dialogues of Saint Gregory*, trans. P. W. [sic], re-ed. Edmund G. Gardner (London: Philip Lee Warner, 1911), Book 2, 51–101. Of particular interest here is Benedict's vision of his sister's soul rising in the form of a dove to Heaven (96).

7 Ian Wood, 'Ripon, Francia and the Franks Casket in the Early Middle Ages', *Northern History* 26 (1990): 14–15. See also Wood, 'The *Vita Columbani* and Merovingian

Hagiography', *Peritia* 1 (1982): 63–80; Barbara Yorke, '"Carriers of Truth": Writing the Biographies of Anglo-Saxon Female Saints', in *Writing Medieval Biography, 750–1250: Essays in Honour of Frank Barlow*, ed. David Bates, Julia Crick and Sarah Hamilton (Woodbridge: Boydell Press, 2006), 52; and Lisa M. C. Weston, 'The Saint-Maker and the Saint: Hildelith Creates Ethelburg', in *Barking Abbey and Medieval Literary Culture*, ed. Brown and Bussell, 56–72. On dreams and visions in early medieval Europe, see Isabel Moreira, *Dreams, Visions, and Spiritual Authority in Merovingian Gaul* (Ithaca, NY: Cornell University Press, 2000).

8   Wood, 'Ripon, Francia and the Franks Casket', 14; see also Wood, 'The *Vita Columbani* and Merovingian Hagiography', 67–8; and Wood, 'The Continental Connections of Anglo-Saxon Courts from Æthelberht to Offa', in *Le relazioni internazionali nell'alto medioevo: Spoleto, 8–12 aprile 2010*, (Spoleto: Fondazione Centro Italiano di Studi sull' alto Medioeva, 2011), 469–70.

9   On these connections, see also Catherine Cubitt, 'St Wilfrid: A Man for his Times', in *Wilfrid: Abbot Bishop Saint: Papers from the 1300th Anniversary Conferences*, ed. N. J. Higham, (Donington: Shaun Tyas, 2013), 320–1; and Ian Wood, 'Quentovic et le Sud-Est britannique (VIe–IXe siècle)', in *Quentovic: Environnement, Archéologie, Histoire*, ed. Stéphane Lebecq, Bruno Béthouart and Laurent Verslype (Lille: Conseil Scientifique de l'Université Charles-de-Gaulle, 2010), 169–70.

10 See Ian N. Wood, 'Differing Emotions in Luxeuil, Bobbio, and Faremoutiers', in *Emotions, Communities, and Difference in Medieval Europe: Essays in Honor of Barbara H. Rosenwein*, ed. Maureen C. Miller and Edward Wheatley (Abingdon: Routledge, 2017), esp. 38–42.

11 Jocelyn Wogan-Browne, 'Dead to the World? Death and the Maiden Revisited in Medieval Women's Convent Culture', in *Guidance for Women in 12th-Century Convents*, trans. Vera Morton with an Interpretative Essay by Jocelyn Wogan-Browne (Cambridge: D.S. Brewer, 2003), 179.

12 Hollis, *Anglo-Saxon Women and the Church*, 111.

13 For an extended analysis, see Elisabeth van Houts, *Memory and Gender in Medieval Europe, 900–1200* (London: Macmillan, 1999), 19–39, and 41–62.

14 *Nova Legenda Anglie: As Collected by John of Tynemouth, John Capgrave, and Others*, ed. Carl Horstman, 2 vols. (Oxford, Clarendon Press, 1901), vol. 2, 34–5.

15 All in-text references to the Latin text of *De Virginitate* are to *Aldhelmi Malmesbiriensis Prosa De Virginitate*, ed. Scott Gwara, Corpus Christianorum Series Latina 124, 2 vols. (Turnhout: Brepols, 2001), vol. 2. All in-text references to the translation are to Aldhelm, *The Prose Works*, trans. Michael Lapidge and Michael Herren (Cambridge: D.S. Brewer, 1979), 51–132.

16 See Michael Lapidge, 'The Career of Aldhelm', *Anglo-Saxon England* 36 (2007): 15–69.

17 Aldhelm, *The Poetic Works*, trans. Michael Lapidge and James L. Rosier, with an appendix by Neil Wright (Cambridge: D.S. Brewer, 1985), 97.

18 Scott Gwara, however, contends that these women may all have been abbesses in Southern England rather than members of the community at Barking: *Aldhelmi Malmesbiriensis Prosa De Virginitate*, ed. Gwara, vol. 1, 47–53.

19 Lapidge, 'Career of Aldhelm', 19.

20 Aldhelm, *Prose Works*, ed. Lapidge and Herren, 194 n.3.

21 Clare A. Lees and Gillian R. Overing, *Double Agents: Women and Clerical Culture in Anglo-Saxon England* (2001, reprinted with a new preface Cardiff: University of Wales Press, 2009); Hollis, *Anglo-Saxon Women and the Church*, 79; Benedicta Ward, '"To My Dearest Sister": Bede and the Educated Woman', in *Women, the Book and the Godly: Selected Proceedings of the St. Hilda's Conference, 1993, vol. 1*, ed. Lesley Smith and Jane H. M. Taylor (Cambridge: D.S. Brewer, 1995), 107.

22 Jane Stevenson, *Women Latin Poets: Language, Gender, and Authority from Antiquity to the Eighteenth Century* (Oxford: Oxford University Press, 2005), 92.

23 See Stevenson, *Women Latin Poets*, 92-96, esp. 92 n.47.

24 Lees and Overing, *Double Agents*, 150–64. See also Carol Braun Pasternack, 'The Sexual Practices of Virginity and Chastity in Aldhelm's *De Virginitate*', in *Sex and Sexuality*, ed. Pasternack and Weston, 93–120.

25 *The Anglo-Saxon Chronicle*, trans. Dorothy Whitelock with David C. Douglas and Susie I. Tucker (1961, rev. ed. London: Eyre and Spottiswoode, 1965), 27; see Aldhelm, *Prose Works*, ed. Lapidge and Herren, 52; and Barbara Yorke, 'The Bonifacian Mission and Female Religious in Wessex', *Early Medieval Europe* 7 (1998): 158-9.

26 Hollis, *Anglo-Saxon Women and the Church*, 84; see also Lees and Overing, 'Women and the Origins of English Literature', in *The History of British Women's Writing, 700-1500*, ed. Liz Herbert McAvoy and Diane Watt (London: Palgrave, 2012), 34.

27 Lees and Overing, *Double Agents*, 151.

28 Heide Estes, 'Feasting with Holofernes: Digesting Judith in Anglo-Saxon England', *Exemplaria* 15 (2003): 327-30.

29 Ambrose, 'On Virgins', translated in Boniface Ramsay, *Ambrose* (London: Routledge, 1997), 71-116. For the original text, see Ambrosius, *De Virginibus Ad Marcellinam Sororem Suam*, in *Patrologiae Cursus Completus, Series Latina*, ed. Jacques-Paul Migne (Paris: Apud Garnier Fratres,1800-76), vol. 16, columns 137-232.

30 For an extended discussion of Aldhelm's metaphor of the spiritual warrior, see Hollis, *Anglo-Saxon Women and the Church*, 82-97.

31 On the bee metaphor, see also Lees and Overing, *Double Agents*, 157-8.

32 'A Letter from Boniface (716/17)' in *Epistolae: Medieval Women's Latin Letters*, available online https://epistolae.ccnmtl.columbia.edu/letter/353.html (accessed 12 April 2017). The text is from 'S.Bonifacii et Lulli Epistolae', in *Epistolae Merowingici et Karolini Aevi*, ed. Ernst Dümmler, MGH Epistolae 3.1.6 (Berlin: Weidmann, 1892), 252-7, available online http://www.dmgh.de/de/fs1/object/

display/bsb00000534_00259.html?sortIndex=040%3A010%3A0003%3A010%3A00
%3A00 (accessed 12 April 2017). The translation is from *The Letters of Saint
Boniface*, trans. Ephraim Emerton, intro. Thomas F. X. Noble (1940, reprinted New
York: Columbia University Press, 2000), 3–9. All in-text quotations and translations
from this letter are from the online version. See also, Patrick Sims-Williams, *Religion
and Literature in Western England 600–800* (Cambridge: Cambridge University
Press, 1990), 243–72.

33 Lees and Overing suggest that Hildelith commissioned the account of the vision of
    the monk ('Women and the Origins', 35), but I see no reason to assume that she did
    not write the text herself.

34 For comparisons with the visions of Dryhthelm and Fursa and the apocryphal
    Vision of St. Paul see: Sims-Williams, *Religion and Literature*, 243–72; and Patrick
    Sims-Williams, 'A Recension of Boniface's Letter to Eadburg about the Monk of
    Much Wenlock's Vision', in *Latin Learning and English Lore: Studies in Anglo-Saxon
    Literature for Michael Lapidge*, ed. Katherine O'Brien O'Keeffe and Andy Orchard
    (Toronto: University of Toronto Press, 2005), vol. 2, 197–8.

35 On these traditions, see in particular, Moreira, *Dreams, Visions, and Spiritual
    Authority*, esp. 136–68. See also Peter Brown, 'The End of the Ancient Otherworld:
    Death and Afterlife Between Late Antiquity and the Early Middle Ages', The Tanner
    Lectures on Human Values, delivered at Yale University, 23 and 24, October 1996,
    available online: https://tannerlectures.utah.edu/_documents/a-to-z/b/Brown99.pdf
    (accessed 19 March 2019); and Marilyn Dunn, *The Vision of St. Fursey and the
    Development of Purgatory* (Norwich: Fursey Pilgrims, 2007).

36 Sims-Williams, *Religion and Literature*, 270.

37 Felix's *Life of Saint Guthlac*, ed. and trans. Bertram Colgrave (Cambridge:
    Cambridge University Press, 1956), 149-151.

38 Boniface, *The English Correspondence of Saint Boniface: Being for the Most Part
    Letters Exchanged between the Apostle of the Germans and his English Friends*, trans.
    Edward Kylie (London: Chatto and Windus, 1911), 169. Kylie's translation is also
    available online: http://elfinspell.com/Boniface6.html (accessed 7 April 2017).

39 Boniface, *Die Briefe des heiligen Bonifatius und Lullus*, ed. Michael Tangl, MGH
    Epistolae Selectae 1 (Berlin: Weidmann, 1916), 152–3, available online at http://www.
    dmgh.de/de/fs1/object/display/bsb00000525_00196.html?sortIndex=040%3A040%3
    A0001%3A010%3A00%3A00&zoom=0.50 (accessed 11 January 2018); Boniface,
    English Correspondence, trans. Kylie, 169.

40 Sims-Williams, 'Boniface's Letter', 197.

41 Charter S1800: 'Ceolred 1', Prosopography of Anglo-Saxon England, available online:
    http://www.pase.ac.uk (accessed 13 January 2011).

42 Sims-Williams, *Religion and Literature*, 270.

43 Sims-Williams, 'Boniface's Letter', 200–01.

44 Boniface, *Die Briefe*, ed. Tangl, vol. 1, 248–9; Boniface, *Letters*, trans Emerton, 168.

45 *Old English Literature: Critical Essays*, ed. R. M. Liuzza (New Haven, CT: Yale University Press, 2012), xi.

46 D. W. Rollason, *The Mildrith Legend: A Study in Early Medieval Hagiography in England* (Leicester: Leicester University Press, 1982), 33–46; and Stephanie Hollis, 'The Minster-in-Thanet Foundation Story', *Anglo-Saxon England* 27 (1998): 44–5.

47 For a translation and edition of the three fragmentary texts discussed in this section, see M. J. Swanton, 'A Fragmentary Life of St. Mildred and other Kentish Royal Saints', *Archæologia Cantiana* 91 (1975): 15–27. All in-text references are to this translation and edition unless otherwise stated.

48 Hollis, 'Minster-in-Thanet', 46 and 44.

49 See *Charters of St Augustine's Abbey, Canterbury and Minster-in-Thanet*, ed. Susan E. Kelly (Oxford: Oxford University Press, 1995), xxv–xxxi and cxii–cxv; and Ian Wood, 'Monastères et Ports dans l'Angleterre du VIIᵉ–VIIIᵉ Siècles', in *Échanges, Communications et Réseaux dans le Haut Moyen Âge: Études et Textes offerts à Stéphane Lebecq*, ed. Alban Gautier and Céline Martin (Turnhout: Brepols, 2011), 90–2. Recent research on Lyminge in Kent, which was very closely associated with Minster-in-Thanet, provides important contextual information about the process of monastic foundation in the period, especially in relation to Frankish influences: see *Early Medieval Monasticism in the North Sea Zone*, ed. Gabor Thomas and Alexandra Knox (Oxford: Oxbow, 2017), especially Barbara Yorke's essay, 'Queen Balthild's "Monastic Policy" and the Origins of Female Religious Houses in Southern England', 7–16.

50 Hollis, 'Minster-in-Thanet', 47.

51 Rollason, *The Mildrith Legend*. For two more recent readings of the legend of Mildrith, see Mary Dockray-Miller, *Motherhood and Mothering in Anglo-Saxon England* (London: Macmillan, 2000), 18–41; and Joshua Davies, 'The Landscapes of Thanet and the Legend of St Mildrith: Human and Nonhuman Voices, Agencies and Histories', *English Studies* 96 (2015): 487–506. Dockray-Miller's analysis focuses on another, more complete, Old English text referred to as *Þá Hálgan*, a version of the Kentish Royal Legend, but she also discusses one of the Lambeth Palace fragments in some detail.

52 Another tradition exists which places the blame on Ecgberht: see Swanton, 'A Fragmentary Life', 18 n.24.

53 Hollis, 'Minster-in-Thanet', 49.

54 Davies, 'Landscapes', 492.

55 Hollis, 'Minster-in-Thanet', 50–1.

56 Davies, 'Landscapes', 494.

57 *OED* sv 'low', 1. See also Davies, 'Landscapes', 495–7.

58 See Stephanie Hollis, 'The Old English "Ritual of the Admission of Mildrith" (London, Lambeth Palace 427, fol. 210)', *Journal of English and Germanic Philology* 97 (1998), 311–21.

59 Dockray-Miller, *Motherhood and Mothering*, 34.

60 Hollis, 'Minster-in-Thanet', 63–4.

61 Hollis, 'Minster-in-Thanet', 42–3.

62 Dockray-Miller, *Motherhood and Mothering*, 9–41.

63 See Dockray-Miller, *Motherhood and Mothering*, 13–14.

64 Hollis, 'The Old English "Ritual"'; Dockray-Miller, *Motherhood and Mothering*, 40. For an earlier and different view, see, for example, Swanton, 'A Fragmentary Life', 22 n.29.

Chapter 3

1 See the entry in Bernhard Bischoff and Birgit Ebersperger, *Katalog der festländischen Handschriften des neunten Jahrhunderts* (Wiesbaden: Harrassowitz, 2017), vol. 3, 482. A facsimile of the manuscript has been edited by Franz Unterkircher: *Sancti Bonifacii Epistolae: Codex Vindobonensis 751 der Österreichischen Nationalbibliothek*, Codices Selecti 24 (Graz, Austria: Akademische Druck und Verlagsanstalt, 1971). Unterkircher's volume does not draw upon the work of Wilhelm Levison, which addresses some key textual issues relating to the Boniface correspondence: *England and the Continent in the Eighth Century* (Oxford: Clarendon Press, 1946), 280–90.

2 The material derived from the earlier lost manuscript ends on fol. 39v. The supplementary letters begin on fol. 42v. A series of poems, mainly by Aldhelm, appear in the intervening folios. See Felice Lifshitz, *Women in Early Carolingian Francia: A Study of Manuscript Transmission and Monastic Culture* (New York: Fordham University Press, 2014), 9.

3 For a full discussion of the collection, see Andy Orchard, 'Old Sources, New Resources: Finding the Right Formula for Boniface', *Anglo-Saxon England* 30 (2001): 15–38.

4 Christine E. Fell, 'Some Implications of the Boniface Correspondence', in *New Readings on Women in Old English Literature*, ed. Helen Damico and Alexandra Hennessey Olsen (Bloomington, IN: Indiana University Press, 1990), 40.

5 Lifshitz, *Religious Women in Early Carolingian Francia*, 211 n.68. Boniface, *Die Briefe des heiligen Bonifatius und Lullus*, ed. Michael Tangl, MGH Epistolae Selectae 1 (Berlin: Weidmann, 1916), available online at http://www.dmgh.de/de/fs1/object/display/bsb00000525_meta:titlePage.html?zoom=0.50&sortIndex=040:040:0001:010:00:00 (accessed 11 January 2018).

6 *The English Correspondence of Saint Boniface*, trans. Edward Kylie, (London: Chatto and Windus, 1911); *The Letters of Saint Boniface*, trans. Ephraim Emerton, intro. Thomas F. X. Noble (1940, reprinted New York: Columbia University Press, 2000); *Berhtgyth's Letters to Balthard*, ed. and trans. Kathryn Maude, *Medieval Feminist*

Forum Subsidia Series 7 (2017), Medieval Texts in Translation 4: 1–24, available online at http://ir.uiowa.edu/cgi/viewcontent.cgi?article=2105&context=mff (accessed 17 January 2018). All references to the Latin text and English translation of Berthgyth's letters are to this edition. Maude points out that the Old English scholar Christine Fell planned to include Berthgyth's correspondence in an edition of early medieval letters but it remained incomplete at the time of her death in 1998 (7).

7 Fell, 'Some Implications', 37.

8 Nicholas Howe, *Migration and Mythmaking in Anglo-Saxon England* (New Haven, CT: Yale University Press, 1989). On Boniface's mission, see also Rosamond McKitterick, *Anglo-Saxon Missionaries in Germany: Personal Connections and Local Influences*, The Eighth Annual Brixworth Lecture, Vaughan Paper 36 (Leicester: Leicester University Press, 1991); and James Palmer, 'Saxon or European? Interpreting and Reinterpreting St Boniface', *History Compass*, 4 (2006): 852–69.

9 'A letter from Boniface (735–36)', in *Epistolae: Medieval Women's Latin Letters*, available online https://epistolae.ccnmtl.columbia.edu/letter/354.html (accessed 12 April 2017). The text of the letters from the Boniface Correspondence in this resource is from 'S.Bonifatii et Lulli Epistolae', in *Epistolae Merowingici et Karolini Aevi*, ed. Ernst Dümmler, MGH Epistolae 3.1.6 (Berlin: Weidmann, 1892), 215–433, available online http://www.dmgh.de/de/fs1/object/display/bsb00000534_00222.htm l?leftTab=toc&sortIndex=040:010:0003:010:00:00 (accessed 12 April 2017). The translations are reproduced (when available) from *The Letters of Saint Boniface*, trans. Emerton, or from *The English Correspondence*, trans. Kylie; otherwise they are original to the online project. As noted, Berthgyth's letters are not included on the *Epistolae* website.

10 Howe, *Migration and Mythmaking*, 141.

11 Jane Stevenson in *Women Latin Poets: Language, Gender, and Authority from Antiquity to the Eighteenth Century* (Oxford: Oxford University Press, 2005), 94. An important study that highlighted the crucial role of women in the Christian missions in Europe in the early Middle Ages was Cordula Nolte's *Conversio und Christianitas: Frauen in der Christianisierung von 5. bis 8. Jahrhundert* (Stuttgart: Hiersemann, 1995).

12 There have been a number of studies of friendship in the women's letters in the Boniface correspondence: see for example, D. Patricia Wallace 'Feminine Rhetoric and the Epistolary Tradition: The Boniface Correspondence', *Women's Studies* 24 (1995): 229–46; Lisa M. C. Weston, 'Reading the Textual Shadows of Anglo-Saxon Monastic Women's Friendships', *Magistra* 14 (2008): 68–78; Lisa M. C. Weston, 'Where Textual Bodies Meet: Anglo-Saxon Women's Epistolary Friendship', in *Friendship in the Middle Ages and Early Modern Age*, ed. Albrecht Classen and Marilyn Sandidge (Berlin: De Gruyter, 2010), 231–46.

13 The influence of Aldhelm is key to the shared literary language: see Orchard, 'Old Sources'; and Weston, 'Where Textual Bodies Meet', 232–4.

14 An important feminist revisioning of these poems is Marilynn Desmond's 'The Voice of Exile: Feminist Literary History and the Anonymous Anglo-Saxon Elegy', *Critical Inquiry* 16 (1990): 572–90. See also Barrie Ruth Straus, 'Women's Words as Weapons: Speech as Action in "The Wife's Lament"', *Texas Studies in Literature and Language* 23 (1981): 268–85; Joyce Hill, '"Þaet Waes Geomuru Ides!" A Female Stereotype Examined', in *New Readings on Women in Old English Literature*, ed. Helen Damico and Alexandra Hennessey Olsen (Bloomington, IN: Indiana University Press, 1990), 235–47; Shari Horner, *The Discourse of Enclosure: Representing Women in Old English Literature* (Albany, NY: State University of New York Press, 2001), 29–63; Patricia Clare Ingham, 'From Kinship to Kingship: Mourning, Gender, and Anglo-Saxon Community', in *Grief and Gender: 700–1700*, ed. Jennifer C. Vaught with Lynne Dickson Bruckner (Basingstoke: Palgrave Macmillan, 2003), 17–31; and Stacy S. Klein, 'Gender and the Nature of Exile in Old English Elegies', in *A Place to Believe In: Locating Medieval Landscapes*, ed. Clare A. Lees and Gillian R. Overing (University Park, PA: Pennsylvania State University Press, 2006), 113–31.

15 For scholarly studies that engage with the emergent new interdisciplinary focus on the history of the emotions and offer culturally specific analyses of affectivity and feelings such as compassion in medieval Europe, see, for example, Allen J. Frantzen, 'Spirituality and Devotion in the Anglo-Saxon Penitentials', *Essays in Medieval Studies,* 22 (2005): 117–28; and Scott DeGregorio, 'Affective Spirituality: Theory and Practice in Bede and Alfred the Great', *Essays in Medieval Studies*, 22 (2005): 129–39.

16 Boniface, *The English Correspondence*, trans. Kylie, 101, available online http://elfinspell. com/MedievalMatter/BonifaceLetters/Letters10-19.html (accessed 22 May 2019).

17 Clare A. Lees and Gillian R. Overing, 'Women and the Origins of English Literature', in *The History of British Women's Writing, 700–1500*, ed. Liz Herbert McAvoy and Diane Watt (Basingstoke: Palgrave Macmillan, 2012), 36.

18 'A letter from Lioba/Leobgytha/Leoba, abbess of Tauberbischofsheim (*c.* 732)', in *Epistolae: Medieval Women's Letters*, available online https://epistolae.ccnmtl. columbia.edu/letter/374.html (accessed 12 April 2017).

19 Lees and Overing, 'Women and the Origins of English Literature', 36; Weston, 'Where Textual Bodies Meet', 236. Weston unpacks Leoba's imitation of Aldhelm in this poem in her essay 'Conceiving the Word(s): Habits of Literacy Among Earlier Anglo-Saxon Monastic Women', in *Nun's Literacies in Medieval Europe: The Hull Dialogue*, ed. Virginia Blanton, Veronica O'Mara and Patricia Stoop (Turnhout: Brepols, 2013), 165–66.

20 Weston, 'Where Textual Bodies Meet', 236

21 'A letter from Lioba (*c.* 732)'.

22 'A letter from Lul (732–55)', in *Epistolae*, available online https://epistolae.ccnmtl. columbia.edu/letter/377.html (accessed 12 April 2017).

23 'A letter from Boniface (735?–55)', in *Epistolae*, available online https://epistolae. ccnmtl.columbia.edu/letter/376.html (accessed 12 April 2017).

24 'A letter from Boniface (742-46)', in *Epistolae*, available online https://epistolae. ccnmtl.columbia.edu/letter/375.html (accessed 12 April 2017).

25 Stevenson, *Women Latin Poets*, 94.

26 Barbara Yorke, 'The Bonifacian Mission and Female Religious in Wessex', *Early Medieval Europe* 7 (1998): 150–2 and 170–2.

27 'A letter from Boniface (735–36)'; cf. Weston 'Conceiving the Word(s)', 152.

28 'A letter from Boniface (*c.* 735)', in *Epistolae*, available online https://epistolae.ccnmtl. columbia.edu/letter/355.html (accessed 12 April 2017).

29 John-Henry Wilson Clay, 'Gift-Giving and Books in the Letters of St. Boniface and Lul', *Journal of Medieval History* 35 (2009): 316.

30 'A letter from Boniface (*c.*742–46)', in *Epistolae*, available online https://epistolae. ccnmtl.columbia.edu/letter/356.html (accessed 12 April 2017).

31 'A letter from Lul (745–46)', in *Epistolae*, available online https://epistolae.ccnmtl. columbia.edu/letter/357.html (accessed 12 April 2017).

32 Yorke, 'The Bonifacian Mission', 148. This Bugga should not be confused with the daughter of King Centwine of Wessex: Yorke, 'The Bonifacian Mission', 157–8.

33 'A letter from Bugga, abbess (*c.* 720)', in *Epistolae*, available online https://epistolae. ccnmtl.columbia.edu/letter/341.html (accessed 12 April 2017).

34 'A letter from Cena (723–55)', in *Epistolae*, available online https://epistolae.ccnmtl. columbia.edu/letter/344.html (accessed 12 April 2017).

35 'A letter from Cuneburg, Cuneburga/Cneuburg (729–44)', in *Epistolae*, available online https://epistolae.ccnmtl.columbia.edu/letter/352.html (accessed 12 April 2017).

36 'A letter from Denehard, Lul, and Burchard (732–42)', in *Epistolae*, available online https://epistolae.ctl.columbia.edu/letter/351.html (accessed 12 April 2017). A fifth-century Italian codex containing the earliest surviving copy of Jerome's *Commenatry on Ecclesiastes*, inscribed with the name of Cneuburg's successor, Cuthswith, made its way to Francia in the eighth century, presumably as a gift from the Inkberrow: Lifshitz, *Women in Early Carolingian Francia*, 30; and Patrick Sims-Williams, 'Cuthswith, Seventh-Century Abbess of Inkberrow, near Worcester, and the Würzburg Manuscript of Jerome on Ecclesiastes', *Anglo-Saxon England* 5 (1976) : 1–21.

37 See also Michael McCormick, 'New Light on the "Dark Ages": How the Slave Trade Fuelled the Carolingian Economy', *Past & Present*, 177 (2002): 17–54.

38 Judith Butler, *Undoing Gender* (London: Routledge, 2004), 17–18.

39 'A letter from Denehard, Lul, and Burchard (732–42)'.

40 'A letter from Denehard, Lul, and Burchard (732–42)'.

41 Fell, 'Some Implications', 32–3.

42 'A letter from Elfled, abbess of Whitby', in *Epistolae*, available online https://epistolae. ccnmtl.columbia.edu/letter/338.html (accessed 12 April 2017).

43 'A letter from Egburg/Egburga/Ecburg (716–20)', in *Epistolae*, available online https://epistolae.ccnmtl.columbia.edu/letter/359.html (accessed 12 April 2017).

44 'A letter from Egburg/Egburga/Ecburg (716–20)'.

45 Weston, 'Where Textual Bodies Meet', 237.

46 'A letter from Eangyth, abbess (719–22)', in *Epistolae*, available online https://epistolae.ccnmtl.columbia.edu/letter/358.html (accessed 12 April 2017).

47 Yorke, 'The Bonifacian Mission', 149.

48 'A letter from Eangyth, abbess (719–22)'.

49 See Weston 'Conceiving the Word(s)', 161.

50 Carolyn Dinshaw, *How Soon is Now? Medieval Texts, Amateur Readers, and the Queerness of Time.* (Durham, NC: Duke University Press, 2012), 4.

51 'A letter from Eangyth, abbess (719–22)'.

52 Howe, *Migration and Mythmaking*, 128.

53 'A letter from Eangyth, abbess (719–2)'.

54 Dorothy Whitelock, 'The Interpretation of *The Seafarer*', in *The Early Cultures of North-West Europe* (*H.M. Chadwick Memorial Studies*), ed. Sir Cyril Fox and Bruce Dickens (Cambridge: Cambridge University Press, 1950), 261–72.

55 'A letter from Boniface (before 738)', in *Epistolae*, available online https://epistolae.ccnmtl.columbia.edu/letter/342.html (accessed 12 April 2017).

56 See, for example, 'A letter from Lul (755–86)', in *Epistolae*, available online https://epistolae.ccnmtl.columbia.edu/letter/382.html (accessed 12 April 2017), and Fell, 'Some Implications', 36–7.

57 Boniface, *English Correspondence*, trans. Kylie, 155, available online http://elfinspell.com/MedievalMatter/BonifaceLetters/Letters10-19.html (accessed 22 May 2019).

58 'A letter from Boniface (732–54)', in *Epistolae*, available online https://epistolae.ccnmtl.columbia.edu/letter/343.html (accessed 12 April 2017).

59 'A letter from Boniface (732–54)'.

60 'A letter from Boniface (732–54)'.

61 'A letter from Boniface (732–54)'.

62 *Old and Middle English: An Anthology*, ed. and trans. Elaine Treharne (Oxford: Blackwell, 2nd edn, 2004), 52–3. All citations, quotations and translations of the Old English elegies are from this edition, but see also Anne L. Klinck, *The Old English Elegies: A Critical Edition and Genre Study* (Montreal: McGill-Queen's University Press, 1992).

63 'A letter from Boniface (732–54)'.

64 *Berhtgyth's Letters*, ed. and trans. Maude, 1–24.

65 Fell, 'Some Implications', 38.

66 *Berhtgyth's Letters*, ed. and trans. Maude, 15.

67 Peter Dronke, *Women Writers of the Middle Ages: A Critical Study of Texts from Perpetua (†203) to Marguerite Porete (†1310)* (Cambridge: Cambridge University Press, 1984), 30–3.

68 *Old and Middle English*, ed. and trans. Treharne, 64–5.

69 See, for example, Dorothy Warwick Frese, '"Wulf and Eadwacer": The Adulterous Woman Reconsidered', *Notre Dame English Journal* 15 (1983): 1–22; Marijane

Osborn, 'The text and context of Wulf and Eadwacer', in *The Old English Elegies: New Essays in Criticism and Research*, ed. by Martin Green (Toronto and London: Fairleigh Dickinson University Press, 1983), 174–89; J. A. Tasioulas, 'The Mother's Lament: Wulf and Eadwacer Reconsidered', *Medium Ævum* 65 (1996): 1–18; and Pat Belanoff, 'Ides…geomrode giddum: The Old English Female Lament', in *Medieval Women's Song: Cross-Cultural Approaches*, ed. by Anne L. Klinck and Ann Marie Rasmussen (Philadelphia: University of Pennsylvania Press, 2002), 29–46.

70 *Berhtgyth's Letters*, ed. and trans. Maude, 16.
71 *Old and Middle English*, ed. and trans. Treharne, 64–5.
72 *Old and Middle English*, ed. and trans. Treharne, 76–7.
73 Howe, *Migration and Mythmaking*, 110.
74 Klein, 'Gender and the Nature of Exile', 115.
75 *Old and Middle English*, ed. and trans. Treharne, 64–5 and 78–9.
76 *Berhtgyth's Letters*, ed. and trans. Maude, 17.
77 Stevenson, *Women Latin Poets*, 95.
78 Jane Stevenson, 'Anglo-Latin Women Poets', in *Latin Learning and English Lore: Studies in Anglo-Saxon Literature for Michael Lapidge*, ed. Katherine O'Brien O'Keeffe and Andy Orchard, 2 vols. (Toronto: University of Toronto Press, 2005), vol.2, 90.
79 Weston, 'Where Textual Bodies Meet', 243.
80 *Old and Middle English*, ed. and trans. Treharne, 76–7.
81 See, for example, Sonja Danielli, '"Wulf, min Wulf": An Eclectic Analysis of the Wolf-man', Neophilologus 91 (2007): 505–24. But see also Eric Stanley, 'Wulf, My Wolf!', in *Old English and New: Studies in Language and Linguistics in Honor of Frederic G. Cassidy*, ed. Joan H. Hall, Nick Doane and Dick Ringler (New York: Garland, 1992), 46–62.
82 *Berhtgyth's Letters*, ed. and trans. Maude, 20.
83 *Berhtgyth's Letters*, ed. and trans. Maude, 18.
84 *Old and Middle English*, ed. and trans. Treharne, 78–9.
85 For the Latin, see *Berhtgyth's Letters*, ed. and trans. Maude, 19. The translation, in this case, is my own. Maude translates '*temporalem vitam*' as 'temporary life'.
86 *Old and Middle English*, ed. and trans. Treharne, 46–7 and 50–1.
87 Stuart Hall, 'Cultural Identity and Diaspora', in *Theorizing Diaspora: A Reader*, ed. Jana Evans Braziel and Anita Mannur (Oxford: Blackwell, 2003), 245.

Chapter 4

1 'Hugeburc' is the most commonly used version of the name and therefore the one used here, but 'Hygeburg' is the Anglo-Saxon form and the one used by Michael Lapidge in his entry in *The Wiley Blackwell Encyclopedia of Anglo-Saxon England*, ed.

Michael Lapidge, John Blair, Simon Keynes and Donald Scragg (Chichester: Wiley Blackwell, 2nd edn, 2014).

2 Hugeburc, 'Vita Willibaldi Episcopi Eichstetensis', in *Vitae Willibaldi et Wynnebaldi Auctore Sanctimoniali Heidenheimensi*, ed. Oswald Holder-Egger, MGH Scriptores 15.1 (Hanover: Hahn, 1887), 80–117 (at 86–106), available online: http://www.dmgh. de/de/fs1/object/display/bsb00000890_00088.html?sortIndex=010%3A050%3A0015 %3A010%3A01%3A00&sort=score&order=desc&context=Vitae+Willibaldi+et+Wy nnebaldi&divisionTitle_str=&hl=false&fulltext=Vitae+Willibaldi+et+Wynnebaldi+ (accessed 12 May 2017); and 'The *Hodoeporicon* of St. Willibald by Huneberc of Heidenheim', in *The Anglo-Saxon Missionaries in Germany*, trans. and ed. C. H. Talbot (London: Sheen and Ward, 1954), 153–77. See also the fully annotated edition, based on Holder-Egger's, with parallel translation into German by Andreas Bauch in his *Quellen zur Geschichte der Diözese Eichstätt, Band 1, Biographien der Gründungszeit* (Eichstätt: Johann Michael Sailer, 1962), 22–122. Unless otherwise stated, all references to the Latin text are to Holder-Egger's edition and all references to the English text are to Talbot's translation.

3 On the complex cross-influences between early monastic foundations in England and continental Europe, see Ian Wood, 'Merovingian Monasticism and England', in *Early Medieval Monasticism in the North Sea Zone*, ed. Gabor Thomas and Alexandra Knox (Oxford: Oxbow, 2017), 17–24.

4 Pauline Head, 'Who is the Nun from Heidenheim? A Study of Hugeburc's *Vita Willibaldi*', *Medium Aevum* 71 (2002): 32. See also Eva Gottschaller, *Hugeburc von Heidenheim. Philologische Untersuchungen zu den Heiligenbiographien einer Nonne des achten Jahrhunderts* (Munich: Arbeo-Gesellschaft, 1973).

5 Bernhard Bischoff and Birgit Ebersperger, *Katalog der festländischen Handschriften des neunten Jahrhunderts*, (Wiesbaden: Harrassowitz, 2004), vol. 2, 222. See also *Quellen zur Geschichte der Diözese Eichstätt*, ed. Bauch, 20–1; and Katharina Bierbrauer, *Die vorkarolingischen und karolingischen Handschriften der Bayerischen Staatsbibliothek* (Wiesbaden: Ludwig Reichert, 1990), vol. 1, 87–8.

6 Bernhard Bischoff, *Manuscripts and Libraries in the Age of* Charlemagne, trans. Michael M. Gorman (Cambridge: Cambridge University Press, 1994), 42.

7 Bauch, *Quellen zur Geschichte der Diözese Eichstätt*, 20.

8 'Vita Leobae Abbatissae Biscofesheimensis Auctore Rudolfo Fuldensis', ed. George Waitz, MGH Scriptores 15.1 (Hanover: Hahn, 1887), 118–31, available online: http:// www.dmgh.de/de/fs1/object/goToPage/bsb00000890.html?pageNo=118&sortIndex =010%3A050%3A0015%3A010%3A01%3A00&sort=score&order=desc&context=Vi tae+Willibaldi+et+Wynnebaldi&hl=false&fulltext=Vitae+Willibaldi+et+Wynnebal di (accessed 1 June 2017); and 'The Life of St. Leoba', in *Anglo-Saxon Missionaries in Germany*, trans. and ed. Talbot, 205–26. Unless otherwise stated, all references to the

Latin text are to Waitz's edition and all references to the English text are to Talbot's translation.

9 Barbara Yorke, 'Rudolf of Fulda's *VITA S. LEOBÆ*: Hagiography and Historical Reality', in *Anglo-Saxon England and the Continent*, ed. Hans Sauer, Joanna Story and Gaby Waxenberger (Tempe, Arizona: ACMRS, 2011), 199–216.

10 See Rosamond McKitterick's exploration of the evidence of women's involvement in book production in 'Nuns' Scriptoria in England and Francia in the Eighth Century', *Francia* 19 (1992): 1–35. On Fulda itself, see Janneke Raaijmakers, *The Making of the Monastic Community of Fulda, c. 744–c. 900* (Cambridge: Cambridge University Press, 2012).

11 McKitterick, 'Nuns' Scriptoria', 24. See also Virginia Blanton and Helene Scheck, 'Leoba and the Iconography of Learning in the Lives of Anglo-Saxon Women Religious, 660–780', in *Nuns' Literacies in Medieval Europe: the Kansas City Dialogue*, ed. Virginia Blanton, Veronica O'Mara and Patricia Stoop (Turnhout: Brepols, 2015), 22–3, esp. 22 n.56. See also Helene Scheck and Virginia Blanton, 'Leoba's Legacy: the Carolingian Transformation of an Iconography of Literacy', in *Nuns' Literacies in Medieval Europe: the Antwerp Dialogue*, ed. Virginia Blanton, Veronica O'Mara and Patricia Stoop (Turnhout: Brepols, 2017), 3–126.

12 Sulpicius Severus, *Vita Sancti Martini*, Praefatio.1, available online: http://www. thelatinlibrary.com/sulpiciusseverusmartin.html (accessed 6 January 2016); *Sulpitius Severus on The Life of St. Martin*, trans. Alexander Roberts (New York: Citadel Press, 1894), available online: http://www.users.csbsju.edu/~eknuth/npnf2-11/sulpitiu/ lifeofst.html (accessed 6 January 2016).

13 See Carolyne Larrington, 'Hugeburc [Huneburc] (*fl.* 760-780)', in the *Oxford Dictionary of National Biography* (2004), available online: http://www.oxforddnb. com/view/article/49413 (accessed 2 October 2015). Larrington compares her style to that of the later medieval writer Hrotsvitha of Gandersheim. See also Head, 'Who was the nun?', 42–3 n.11. In one edition of extracts of the text, the translator claims to be able to distinguish the parts of the text composed by Hugeburc, stating that 'she wrote in long sentences with a good many alliterative words and many similes' with considerable 'padding', in comparison with Willibald, whose dictated words are, so he claims, identifiable by their clarity: *Jerusalem Pilgrimages Before the Crusades*, trans. John Wilkinson (Warminster: Aris & Phillips, 2002), 22. For a reading of the text that views it as an almost verbatim transcription, see Rodney Aist, 'Images of Jerusalem: the Religious Imagination of Willibald of Eichstätt', in *Anglo-Saxon England and the Continent*, ed. Sauer and Story with Waxenberger, 179–98. Other recent studies of Hugeburc's work include Katharine Scarfe Beckett, *Anglo-Saxon Perceptions of the Islamic World* (Cambridge: Cambridge University Press, 2003), 46–52; Ora Limor, 'Pilgrims and Authors: Adomnán's *De locis sanctis* and Hugeburc's *Hodoeporicon Sancti Willibaldi*', *Revue Bénédictine* 114 (2004): 253–75; Aist, *The*

Christian Topography of Early Islamic Jerusalem: The Evidence of Willibald of Eichstätt (700–787 CE) (Turnhout: Brepols, 2009); and James Palmer, *Anglo-Saxons in a Frankish World, 690–900* (Turnhout: Brepols, 2009), esp. 249–50. For a sophisticated analysis based on the assumption that 'a feminist reading of Hugeburc should foreground her role in the cultural production of her work', see Aidan Conti, 'The Literate Memory of Hugeburc of Heidenheim', in *Feminist Approaches* to Anglo-Saxon Studies, ed. Robin Norris, Rebecca Stephenson and Renée Trilling (Tempe, AZ: Arizona Center for Medieval Studies, forthcoming).

14 *The Writings of Julian of Norwich*, ed. Nicholas Watson and Jacqueline Jenkins (Turnhout: Brepols, 2006), 75; the translation is my own.

15 Head, 'Who is the nun?', 29; the translation is my own. For the identification of Hugeburc, see Bernhard Bischoff, 'Wer ist die Nonne von Heidenheim?', *Studien und Mitteilungen zur Geschichte des Benediktinerordens und seiner Zweige* 49 (1931): 387–88. See also Joachim von zur Gathen, *CryptoSchool* (Berlin: Springer-Verlag, 2015), 78–9.

16 Head, 'Who is the nun?', 30.

17 Lisa M. C. Weston, 'Saintly Lives: Friendship, Kinship, Gender and Sexuality', in *The Cambridge History of Early Medieval English Literature,* ed. Clare A. Lees (Cambridge: Cambridge University Press, 2013), 385.

18 Stephanie Hollis, *Anglo-Saxon Women and the Church: Sharing a Common Fate* (Woodbridge: Boydell Press, 1992), 145–6; cf. also Jane Stevenson, 'Brothers and Sisters: Women and Monastic Life in Eighth-Century England and Frankia', *Nederlandsch archief voor kerkgeschiedenis* 82 (2002): 11.

19 Conti, 'The Literate Memory of Hugeburc of Heidenheim'.

20 John A. Burrow, *The Ages of Man: A Study in Medieval Writing and Thought* (Oxford: Clarendon Press, 1986).

21 Sulpicius Severus, *Vita Sancti Martini,* 2.3–4, available online: http://www.thelatinlibrary.com/sulpiciusseverusmartin.html (accessed 6 January 2016); *Life of St. Martin*, ed. and trans. Roberts, available online: http://www.users.csbsju.edu/~eknuth/npnf2-11/sulpitiu/lifeofst.html (accessed 6 January 2016).

22 *Egeria's Travels*, ed. and trans. John Wilkinson (Oxford: Oxbow, 1999).

23 See Head, 'Who was the nun?', 28.

24 On the connections between the *sanctorale,* the *temporale,* and seasonal activities within saints' lives, see Weston, 'Saintly Lives', 382.

25 *The Life of St Eligius, 588-660,* trans. Jo Ann McNamara, available online: https://sourcebooks.fordham.edu/basis/eligius.asp (accessed 24 October 2018). The *Vita Eligii* is however interpolated and this passage on paganism was a later addition: see Yitzhak Hen, *Culture and Religion in Merovingian Gaul: A.D. 481–751* (Leiden: Brill, 1995), 230.

26 See Jerome's *Life of Paul of Thebes* in *Early Christian Lives*, ed. and trans. Caroline White (Harmondsworth: Penguin, 1998), 75–84; and *The Old English Life of St. Mary of Egypt*, ed. and trans. Hugh Magennis (Exeter: University of Exeter Press, 2002).

27 For a perceptive analysis of this episode 'as a raconteur's tale of purloined contraband', see Conti, 'The Literate Memory of Hugeburc of Heidenheim'.

28 Barbara Yorke, 'Rudolf of Fulda's *VITA S. LEOBÆ*', 206. See also Frederick S. Paxton, *Anchoress and Abbess in Ninth-Century Saxony: The* Lives *of Liutbirga of Wendhausen and Hathumoda of Gandersheim* (Washington, DC: The Catholic University of America Press, 2009), 43 and 74. The earliest manuscript, dating to the tenth century, is Munich, Bayerische Staatsbibliothek, Codex latinus monacensis (Clm) 18897, fols. 3r–42v.

29 Elizabeth Alvilda Petroff, *Medieval Women's Visionary Literature* (Oxford: Oxford University Press, 1986), 85; see also Yorke, 'Rudolf of Fulda's *VITA S. LEOBÆ*', 210–11.

30 Lisa M. C. Weston, '*Sanctimoniales Cum Sanctimoniale*: Particular Friendships and Female Community in Anglo-Saxon England', in *Sex and Sexuality in Anglo-Saxon England: Essays in Memory of Daniel Gillmore Calder*, ed. Carol Braun Pasternack and Lisa M. C. Weston (Tempe, AZ: Arizona Center for Medieval and Renaissance Studies, 2004), 51.

31 Clare A. Lees and Gillian R. Overing, 'Women and the Origins of English Literature', in *The History of British Women's Writing, 700–1500*, ed. Liz Herbert McAvoy and Diane Watt (Basingstoke: Palgrave Macmillan, 2012), 36. See also Blanton and Scheck, 'Leoba and the Iconography of Learning', 23.

32 Blanton and Scheck, 'Leoba and the Iconography of Learning', 23.

33 Blanton and Scheck, 'Leoba and the Iconography of Learning', 25. Blanton and Scheck challenge readings that suggest that the *Life of Leoba* is heavily derivative of other *vitae*, such as those of St Martin of Tours, St Germain and Gregory's *Dialogues*: 'Leoba and the Iconography of Learning', 7.

34 Ian Wood locates Rudolf's text within a tradition of lives associated with the Boniface circle, which includes the writing of Hugeburc, and he states that Rudolf, like Hugeburc, was influenced by Willibald's *Life of Boniface*: 'Missionary Hagiography in the Eighth and Ninth Centuries', in *Ethnogenese und Überlieferung: Angewandte Methoden der Frühmittelalterforschung*, ed. Karl Brunner and Brigitte Merta (Vienna: R. Oldenbourg, 1994), 189.

35 'The Life of the Holy Radegund by Venantius Fortunatus', in *Sainted Women of the Dark Ages*, ed. and trans. Jo Ann McNamara, John E. Halborg, with E. Gordon Whatley (Durham, NC: Duke University Press, 1992), 70–86, available online: http://mw.mcmaster.ca/scriptorium/radegund.html (accessed 6 January 2016).

36 *The Book of Margery Kempe*, ed. Sanford Brown Meech and Hope Emily Allen, EETS o.s. 212 (Oxford: Oxford University Press, 1940).

37 See the discussion in Diane Watt, *Medieval Women's Writing: Works by and for Women in England, 1100–1500* (Cambridge: Polity, 2007), 118-124; and Sebastian Sobecki, '"The writyng of this tretys": Margery Kempe's Son and the Authorship of Her Book', *Studies in the Age of Chaucer* 37 (2015): 257–83.

38 On Tetta, see Hollis, *Anglo-Saxon Women*, 275–6.

39 See Hollis, *Anglo-Saxon Women*, 272–4; and Yorke, 'Rudolf of Fulda's *VITA S. LEOBÆ*', 199–202.

40 Blanton and Scheck, 'Leoba and the Iconography of Learning', 23–4.

41 *Cf.* Pauline Head, '"Integras" in Rudolf of Fulda's *Vita Leobae Abbatissae*', *Parergon* 13 (1995): 33-51, esp. 44–51.

42 Hollis, *Anglo-Saxon Women*, 274. See also Margaret Cotter-Lynch, 'Rereading Leoba, or Hagiography as Compromise', *Medieval Feminist Forum* 46.1 (2010): 14–37.

43 See also Hollis, *Anglo-Saxon Women*, 277–8.

44 For a detailed recent exposition of this dream, see Blanton and Scheck, 'Leoba and the Iconography of Learning', 3–6.

45 Lees and Overing, 'Women and the Origins', 37.

46 See, for example, Caroline Walker Bynum's classic study, *Holy Feast and Holy Fast: The Religious Significance of Food to Medieval Women* (Los Angeles: University of California Press, 1988), which however focuses primarily on women's religious experience in the later Middle Ages.

47 Diane Watt, 'Mary the Physician: Women, Religion and Medicine in the Middle Ages', in *Medicine, Religion and Gender in Medieval Culture*, ed. Naoë Kukita Yoshikawa (Cambridge: D.S. Brewer, 2015), 33–7.

48 Jane Tibbetts Schulenburg, *Forgetful of Their Sex: Female Sanctity and Society, Ca. 500–1100* (Chicago: University of Chicago Press, 1998), 357.

49 Marion Grau, *Rethinking Mission in the Postcolony: Salvation, Society and Subversion* (New York: T&T Clarke International, 2011)*,* 128; see also Lisa M. C. Weston, 'Where Textual Bodies Meet: Anglo-Saxon Women's Epistolary Friendships', in *Friendship in the Middle Ages and Early Modern Age*, ed. Albrecht Classen and Marilyn Sandidge ((Berlin: De Gruyter, 2010), 231–46, esp. 244–45; and Valerie Garver, *Women and Aristocratic Culture in the Carolingian World* (Ithaca: Cornell University Press, 2009), 126–7.

50 Blanton and Scheck, 'Leoba and the Iconography of Learning', 24.

51 See Schulenburg, *Forgetful of Their Sex*, 357–8.

52 Weston, '*Sanctimoniales Cum Sanctimoniale*', 61; see also Hollis, *Anglo-Saxon Women*, 297–300.

53 'A letter from Lioba/Leobgytha/Leoba, abbess of Tauberbischofsheim (c.732)', in *Epistolae: Medieval Women's Letters*, available online https://epistolae.ccnmtl. columbia.edu/letter/374.html (accessed 12 April 2017). See also Yorke, 'Rudolf of Fulda's *VITA S. LEOBÆ*', 204 and 211–12.

54 On Leoba's burial, see Lees and Overing, *Double Agents: Women and Clerical Culture in Anglo-Saxon England* (2001, reprinted with a new preface Cardiff: University of Wales Press, 2009), 223–4.

55 Hollis, *Anglo-Saxon Women*, 273 and 283–7.

56 Ian Wood, *The Missionary Life: Saints and the Evangelisation of Europe 400–1050* (Harlow, Essex: Longman, 2001), 68.

57 Hollis, *Anglo-Saxon Women*, 282.

Chapter 5

1 Goscelin of St Bertin, *The Hagiography of the Female Saints of Ely*, ed. and trans. Rosalind C. Love (Oxford: Clarendon Press, 2004).

2 Goscelin of St Bertin, 'Texts of Jocelyn of Canterbury which Relate to the History of Barking Abbey', ed. Marvin L. Colker, *Studia Monastica* 7 (1965): 383–460. This edition is based on the Barking texts in Dublin, Trinity College Library, MS 167 and the *Life of Æthelburh* lections for St Hildelith found in Cardiff, Central Library, MS 1.381, fols. 84r–94r and 94r–96v. Colker was, at the time of editing, unaware of the texts in Gotha, Forschungsbibliothek, Codex Memb. I.81: see Marvin L. Colker, 'A Gotha Codex Dealing with the Saints of Barking Abbey', *Studia Monastica* 10 (1968), 321–4.

3 D. W. Rollason, 'Goscelin of Canterbury's Account of the Translation and Miracles of St Mildrith (BHL 5961/4). An Edition with Notes', *Mediaeval Studies* 48 (1986): 139–210; D.W. Rollason, *The Mildrith Legend: A Study in Early Medieval Hagiography in England* (Leicester: Leicester University Press, 1982), 105–43. On Goscelin's representation of female saints more generally, see Rosalind Love, '"Torture Me, Rend Me, Burn Me, Kill Me!" Goscelin of Saint-Bertin and the Depiction of Female Sanctity', in *Writing Women Saints in Anglo-Saxon England*, ed. Paul E. Szarmach (Toronto: University of Toronto Press, 2013), 274–306.

4 Sarah Foot, '*Flores ecclesiae*: Women in Early Anglo-Saxon Monasticism', in *Female* vita religiosa *between Late Antiquity and the High Middle Ages: Structures, Developments and Spatial Contexts*, ed. Gert Melville and Anne Müller (Berlin: LIT Verlag, 2011), 181–2.

5 *Writing the Wilton Women: Goscelin's Legend of Edith and* Liber confortatorius, ed. Stephanie Hollis, with W. R. Barnes, Rebecca Hayward, Kathleen Loncar and Michael Wright (Turnhout: Brepols, 2004), 7; and see Hollis, 'Wilton as a Centre of Learning', in *Writing the Wilton Women*, ed. Hollis *et al*, 307–08.

6 See further Elizabeth M. Tyler, *England in Europe: Royal Women and Literary Patronage c. 1000–c. 1150* (Toronto: Toronto University Press, 2017).

7 Hollis, 'Wilton as a Centre of Learning', 308–09. On the literary culture of Barking Abbey in this period, see also the collection *Barking Abbey and Medieval Literary*

Culture: Authorship and Authority in a Female Community, ed. Jennifer N. Brown and Donna Alfano Bussell, (York: York Medieval Press, 2012).

8 Katie Ann-Marie Bugyis, 'Recovering the Histories of Women Religious in England in the Central Middle Ages: Wilton Abbey and Goscelin of Saint-Bertin', *Journal of Medieval History* 42 (2016), 286 and n.7; Jane Stevenson, 'Anglo-Latin Women Poets', in *Latin Learning and English Lore: Studies in Anglo-Saxon Literature for Michael Lapidge*, ed. Katherine O'Brien O'Keeffe and Andy Orchard, 2 vols. (Toronto: University of Toronto Press, 2005), vol.2, 95; J. S. P. Tatlock, 'Muriel: The Earliest English Poetess', *PMLA* 48 (1933): 317–21; Tyler, *England in Europe*, 318–24.

9 Bugyis, 'Recovering the Histories', 286–7.

10 Bugyis, 'Recovering the Histories', 288.

11 *Edward King and Martyr*, ed. Christine E. Fell, (Leeds: University of Leeds, 1971); Paul Antony Hayward, 'Translation-Narratives in Post-Conquest Hagiography and English Resistance to the Norman Conquest', *Anglo-Norman Studies* 21 (1998), 85.

12 See Diane Watt, *Medieval Women's Writing: Works by and for Women in England, 1100–1500* (Cambridge: Polity, 2007), 71-81; and Bugyis, 'Recovering the Histories', 287–8.

13 Goscelin, 'Texts of Jocelyn of Canterbury', trans. Colker; Hayward, 'Translation-Narratives', 81–3; and Georges Whalen, 'Patronage Engendered: How Goscelin Allayed the Concerns of Nuns' Discriminatory Publics', in *Women, the Book and the Godly: Selected Proceedings of the St Hilda's Conference, 1993*, ed. Lesley Smith and Jane H. M. Taylor (Cambridge: D.S. Brewer, 1995), vol. 1, 129–30.

14 Goscelin of St Bertin, 'Goscelin of St Bertin: lives of the abbesses at Barking', trans. Vera Morton in *Guidance for Women in Twelfth-Century convents*, trans. Vera Morton, with an interpretative essay by Jocelyn Wogan-Browne (Cambridge: D.S. Brewer, 2003), 146 and 149.

15 Bugyis, 'Recovering the Histories', 289.

16 Bugyis, 'Recovering the Histories', 289; cf. Diane Watt, 'Literature in Pieces: Female Sanctity and the Relics of Early Women's Writing', in *The Cambridge History of Early Medieval English Literature*, ed. Clare A. Lees (Cambridge: Cambridge University Press, 2012), 357–80.

17 Cynthia Turner Camp, *Anglo-Saxon Saints' Lives as History Writing in Late Medieval England* (Cambridge: D.S. Brewer, 2015), 3–6; at 4.

18 See Susan J. Ridyard, *The Royal Saints of Anglo-Saxon England: a Study of West Saxon and East Anglian Cults* (Cambridge: Cambridge University Press, 1988), 153.

19 Goscelin of St Bertin, 'La Légende de Ste Édith en Prose et Verse par le Moine Goscelin', ed. A. Wilmart, *Analecta Bollandiana* 56 (1938): 5–101 and 265–307. All in-text references to the Latin text of the *Vita* and the *Translatio* are to these editions.

20 'The *Vita* of Edith', trans. Michael Wright and Kathleen Loncar, in *Writing the Wilton Women,* ed. Hollis *et al*, 23–67. 'The *Translatio* of Edith', trans. Wright and Loncar, is

found at 69–93. All in-text references to the English translations of the *Vita* and the *Translatio* are to these versions. Significant differences between the Latin texts of the *Vita*, edited by Wilmart, and based on the Rawlinson manuscript, and the English translation cited here, and based on the Cardiff manuscript, are noted.

21 Discussed by Hollis, 'Goscelin's Writings and the Wilton Women', in *Writing the Wilton Women*, ed. Hollis *et al*, 235. See also Paul Grosjean, 'De Codice Hagiogaphica Gothano', *Analecta Bollandiana* 58 (1940): 90–103.

22 Hayward, 'Translation-Narratives', 77.

23 Ridyard, *Royal Saints*, 147–8; 152–3.

24 Hollis, 'St Edith and the Wilton Community', in *Writing the Wilton Women*, ed. Hollis *et al*, 246.

25 Hollis, 'St Edith and the Wilton Community', 252–4 and Tyler, *England in Europe*, 231–2. On the patronage of the West Saxon royal family more widely, see Sarah Foot, *Veiled Women II: Female Religious Communities in England, 871–1066* (Aldershot: Ashgate, 2000), 221–37; esp. 224–5.

26 Hollis, 'St Edith and the Wilton Community', 254.

27 Goscelin of St Bertin, *Hagiography*, ed. and trans. Love, civ.

28 Hollis, 'St Edith and the Wilton Community', 273.

29 See Hollis, 'Wilton as a Centre of Learning', 330.

30 '*Vita*', trans. Wright and Loncar, 25 n.4.

31 See Mary Dockray-Miller, *Saints Edith and Æthelthryth: Princesses, Miracle Workers, and Their Late Medieval Audience* (Turnhout: Brepols, 2009), 8–9.

32 Bugyis, 'Recovering the Histories', 285–303. Barbara Yorke is also of the view that Goscelin was working from a lost life of Edith: '"Carriers of Truth": Writing the Biographies of Anglo-Saxon Female Saints', in *Writing Medieval Biography, 750–1250: Essays in Honour of Frank Barlow*, ed. David Bates, Julia Crick and Sarah Hamilton (Woodbridge: Boydell Press, 2006), 51–2.

33 Katherine O'Brien O'Keeffe, *Stealing Obedience: Narratives of Agency and Identity in Later Anglo-Saxon England* (Toronto: University of Toronto Press, 2012), 159.

34 *Bede's Ecclesiastical History of the English People*, ed. and trans. Bertram Colgrave and R. A. B. Mynors (Oxford: Clarendon Press, 1969), 4.23, pp. 410–11.

35 Clare A. Lees and Gillian R. Overing, *Double Agents: Women and Clerical Culture in Anglo-Saxon England* (2001, reprinted with a new preface Cardiff, University of Wales Press, 2009), 28.

36 Lees and Overing, *Double Agents*, 28.

37 O'Brien O'Keeffe, *Stealing Obedience,* 160.

38 O'Brien O'Keeffe, *Stealing Obedience*, 152.

39 Tom Licence, *Hermits and Recluses in English Society, 950–1200* (Oxford: Oxford University Press, 2011), 61.

40 See Stephanie Hollis and Jocelyn Wogan-Browne, 'St Albans and Women's Monasticism: Lives and their Foundations in Christina's World', in *Christina of Markyate: A Twelfth-Century Holy Woman*, ed. Samuel Fanous and Henrietta Leyser (London: Routledge, 2005), 32.

41 See Kathryn Maude, '"Look at my Hands": Physical Presence and the Saintly Intercessor at Wilton', in *Dealing With The Dead: Mortality and Community in Medieval and Early Modern Europe*, ed. Thea Tomaini (Leiden, the Netherlands: Brill, 2018), 129–47.

42 See L. M. C. Weston, 'Saintly Lives: Friendship, Kinship, Gender and Sexuality', in *The Cambridge History of Early Medieval English Literature*, ed. Clare A. Lees (Cambridge: Cambridge University Press, 2013), 385.

43 Hollis, 'Goscelin's Writing and the Wilton Women', 239.

44 Hollis, 'Wilton as a Centre of learning', 310.

45 Catherine E. Karkov, *The Ruler Portraits of Anglo-Saxon England* (Woodbridge: the Boydell Press, 2004), 115.

46 Karkov, *Ruler Portraits*, 116.

47 See Catherine E. Karkov, 'Pictured in the Heart: the Ediths at Wilton', in *Intertexts: Studies in Anglo-Saxon Culture Presented to Paul E. Szarmach*, ed. Virginia Blanton and Helene Scheck (Turnhout: Brepols, 2008), 273–85.

48 See Hollis, 'Edith as Contemplative and Bride of Christ', in *Writing the Wilton Women*, ed. Hollis *et al*, 291–4; Hollis, 'Strategies of Emplacement and Displacement: St. Edith and the Wilton Community in Goscelin's *Legend of Edith* and *Liber confortatorius*', in *A Place to Believe In: Locating Medieval Landscapes*, ed. Clare A. Lees and Gillian R. Overing (University Park, PA: Pennsylvania State University Press, 2006), 159–61.

49 Hollis, 'St Edith and the Wilton Community', 260.

50 Hollis, 'St Edith and the Wilton Community', 258; Ridyard, *Royal Saints*, 141 n. 5.

51 Hollis, 'St Edith and the Wilton Community', 275.

52 See Hollis, 'St Edith and the Wilton Community', 270–1.

53 See Diane Watt, 'Mary the Physician: Women, Religion and Medicine in the Middle Ages', in *Medicine, Religion and Gender in Medieval Culture*, ed. Naoë Kukita Yoshikawa (Cambridge: D.S. Brewer, 2015), 27.

54 *The Life of King Edward Who Rests at Westminster Attributed to a Monk of Saint-Bertin*, ed. and trans. Frank Barlow (Oxford: Clarendon Press, 2nd edn, 1992), 93–5; *cf.* Frank Barlow, 'The King's Evil', *English Historical Review* 95 (1980): 3–27.

55 *The Life of King Edward*, ed. and trans. Barlow, 71–3; *cf.* Hollis, 'St Edith and the Wilton Community', 253. On the influence of *The Life of King Edward* on Edith's *Legend*, see Tyler, *England in Europe*, 225–8. Tyler suggests that Goscelin had read the *The Life of King Edward* at Wilton and that it too was written for the Abbey (228).

56 Hollis, 'Goscelin's Writing and the Wilton Women', 239–42.

57 Bugyis, 'Recovering the Histories', 294.

58 Hollis summarizes the main changes made to the text in the Cardiff *Vita* in 'Goscelin's Writing and the Wilton Women', 238–44.

59 Hollis, 'Goscelin's Writing and the Wilton Women', 240.

60 Hollis, 'Goscelin's Writing and the Wilton Women', 244. Hollis develops this argument in her essay, 'Strategies of Displacement'.

61 Hollis and Wogan-Browne, 'St Albans and Women's Monasticism', 33–4.

62 See N. R. Ker, *Medieval Manuscripts in British Libraries II, Abbotsford-Keele* (Oxford: Clarendon Press, 1977), 348–9.

63 See *Edward King and Martyr*, ed. Christine E. Fell (Leeds: University of Leeds, 1971), v–vi and xvii–xx; Hayward, 'Translation-narratives', 85; and Elizabeth M. Tyler, 'From Old English to Old French', in *Language and Culture in Medieval Britain: The French of England, c. 1100–c. 1500*, ed. Jocelyn Wogan-Browne with Carolyn Collette, Maryanne Kowaleski, Linne Mooney, Ad Putter and David Trotter (Woodbridge, Suffolk: York Medieval Press, 2009), 175.

64 Hollis, 'St. Edith and the Wilton Community', 237–8.

65 See Diane Watt and Clare A. Lees, 'Age and Desire in the Old English Mary of Egypt: A Queerer Time and Place?', in *Middle-Aged Women in the Middle Ages,* ed. Sue Niebrzydowski (Cambridge: D.S. Brewer, 2011), 53–67; see also Tyler, 'From Old French to Old English,' 166–7.

66 Ker, *Medieval Manuscripts II*, 349. This is, however, disputed by Colker in his edition, 'Texts of Jocelyn of Canterbury', 394. Colker suggests that the manuscript was owned by St Martin's Priory, Dover.

Chapter 6

1 Goscelin of St Bertin, *Liber confortatorius*, ed. C. H. Talbot, *Studia Anselmiana* 37 (1955): 1–117. All in-text references to the Latin text are to this edition. Goscelin of St Bertin, *The Book of Encouragement and Consolation (Liber Confortatorius)*, trans. Monika Otter (Cambridge: D.S. Brewer, 2004). Unless otherwise stated, all in-text references to the modern English are to this translation.

2 For a recent account of Wilton as an intellectual centre, see Elizabeth M. Tyler, *England in Europe: Royal Women and Literary Patronage c. 1000–c. 1150* (Toronto: Toronto University Press, 2017), 202–59.

3 The translation of '*unanimis tuus*' (*Liber confortatorius*, ed. Talbot, 27) is 'your soul-friend' in Goscelin's *Liber confortatorius*, trans. W. R Barnes and Rebecca Hayward, in *Writing the Wilton Women: Goscelin's* Legend of Edith *and* Liber confortatorius, ed. Stephanie Hollis, with W. R. Barnes, Rebecca Hayward, Kathleen Loncar and Michael Wright (Turnhout: Brepols, 2004), 101. Monika Otter's

translation has 'soulmate', which frames the relationship more in terms of secular love: *Book of Encouragement*, trans. Otter, 21.

4   Stephanie Hollis, 'Goscelin's Writings and the Wilton Women', in *Writing the Wilton Women*, ed. Hollis *et al*, 237; Mari Hughes-Edwards, 'The Role of the Anchoritic Guidance Writer: Goscelin of St Bertin', in *Anchoritism in the Middle Ages: Text and Traditions*, ed. Catherine Innes-Parker and Naoë Kukita Yoshikawa (Cardiff: University of Wales Press, 2013), 32 and 41.

5   Hollis, 'Goscelin's Writings', 236–7.

6   Hayward and Hollis, 'The Female Reader in the *Liber confortatorius*', in *Writing the Wilton Women*, ed. Hollis *et al*, 385.

7   *The Book of Encouragement*, trans. Otter, 6–11. For the complex and conflicting relationship between education and desire in early medieval England, see Irina Dumitrescu, *The Experience of Education in Anglo-Saxon Literature* (Cambridge: Cambridge University Press, 2018). Tyler offers a nuanced but uncompromising reading of the relationship between Goscelin and Eve: *England in Europe*, 237–8.

8   *The Letter Collection of Peter Abelard and Heloise*, ed. David Luscombe, trans. Betty Radice and rev. David Luscombe (Oxford: Oxford University Press, 2013), 28–9.

9   Dante Alighieri, *Inferno* 5.121–38, from *The Divine Comedy of Dante Alighieri*, vol. 1, trans. Courtney Langdon (Cambridge, MA: Harvard University Press, 1918), available online http://oll.libertyfund.org/titles/alighieri-the-divine-comedy-vol-1-inferno-bilingual-edition (accessed 7 April 2016). See Mark Balfour, 'Francesca da Rimini and Dante's Women Readers', in *Women, the Book and the Worldly*, ed. Lesley Smith and Jane H. M. Taylor (Cambridge: D.S. Brewer, 1995), 71–83.

10   *Book of Encouragement*, trans. Otter, 11.

11   'Goscelin expects Eve to cope with his own fairly difficult Latin, and to understand his allusions to classical literature, as well as following a demanding programme of Latin reading' according to Bella Millett, 'Women in No Man's Land: English Recluses and the Development of Vernacular Literature in the Twelfth and Thirteenth Centuries', in *Women and Literature in Britain, 1150–1500*, ed. Carole M. Meale (Cambridge: Cambridge University Press, 1993), 88. See also Linda Olson, 'Did Medieval English Women Read Augustine's *Confessiones*? Constructing Female Interiority and Literacy in the Eleventh and Twelfth Centuries', in *Learning and Literacy in Medieval England and Abroad*, ed. Sarah Rees Jones (Turnhout: Brepols, 2003), 69–96; and Tyler, *England in Europe*, 233–6.

12   Hughes-Edwards 'Role', 36.

13   Hollis, 'Wilton as a Centre of Learning', in *Writing the Wilton Women*, ed. Hollis *et al*, 312.

14   Hollis, 'Wilton as a Centre of Learning', 312.

15   Tom Licence, *Hermits and Recluses in English Society, 950–1200* (Oxford: Oxford University Press, 2011), 106.

16 Licence, *Hermits and Recluses*, 159–60.

17 Hollis, 'Introduction', in *Writing the Wilton Women*, ed. Hollis *et al*, 10.

18 Licence, *Hermits and Recluses*, 115.

19 Hughes-Edwards, 'Role', 40.

20 Licence, *Hermits and Recluses*, 118.

21 Jane Tibbetts Schulenburg, *Forgetful of Their Sex: Female Sanctity and Society, ca. 500–1100* (Chicago: University of Chicago Press, 1998), 360.

22 Schulenburg, *Forgetful of Their Sex*, 361.

23 For the last two examples, see Hayward and Hollis, 'The Female Reader', 398–9.

24 See Kathryn Maude, '"She Fled from the Uproar of the World": Eve of Wilton and the Rhetorics of Solitude', *Magistra* 21.1 (2015), 37. On the communal aspects of the reclusive life and the idea of the social solitary, see Cate Gunn and Liz Herbert McAvoy, eds., *Medieval Anchorites in their Communities* (Cambridge: D.S. Brewer, 2017).

25 Licence, *Hermits and Recluses*.

26 Tyler, *England in Europe*, 242–8.

27 See Maude, 'Rhetorics of Solitude', 37.

28 Hughes-Edwards, 'Role', 35.

29 See Hughes-Edwards, 'Role', 38; Licence, *Hermits and Recluses*, 78–9.

30 *Liber confortatorius*, ed. Talbot, 67 n.88.

31 *Liber confortatorius*, trans. Barnes and Hayward, 149 n.62.

32 *Book of Encouragement*, trans. Otter, 113 n.10. See also Tyler, *England in Europe*, 246–7.

33 Tyler, *England in Europe*, 242–8; Hollis, 'Goscelin's Writings', 229.

34 Hollis, 'Goscelin's Writings', 229.

35 Barbara Newman, 'Liminalities: Literate Women in the Long Twelfth Century', in *European Transformations: The Long Twelfth Century*, ed. Thomas F.X. Noble and John van Engen (Notre Dame, IN: University of Notre Dame Press, 2012), 359.

36 See Dyan Elliott, 'Alternative Intimacies: Men, Women and Spiritual Direction in the Twelfth Century', in *Christina of Markyate: A Twelfth-Century Holy Woman*, ed. Samuel Fanous and Henrietta Leyser (London: Routledge, 2005), 167.

37 Hilary of Orléans, 'Die Gedichte und Mysterienspiele des Hilarius von Orléans', ed. Nikolaus M. Häring, *Studi Medievali*, 3rd Series, 17.2 (1976), 928.

38 Translated in Maude, 'Rhetorics of Solitude', 48.

39 Maude, 'Rhetorics of Solitude', 47.

40 Hilary of Orléans, 'Die Gedichte', ed. Häring, 929; trans. Maude, 'Rhetorics of Solitude', 49.

41 Hughes-Edwards, 'Role', 39.

42 See Diane Watt and Clare A. Lees, 'Age and Desire in the Old English *Life of St Mary of Egypt*: A Queerer Time and Place?', in *Middle-Aged Women in the Middle Ages*, ed. Sue Niebrzydowski (Cambridge: D.S. Brewer, 2011), 53–68.

43 See also Hollis, 'Goscelin's Writings', 225–9.

44 Licence, *Hermits and Recluses*, 143.

45 See Liz Herbert McAvoy, *Medieval Achoriticisms: Gender, Space and the Solitary Life* (Woodbridge: D.S. Brewer, 2011), 87–9. McAvoy argues that this depiction of the female anchorite as the *miles Christi* is unusual. Barbara Newman is of the opinion that Goscelin is not concerned with gender: see *From Virile Woman to WomanChrist: Studies in Medieval Religion and Literature* (Philadelphia: University of Pennsylvania Press, 1995), 28.

46 See Diane Watt, 'Small Consolation?': Goscelin of St. Bertin's *Liber confortatorius* and the Middle English *Pearl*', *Chaucer Review* 51 (2016): 31–48.

47 Hayward and Hollis suggest that this may actually refer to the church built by St Edith, that Goscelin describes in his *Legend of Edith*: 'The Anchorite's Progress: Structure and Motif in the *Liber confortatorius*', in *Writing the Wilton Women*, ed. Hollis *et al*, 369–83, 379 and 380–1.

48 See Hollis, 'Strategies of Emplacement and Displacement: St. Edith and the Wilton Community in Goscelin's Legend of Edith and *Liber confortatorius*', in *A Place to Believe In: Locating Medieval Landscapes*, ed. Clare A. Lees and Gillian R. Overing (University Park, PA: Pennsylvania State University Press, 2006), 168.

49 'The *Translatio* of Edith', trans. Michael Wright and Kathleen Loncar, in *Writing the Wilton Women*, ed. Hollis *et al*, 75.

Coda

1 I first discussed Christina of Markyate and the texts associated with her in detail in my study *Medieval Women's Writing: Works by and for Women in England, 1100–1500* (Cambridge: Polity, 2007), 19–38. Here I revisit some of arguments in the light of further research and recent scholarship.

2 The digitized text of the St Albans Psalter is available online: http://www.abdn.ac.uk/ stalbanspsalter/ (accessed 1 December 2016).

3 The dating of the psalter and its production and ownership are widely debated. In recent years it has been variously dated to between the 1120s and the 1150s or even later. The claim that the psalter was produced for Christina was made by Otto Pächt, C.R. Dodwell and Francis Wormald, *The St Albans Psalter (Albani Psalter)* (London: Warburg Institute, 1960). For more recent readings that assume an early date for the psalter, see, for example: Jane Geddes, *The St Albans Psalter: A Book for Christina of Markyate* (London, British Library, 2005); Morgan Powell, 'Making the Psalter of Christina of Markyate (The St Albans Psalter)', *Viator* 36 (2005): 293–335; Watt, *Medieval Women's Writing*, 21–6; Powell, 'The Visual, the Visionary, and Her Viewer: Media and Presence in the Psalter of Christina of Markyate (The St Albans Psalter)',

Word and Image 22 (2006): 340–62. There are, however, a number of critics and historians who disagree, offering a range of counter arguments and alternative owners and functions. These include Donald Matthew, 'The Incongruities of the St Albans Psalter', *Journal of Medieval History* 34 (2008): 396–416; Kathryn Gerry, 'The Alexis quire and the Cult of Saints at St Albans', *Historical Research* 82 (2009): 593–612; Gerry, 'Cult and Codex: Alexis, Christina and the Saint Albans Psalter', in *Der Albani-Psalter: Stand und Perspektiven der Forschung/The St Albans Psalter: Current Research and Perspectives*, ed. Jochen Bepler and Christian Heitzmann (Hildesheim: Georg Olms Verlag, 2013), 69–95; Robert Thompson, 'The St Albans Psalter: Abbot Geoffrey's Book?', in *Der Albani-Psalter*, ed. Bepler and Heitzmann, 57–68; Bernhard Gallistl, 'Codex and Room: The St Albans Psalter', *European Research Centre for Book and Paper Conservation Preservation Newsletter* 2 (2015): 4–17. These critics also remain divided over whether the psalter is intended for personal or communal use, whether it was planned as a single codex or is a composite manuscript which brings together disparate elements, and whether it was even produced at St Albans Abbey. A recent work that allows for the possibility of Christina's ownership at some point is Kirsten Collins, 'Pictures and the Devotional Imagination in the St Albans Psalter', in Kirsten Collins, Peter Kidd and Nancy K. Turner, *The St Albans Psalter: Painting and Prayer in Medieval England* (Los Angeles: The J. Paul Getty Museum, 2013), 9–63.

4 *The Life of Christina of Markyate: A Twelfth Century Recluse*, ed. and trans. C. H. Talbot (1959, reprinted Toronto: University of Toronto Press/Medieval Academy of America, 1998). All in-text references to *The Life of Christina of Markyate* are to this edition. It is dated to *c.* 1140–50 by Rachel M. Koopmans, 'The Conclusion of Christina of Markyate's *Vita*', *Journal of Ecclesiastical History* 51 (2000): 663–98. For the identification of Robert de Gorran as the hagiographer responsible for writing down the *Life,* see Katie Ann-Marie Bugyis, 'The Author of the *Life of Christina of Markyate*: The Case for Robert de Gorron (*d.* 1166)', *Journal of Ecclesiastical History* 68 (2017): 719–46. Bugyis follows Paulette L'Hermite-Leclerq in dating the *Life* to the 1130s.

5 Koopmans argues that the *Life* was probably never finished ('Conclusion'). For Roscarrock's summary, see *Nova Legenda Anglie: As Collected by John of Tynemouth, John Capgrave, and Others*, ed. Carl Horstman, 2 vols. (Oxford, Clarendon Press, 1901), vol. 2, 532–7.

6 For Walsingham's extracts, see *Gesta abbatum monasterii Sancti Albani a Thoma Walsingham*, vol. 1: AD 793–1290, ed. Henry Thomas Riley (London: Longman, Green, Reader, and Dyer, 1867), 98–105.

7 Koopmans, 'Conclusion', 669–74.

8 *Gesta abbatum*, ed. Riley, 104–05.

9 For a recent discussion of Geoffrey's role specifically in relation to the Alexis quire, see Powell 'The Visual, the Visionary and Her Viewer', 348; and Collins, 'Pictures and

the Devotional Imagination', 41–2. For the counter-arguments, see, for example, Gerry, 'The Alexis quire'; Gerry, 'Cult and Codex'; and Matthew, 'Incongruities'. Jane Geddes discusses the *psychomachia* in 'The St Albans Psalter: Sex, Desire and the Middle-Aged Woman', in *Middle-Aged Women in the Middle Ages*, ed. Sue Niebrzydowski (Cambridge: Brewer, 2011), 71–5.

10 A mid-twelfth century Anglo-Norman prose psalter known as the Oxford Psalter, Oxford, Bodleian Library, MS Douce 320, fols. 37r–75v, has also been connected with Markyate Priory. The St Albans Psalter appears to have provided the base text for this translation. Like the St Albans Psalter, the Oxford Psalter, which is, however, relatively undecorated, may have been presented to Christina and her community. Ian Short, in the introduction to his recent edition of the text, makes the case that the Oxford Psalter was produced at St Albans specifically for the Markyate Priory around 1145, in other words at the time of its foundation: *The Oxford Psalter (Bodleian MS Douce 320)*, ed. Ian Short, Anglo-Norman Text Society 72 (Oxford: Anglo-Norman Text Society, 2015), 9–10. As Short points out, Douce 320 was copied by the same scribe responsible for many St Albans productions in this period, including Markyate Priory's foundation charter.

11 Clarissa Atkinson, 'Authority, Virtue, and Vocation: The Implications of Gender in Two Twelfth-Century Lives', in *Religion, Text, and Society in Medieval Spain and Northern Europe: Essays in Honor of J.N. Hillgarth*, ed. Thomas E. Burman, Mark D. Meyerson and Leah Shopkow (Toronto: Pontifical Institute of Mediaeval Studies, 2002), 181. Katie Bugyis argues that the *Life* was written to support St Albans' ambitions for independence: 'Envisioning Episcopal Exemption: *The Life of Christina of Markyate*', *Church History* 84 (2015): 32–63.

12 Douglas Gray, 'Christina of Markyate: The Literary Background', in *Christina of Markyate: A Twelfth-Century Holy Woman*, ed. Samuel Fanous and Henrietta Leyser (London: Routledge, 2005), 17.

13 Bugyis, 'Envisioning Episcopal Exemption', 59.

14 Bugyis, 'Envisioning Episcopal Exemption', 59 and n.115. See also Bugyis, 'The Author of the *Life of Christina of Markyate*', 722.

15 In addition to the references in Chapter 6 n.15, see also Jane Geddes's 'Introduction to the St Albans Psalter', available online: https://www.abdn.ac.uk/stalbanspsalter/english/essays/introduction.shtml (accessed 1 December 2016).

16 Geddes, 'The St Albans Psalter: The Abbot and the Anchoress', in *Christina of Markyate*, ed. Fanous and Leyser, 198–9 and 205; and Geddes, 'The St Albans Psalter: Sex, Desire and the Middle-Aged Woman', 69–82.

17 Niebrzydowski, 'The Text of the Canticles', available online: http://www.abdn.ac.uk/stalbanspsalter/english/essays/calendar.shtml#textcanticles (accessed 1 December 2016); Geddes, 'The Significance of the Litany', available online: http://www.abdn.ac.uk/stalbanspsalter/english/essays/calendar.shtml#textlitany (accessed 1 December 2016);

and Niebrzydowski 'The Collects or Prayers', available online: http://www.abdn.ac.uk/
stalbanspsalter/english/essays/calendar.shtml#collects (accessed 1 December 2016).

18 Kathryn Gerry argues, in contrast, that the Alexis quire and the St Albans Psalter
were only adapted much later to represent the interests of Christina and her
supporters: 'Cult and Codex', 69–95. In her analysis of the Alexis quire, Gerry does
not discuss the psychomachia in any detail. Gerry's resistance to the idea of
Christina's ownership has hardened since her earlier article 'The Alexis quire and the
Cult of Saints', in which she suggests that rather than being presented to Christina at
her own consecration, the psalter might have been presented to Markyate Priory at
its dedication in 1145 or after Christina's death (598).

19 Geddes, 'The Calendar and Liturgical Apparatus', available online: http://www.abdn.
ac.uk/stalbanspsalter/english/essays/calendar.shtml#signifilitany (accessed 1
December 2016).

20 Geddes, 'The Later Obits', available online: http://www.abdn.ac.uk/stalbanspsalter/
english/essays/calendar.shtml#laterobits (accessed 1 December 2016).

21 Bugyis, 'The Author of the *Life of Christina of Markyate*', 728–37.

22 Geddes, 'Abbess and Anchoress', 204.

23 Goscelin of St Bertin, *The Book of Encouragement and Consolation (Liber
Confortatorius)*, trans. Monika Otter (Cambridge: D.S. Brewer, 2004), 42.

24 Stephanie Hollis and Jocelyn Wogan-Browne, 'St Albans and Women's Monasticism:
Lives and Their Foundations in Christina's World', in *Christina of Markyate*, ed.
Fanous and Leyser, 35–6.

25 See Sarah Foot, *Veiled Women 1: the Disappearance of Nuns from Anglo-Saxon
England* (Aldershot: Ashgate, 2000), 104–10.

26 Hollis and Wogan-Browne comment that 'Christina's world must already have been
aurally trilingual': 'St Albans and Women's Monasticism', 26.

27 Bugyis, 'The Author of the *Life of Christina of Markyate*', 743.

28 Goscelin of St Bertin, 'Goscelin's Legend of Edith', trans. Michael Wright and
Kathleen Loncar in *Writing the Wilton Women: Goscelin's Legend of Edith and* Liber
confortatorius, ed. Stephanie Hollis, with W. R. Barnes, Rebecca Hayward, Kathleen
Loncar and Michael Wright (Turnhout: Brepols, 2004), 38–9 and 48.

29 For a description, see the entry in the British Library online Archives and
Manuscripts Catalogue http://searcharchives.bl.uk/primo_library/libweb/action/
display.do?tabs=detailsTab&ct=display&fn=search&doc=IAMS040–
001102290&indx=1&recIds=IAMS040–001102290&recIdxs=0&elementId=0&rende
rMode=poppedOut&displayMode=full&frbrVersion=&dscnt=2&scp.scps=scope%2
53A%2528BL%2529&frbg=&tab=local&dstmp=1481022907884&srt=rank&mode=
Basic&dum=true&fromLogin=true&vl(freeText0)=Cotton%20MS%20Tiberius%20
E%20I&vid=IAMS_VU2 (accessed 1 December 2016). The *Sanctilogium Anglie* was
a popular text. It was, for example, adapted to become the *De sanctis Anglie* and the

Nova Legenda Anglie (the latter was misattributed to John Capgrave, and subsequently printed by Richard Pynson in the early sixteenth century), but these later versions did not include the additional *Life of Christina of Markyate*: see *Nova Legenda Anglie*, ed. Horstman, vols. 1 and 2, Koopmans, 'Conclusion', 696–7, and Catherine Sanock, *Her Life Historical: Exemplarity and Female Saints' Lives in Late Medieval England* (Philadelphia: University of Pennsylvania Press, 2007), 86.

30 For the different versions of Edith's legend, see Cynthia Turner Camp, *Anglo-Saxon Saints Lives as History Writing in Late Medieval England* (Cambridge: D.S. Brewer, 2015), 25–63.

31 See further Shari Horner, *The Discourse of Enclosure: Representing Women in Old English Literature* (Albany, NY: SUNY Press, 2001), 173–85. I also discuss this at greater length in *Medieval Women's Writing: Works by and for Women in England, 1100–1500* (Cambridge: Polity, 2007), 27–31 and 63–71.

32 Bugyis, 'The Author of the *Life of Christina of Markyate*', 728–37.

33 Geddes, 'The Remaining Saints', available online: http://www.abdn.ac.uk/ stalbanspsalter/english/essays/calendar.shtml#remainingsaints (accessed 1 December 2016).

34 Bugyis, 'Envisioning Episcopal Exemption', 55; and see also Hollis and Wogan-Browne, 'St Albans and Women's Monasticism', 42.

35 'Life of Edith', trans. Wright and Loncar, 29.

36 *Bede's Ecclesiastical History of the English People*, ed. and trans. Bertram Colgrave and R. A. B. Mynors (Oxford: Clarendon Press, 1969), 4.23.

37 'Life of Edith', trans. Wright and Loncar, 27.

38 'Life of Edith', trans. Wright and Loncar, 54.

39 Hollis and Wogan-Browne, 'St Albans and Women's Monasticism', 33–4.

40 'The Descent From the Cross', The St Albans Psalter, 47. Available online: https:// www.abdn.ac.uk/stalbanspsalter/english/commentary/page047.shtml (accessed 1 December 2016). Strikingly there is no illustration of the Crucifixion itself in the St Albans Psalter. See further John Munns, *Cross and Culture in Anglo-Norman England: Theology, Imagery, Devotion* (Woodbridge: Boydell Press, 2016).

41 Elaine Treharne, *Living Through Conquest: The Politics of Early English, 1020–1220* (Oxford, Oxford University Press, 2012), 2.

42 Katie Ann-Marie Bugyis, 'Recovering the Histories of Women Religious in England in the Central Middle Ages: Wilton Abbey and Goscelin of Saint-Bertin', *Journal of Medieval History* 48 (2016), 286.

Bibliography

Manuscripts

Cambridge, Cambridge University Library, MS Add. 3041.

Cardiff, Central Library, MS 1.381.

Dublin, Trinity College Library, MS 176.

Gotha, Forschungs-und Landesbibliothek, MS I.81.

Hildesheim, Dombibliothek, MS St Godehard 1.

Karlsruhe, Badische Landesbibliothek, Cod. Rastatt 22.

London, British Library, MS Cotton Caligula A.XIV.

London, British Library, MS Cotton Claudius E.IV.

London, British Library, MS Cotton Tiberius E.I.

London, British Library, MS Sloane 3103.

London, Lambeth Palace, MS 427.

Munich, Bayerische Staatsbibliothek, Codex latinus monacensis (Clm) 1086.

Munich, Bayerische Staatsbibliothek, Codex latinus monacensis (Clm) 8112.

Munich, Bayerische Staatsbibliothek, Codex latinus monacensis (Clm) 11321.

Munich, Bayerische Staatsbibliothek, Codex latinus monacensis (Clm) 18897.

Oxford, Bodleian Library, MS Douce 320.

Oxford, Bodleian Library, MS Rawlinson C.938.

St Gallen, Stiftsbibliothek, Codex Sangallensis 567.

Vienna, Österreichische Nationalbibliothek, Cod. Lat. Vindobonensis 751.

Primary material

Abelard, Peter, and Heloise, *The Letter Collection of Peter Abelard and Heloise*, ed. David Luscombe, trans. Betty Radice and rev. David Luscombe (Oxford: Oxford University Press, 2013).

Ælfric, *Ælfric's Lives of Saints*, ed. Walter W. Skeat, Early English Text Society 76, 82 (London: N. Trübner, 1881), vol. 1.

Ælfric, *Ælfric's Lives of Saints*, ed. Walter W. Skeat, Early English Text Society 94, 114 (London: Kegan Paul, Trench, Trübner, 1890), vol. 2.

Aldhelm, *The Poetic Works*, trans. Michael Lapidge and James L. Rosier, with an appendix by Neil Wright (Cambridge: D.S. Brewer, 1985).

Aldhelm, *The Prose Works*, trans. Michael Lapidge and Michael Herren (Cambridge: D.S. Brewer, 1979).

Aldhelmi Malmesbiriensis Prosa De Virginitate, ed. Scott Gwara, Corpus Christianorum Series Latina 124, 2 vols. (Turnhout: Brepols, 2001).

Ambrose, St, 'On Virgins', trans. in Boniface Ramsay, *Ambrose* (London: Routledge, 1997), 71–116.

Ambrosius, *De Virginibus Ad Marcellinam Sororem Suam*, in *Patrologiae Cursus Completus, Series Latina*, ed. Jacques-Paul Migne (Paris: Apud Garnier Fratres,1800–76), vol. 16, columns 137–232.

The Anglo-Saxon Chronicle, trans. Dorothy Whitelock with David C. Douglas and Susie I. Tucker (London: Eyre and Spottiswoode, rev. edn 1965).

The Anglo-Saxon Missionaries in Germany, trans. and ed. C. H. Talbot (London: Sheed and Ward, 1954).

Anonymous, *Life of Cuthbert*, in *Two Lives of St. Cuthbert: A Life by an Anonymous Monk of Lindisfarne and Bede's Prose Life*, ed. and trans. Bertram Colgrave (1940, Cambridge: Cambridge University Press, 1985), 60–139.

Bede, *Bede's Ecclesiastical History of the English People*, ed. Bertram Colgrave and R. A. B. Mynors (Oxford: Clarendon Press, 1969).

Bede, *The Old English Version of Bede's Ecclesiastical History of the English People*, ed. and trans. Thomas Miller, Early English Text Society 95 and 96 (London: N. Trübner, 1890), part 1.

Bede, *The Old English Version of Bede's Ecclesiastical History of the English people*, ed. and trans. Thomas Miller, Early English Text Society 110 and 111 (London: Kegan Paul, Trench, Trübner, 1898), part 2.

Bede, prose *Life of Cuthbert*, in *Two Lives of St. Cuthbert: A Life by an Anonymous Monk of Lindisfarne and Bede's Prose Life*, ed. and trans. Bertram Colgrave (1940, Cambridge: Cambridge University Press, 1985), 142–307.

Berthgyth, *Berhtgyth's Letters to Balthard*, ed. and trans. Kathryn Maude, *Medieval Feminist Forum* Subsidia Series 7 (2017), Medieval Texts in Translation 4: 1–24, available online at http://ir.uiowa.edu/cgi/viewcontent.cgi?article=2105&context=mff (accessed 17 January 2018).

Boniface, *Die Briefe des heiligen Bonifatius und Lullus*, ed. Michael Tangl, MGH Epistolae Selectae 1 (Berlin: Weidmann, 1916), available online at http://www.dmgh.de/de/fs1/object/display/bsb00000525_meta:titlePage.html?zoom=0.50&sortIndex=040:040:0001:010:00:00 (accessed 11 January 2018).

Boniface, *The English Correspondence of Saint Boniface*, trans. Edward Kylie (London: Chatto and Windus, 1911), available online http://elfinspell.com/MedievalMatter/BonifaceLetters/Letters10-19.html (accessed 22 May 2019).

Boniface, *The Letters of Saint Boniface*, trans. Ephraim Emerton, intro. Thomas F. X. Noble (1940, reprinted New York: Columbia University Press, 2000).

Boniface, 'S.Bonifatii et Lulli Epistolae', in *Epistolae Merowingici et Karolini Aevi*, ed. Ernst Dümmler, MGH Epistolae 3.1.6 (Berlin: Weidmann, 1892), 215–433, available

online http://www.dmgh.de/de/fs1/object/display/bsb00000534_00222.html?leftTab
=toc&sortIndex=040:010:0003:010:00:00 (accessed 12 April 2017).

Boniface, *Sancti Bonifacii Epistolae: Codex Vindobonensis 751 der Österreichischen Nationalbibliothek*, Codices Selecti 24, ed. Franz Unterkircher (Graz, Austria: Akademische Druck und Verlagsanstalt, 1971).

The Book of Margery Kempe, ed. Sanford Brown Meech and Hope Emily Allen, EETS o.s. 212 (Oxford: Oxford University Press, 1940).

Charter S1800: 'Ceolred 1', Prosopography of Anglo-Saxon England, http://www.pase. ac.uk (accessed 13 January 2011).

Charters of St Augustine's Abbey, Canterbury and Minster-in-Thanet, ed. Susan E. Kelly (Oxford: Oxford University Press, 1995).

Clemence of Barking, *The Life of St Catherine*, ed. William MacBain, Anglo-Norman Text Society 18 (Oxford: Blackwell, 1964).

Clemence of Barking, 'The Life of St Catherine', in *Virgin Lives and Holy Deaths: Two Exemplary Biographies for Anglo-Norman Women*, trans. Jocelyn Wogan-Browne and Glyn S. Burgess (London: Everyman, 1996), 1–43.

Dante Alighieri, *The Divine Comedy of Dante Alighieri*, trans. Courtney Langdon (Cambridge, MA: Harvard University Press, 1918, 1920, 1921), 3 vols., available online http://oll.libertyfund.org/titles/alighieri-the-divine-comedy-in-3-vols-langdon-trans (accessed 21 September 2017).

The Earliest Life of Gregory the Great by an Anonymous Monk of Whitby, ed. and trans. Bertram Colgrave (Lawrence: University of Kansas Press, 1968).

Edward King and Martyr, ed. Christine E. Fell (Leeds: University of Leeds, 1971).

Egeria, *Egeria's Travels*, ed. and trans. John Wilkinson (Oxford: Oxbow, 1999).

Encomium Emmae Reginae, ed. Alistair Campbell, reprinted edition with a supplementary introduction by Simon Keynes (1949, Cambridge: Cambridge University Press, 1998).

Epistolae: Medieval Women's Latin Letters, available online https://epistolae.ccnmtl. columbia.edu (accessed 12 April 2017).

Felix's Life of Saint Guthlac, ed. and trans. Bertram Colgrave (Cambridge: Cambridge University Press, 1956).

Goscelin of St Bertin, *The Book of Encouragement and Consolation (Liber Confortatorius)*, trans. Monika Otter (Cambridge: D.S. Brewer, 2004).

Goscelin of St Bertin, 'Goscelin of St Bertin: Lives of the Abbesses at Barking', trans. Vera Morton in *Guidance for Women in Twelfth-Century Convents*, trans. Vera Morton, with an interpretative essay by Jocelyn Wogan-Browne (Cambridge: D.S. Brewer, 2003), 139–55.

Goscelin of St Bertin, 'Goscelin's Legend of Edith', trans. Michael Wright and Kathleen Loncar, in *Writing the Wilton Women: Goscelin's Legend of Edith and* Liber confortatorius, ed. Stephanie Hollis, with W. R. Barnes, Rebecca Hayward, Kathleen Loncar and Michael Wright, Medieval Women: Texts and Context vol. 9 (Turnhout: Brepols, 2004), 15–93.

Goscelin of St Bertin, 'Goscelin's *Liber confortatorius*', trans. W. R. Barnes and Rebecca Hayward, in *Writing the Wilton Women: Goscelin's Legend of Edith and* Liber confortatorius, ed. Stephanie Hollis, with W. R. Barnes, Rebecca Hayward, Kathleen Loncar and Michael Wright (Turnhout: Brepols, 2004), 95–212.

Goscelin of St Bertin, *The Hagiography of the Female Saints of Ely*, ed. and trans. Rosalind C. Love (Oxford: Clarendon Press, 2004).

Goscelin of St Bertin, 'La Légende de Ste Édith en Prose et Verse par le Moine Goscelin', ed. A. Wilmart, *Analecta Bollandiana* 56 (1938): 5–101 and 265–307.

Goscelin of St Bertin, 'The Liber confortatorius of Goscelin of Saint-Bertin', ed. C. H. Talbot, *Studia Anselmiana* 37 (1955): 1–117.

Goscelin of St Bertin, 'Texts of Jocelyn of Canterbury which Relate to the History of Barking Abbey', ed. Marvin L. Colker, *Studia Monastica* 7 (1965): 383–460.

Goscelin of St Bertin, 'The *Translatio* of Edith', trans. Michael Wright and Kathleen Loncar, in *Writing the Wilton Women: Goscelin's Legend of Edith and* Liber confortatorius, ed. Stephanie Hollis, with W. R. Barnes, Rebecca Hayward, Kathleen Loncar and Michael Wright (Turnhout: Brepols, 2004), 69–93.

Goscelin of St Bertin, 'The *Vita* of Edith', trans. Michael Wright and Kathleen Loncar, in *Writing the Wilton Women: Goscelin's Legend of Edith and* Liber confortatorius, ed. Stephanie Hollis, with W. R. Barnes, Rebecca Hayward, Kathleen Loncar and Michael Wright (Turnhout: Brepols, 2004), 23–67.

Gregory, *The Dialogues of Saint Gregory*, trans. P. W., re-edited by Edmund G. Gardner (London: Philip Lee Warner, 1911).

Hilary of Orléans, 'Die Gedichte und Mysterienspiele des Hilarius von Orléans,' ed. Nikolaus M. Häring, *Studi Medievali*, 3rd Series, 17.2 (1976): 915–68.

Hugeburc, 'The *Hodoeporicon* of St. Willibald by Huneberc of Heidenheim', in *The Anglo-Saxon Missionaries in Germany*, trans. and ed. C. H. Talbot (London: Sheen and Ward, 1954), 153–77.

Hugeburc, 'Vita Willibaldi Episcopi Eichstetensis', in *Quellen zur Geschichte der Diözese Eichstätt, Band 1, Biographien der Gründungszeit*, ed. and trans. Andreas Bauch (Eichstätt: Johann Michael Sailer, 1962), 22–122.

Hugeburc, 'Vita Willibaldi Episcopi Eichstetensis', in *Vitae Willibaldi et Wynnebaldi Auctore Sanctimoniali Heidenheimensi*, ed. Oswald Holder-Egger, MGH Scriptores 15.1 (Hanover: Hahn, 1887), 80–117 (at 86–106), available online: http://www.dmgh. de/de/fs1/object/display/bsb00000890_00088.html?sortIndex=010%3A050%3A0015 %3A010%3A01%3A00&sort=score&order=desc&context=Vitae+Willibaldi+et+Wy nnebaldi&divisionTitle_str=&hl=false&fulltext=Vitae+Willibaldi+et+Wynnebaldi+ (accessed 12 May 2017).

Jerome, *Life of Paul of Thebes* in *Early Christian Lives*, ed. and trans. Caroline White (Harmondsworth: Penguin, 1998), 75–84.

Jerusalem Pilgrimages Before the Crusades, trans. John Wilkinson (Warminster: Aris & Phillips, 2002).

Julian of Norwich, *The Writings of Julian of Norwich*, ed. Nicholas Watson and
   Jacqueline Jenkins (Turnhout: Brepols, 2006).
*Leechdoms, Wortcunning, and Starcraft of Early England: The History of Science Before
   the Norman Conquest*, ed. and trans. Oswald Cockayne, 3 vols. (1864–6, Bristol:
   Thoemmes Press, 2001).
Liber Eliensis: A History of the Isle of Ely from the Seventh Century to the Twelfth, trans.
   Janet Fairweather (Woodbridge: Boydell Press, 2005).
The Life of Christina of Markyate: a Twelfth-Century Recluse, ed. and trans. C. H. Talbot
   (1959, reprinted Toronto: University of Toronto Press/Medieval Academy of
   America, 1998).
'The Life of the Holy Radegund by Venantius Fortunatus', in *Sainted Women of the Dark
   Ages*, ed. and trans. Jo Ann McNamara, John E. Halborg, with E. Gordon Whatley
   (Durham, NC.: Duke University Press, 1992), 70–86, available online: http://mw.
   mcmaster.ca/scriptorium/radegund.html (accessed 6 January 2016).
The Life of King Edward Who Rests at Westminster Attributed to a Monk of Saint-Bertin,
   ed. and trans. Frank Barlow (Oxford: Clarendon Press, 2nd edition, 1992).
The Life of St Eligius, 588–660, trans. Jo Ann McNamara, available online: https://
   sourcebooks.fordham.edu/basis/eligius.asp (accessed 24 October 2018).
Nova Legenda Anglie: As Collected by John of Tynemouth, John Capgrave, and Others, ed.
   Carl Horstman, 2 vols. (Oxford: Clarendon Press, 1901), vols. 1 and 2.
Old and Middle English: An Anthology, ed. and trans. Elaine Treharne (Oxford:
   Blackwell, 2nd edn, 2004).
The Old English Life of St. Mary of Egypt, ed. and trans. Hugh Magennis (Exeter:
   University of Exeter Press, 2002).
The Old English Martyrology: Edition, Translation and Commentary, ed. and trans.
   Christine Rauer (Cambridge: D.S. Brewer, 2013).
The Oxford Psalter (Bodleian MS Douce 320), ed. Ian Short, Anglo-Norman Text Society
   72 (Oxford: Anglo-Norman Text Society, 2015).
Rudolf of Fulda, 'The Life of St. Leoba', in *The Anglo-Saxon Missionaries in Germany*,
   trans. and ed. C. H. Talbot (London: Sheen and Ward, 1954), 205–26.
Rudolf of Fulda, 'Vita Leobae Abbatissae Biscofesheimensis Auctore Rudolfo Fuldensis',
   ed. George Waitz, MGH Scriptores 15.1 (Hanover: Hahn, 1887), 118–31, available
   online: http://www.dmgh.de/de/fs1/object/goToPage/bsb00000890.html?pageNo=11
   8&sortIndex=010%3A050%3A0015%3A010%3A01%3A00&sort=score&order=desc
   &context=Vitae+Willibaldi+et+Wynnebaldi&hl=false&fulltext=Vitae+Willibaldi+et
   +Wynnebaldi (accessed 1 June 2017).
Soldiers of Christ: Saints and Saints' Lives from Late Antiquity and the Early Middle Ages,
   ed. Thomas F. X. Noble and Thomas Head (London: Sheed & Ward, 1995).
The St Albans Psalter, available online: http://www.abdn.ac.uk/stalbanspsalter (accessed
   1 December 2016).
Stephen of Ripon, *The Life of Bishop Wilfrid by Eddius Stephanus*, ed. and trans. Bertram
   Colgrave (1927, Cambridge: Cambridge University Press, 1985).

Sulpitius Severus on The Life of St. Martin, trans. Alexander Roberts (New York: Citadel Press, 1894), available online: http://www.users.csbsju.edu/~eknuth/npnf2-11/sulpitiu/lifeofst.html (accessed 6 January 2016).

Sulpicius Severus, *Vita Sancti Martini*, Praefatio.1, available online: http://www.thelatinlibrary.com/sulpiciusseverusmartin.html (accessed 6 January 2016).

Walsingham, Thomas, *abbatum monasterii Sancti Albani a Thoma Walsingham*, vol. 1: AD 793–1290, ed. Henry Thomas Riley (London: Longman, Green, Reader, and Dyer, 1867).

Secondary material

Aist, Rodney, *The Christian Topography of Early Islamic Jerusalem: The Evidence of Willibald of Eichstätt (700–787 CE)* (Turnhout: Brepols, 2009).

Aist, Rodney, 'Images of Jerusalem: the Religious Imagination of Willibald of Eichstätt', in *Anglo-Saxon England and the Continent*, ed. Hans Sauer and Joanna Story with Gaby Waxenberger (Tempe, AZ: ACMRS, 2011), 179–98.

Ashe, Laura, *Conquest and Transformation, 1000-1350*, The Oxford English Literary History Vol. 1 (Oxford: Oxford University Press, 2017).

Atkinson, Clarissa, 'Authority, Virtue, and Vocation: The Implications of Gender in Two Twelfth-Century Lives', in *Religion, Text, and Society in Medieval Spain and Northern Europe: Essays in Honor of J.N. Hillgarth*, ed. Thomas E. Burman, Mark D. Meyerson and Leah Shopkow (Toronto: Pontifical Institute of Mediaeval Studies, 2002), 169–82.

Backhouse, Janet, 'Literature, Learning and Documentary Sources', in *The Golden Age of Anglo-Saxon Art and Culture, 966–1066*, ed. Janet Backhouse, D. H. Turner and Leslie Webster (Bloomington, IN: Indiana University Press, 1984),143–71.

Balfour, Mark, 'Francesca da Rimini and Dante's Women Readers', in *Women, the Book and the Worldly*, ed. Lesley Smith and Jane H. M. Taylor (Cambridge: D.S. Brewer, 1995), 71–83.

Barlow, Frank, 'The King's Evil', *English Historical Review* 95 (1980): 3–27.

Barratt, Alexandra, ed. *Women's Writing in Middle English* (London: Longman, 1992).

Bauch, Andreas, ed. and trans., *Quellen zur Geschichte der Diözese Eichstätt, Band 1, Biographien der Gründungszeit* (Eichstätt: Johann Michael Sailer, 1962).

Beach, Alison I., *Women as Scribes: Book Production and Monastic Reform in Twelfth-Century Bavaria* (Cambridge: Cambridge University Press, 2004).

Beckett, Katharine Scarfe, *Anglo-Saxon Perceptions of the Islamic World* (Cambridge: Cambridge University Press, 2003).

Belanoff, Pat, 'Ides . . . geomrode giddum: The Old English Female Lament', in *Medieval Women's Song: Cross-Cultural Approaches*, ed. by Anne L. Klinck and Ann Marie Rasmussen (Philadelphia, PA: University of Pennsylvania Press, 2002), 29–46.

Bennett, Judith M., *History Matters: Patriarchy and the Challenge of Feminism* (Manchester: Manchester University Press, 2006).

Bierbrauer, Katharina, *Die vorkarolingischen und karolingischen Handschriften der Bayerischen Staatsbibliothek*, 2 vols (Wiesbaden: Ludwig Reichert, 1990).

Bischoff, Bernhard, *Manuscripts and Libraries in the Age of* Charlemagne, trans. Michael M. Gorman (Cambridge: Cambridge University Press, 1994).

Bischoff, Bernhard, 'Wer ist die Nonne von Heidenheim?', *Studien und Mitteilungen zur Geschichte des Benediktinerordens und seiner Zweige* 49 (1931): 387–88.

Bischoff, Bernhard, and Birgit Ebersperger, *Katalog der festländischen Handschriften des neunten Jahrhunderts*, 3 vols (Wiesbaden: Harrassowitz, 1998–2017).

Black, John, '"*Nutrix* pia": The Flowering of the Cult of St Æthelthryth in Anglo-Saxon England', in *Writing Women Saints in Anglo-Saxon England*, ed. Paul E. Szarmach (Toronto: University of Toronto Press, 2013), 167–90.

Blair, John, 'Saint Frideswide Reconsidered', *Oxoniensia* 52 (1987): 71–27.

Blair, Peter Hunter, 'Whitby as a Centre of Learning in the Seventh Century', in *Learning and Literature in Anglo-Saxon England: Studies Presented to Peter Clemoes on the Occasion of his Sixty-fifth Birthday*, ed. Michael Lapidge and Helmut Gneuss (Cambridge: Cambridge University Press, 1985), 3–32.

Blanton, Virginia, 'Presenting the Sister Saints of Ely, or Using Kinship to Increase a Monastery's Status as a Cult Center', *Literature Compass* 5.4 (2008): 755–71.

Blanton, Virginia, *Signs of Devotion: the Cult of St. Æthelthryth in Medieval England, 695–1615* (University Park, PA: Pennsylvania State University Press, 2007).

Blanton, Virginia, and Helene Scheck, 'Leoba and the Iconography of Learning in the Lives of Anglo-Saxon Women Religious, 660–780', in *Nuns' Literacies in Medieval Europe: the Kansas City Dialogue*, ed. Virginia Blanton, Veronica O'Mara and Patricia Stoop (Turnhout: Brepols, 2015), 3–26.

Breeze, Andrew, 'Did a Woman Write the Whitby Life of St Gregory?', *Northern History* 49 (2012): 345–50.

Brown, Jennifer N., and Donna Alfano Bussell, eds., *Barking Abbey and Medieval Literary Culture: Authorship and Authority in a Female Community* (York: York Medieval Press, 2012).

Brown, Michelle P., *Anglo-Saxon Manuscripts* (London: The British Library, 1991).

Brown, Michelle P., 'Female Book-Ownership and Production in Anglo-Saxon England: The Evidence of the Ninth-Century Prayerbooks', in *Lexis and Texts in Early English: Studies Presented to Jane Roberts*, ed. Christian. Kay and L. Sylvester (Amsterdam: Rodolpi, 2001), 45–67.

Brown, Peter, 'The End of the Ancient Otherworld: Death and Afterlife Between Late Antiquity and the Early Middle Ages', The Tanner Lectures on Human Values, delivered at Yale University, 23 and 24 October 1996, available online: https://tannerlectures.utah.edu/_documents/a-to-z/b/Brown99.pdf (accessed 19 March 2019).

Bugyis, Katie Ann-Marie, 'The Author of the *Life of Christina of Markyate*: The Case for Robert de Gorron (*d.* 1166)', *Journal of Ecclesiastical History* 68 (2017): 719–46.

Bugyis, Katie [Ann-Marie], 'Envisioning Episcopal Exemption: *The Life of Christina of Markyate*', *Church History* 84 (2015): 32–63.

Bugyis, Katie Ann-Marie, 'Recovering the Histories of Women Religious in England in the Central Middle Ages: Wilton Abbey and Goscelin of Saint-Bertin', *Journal of Medieval History* 42 (2016): 285–303.

Burrow, John A., *The Ages of Man: A Study in Medieval Writing and Thought* (Oxford: Clarendon Press, 1986).

Bussell, Donna Alfano, with Jennifer N. Brown, 'Introduction: Barking's Lives, the Abbey and its Abbesses', in *Barking Abbey and Medieval Literary Culture: Authorship and Authority in a Female Community* (York: York Medieval Press, 2012), ed. Jennifer R. Brown and Donna Alfano Bussell, 1–30.

Butler, Judith, *Undoing Gender* (London: Routledge, 2004).

Bynum, Caroline Walker, *Holy Feast and Holy Fast: The Religious Significance of Food to Medieval Women* (Los Angeles: University of California Press, 1988).

Camp, Cynthia Turner, *Anglo-Saxon Saints Lives as History Writing in Late Medieval England* (Cambridge: D.S. Brewer, 2015).

Campbell, Emma, 'Clerks and Laity', in *The Cambridge Companion to Medieval French Literature*, ed. Simon Gaunt and Sarah Kay (Cambridge: Cambridge University Press, 2008), 210–24.

Cannon, Christopher, *The Grounds of English Literature* (Oxford: Oxford University Press, 2004).

Chance, Jane, *Woman as Hero in Anglo-Saxon Literature* (Syracuse, NY: Syracuse University Press, 1986).

Clarke, Catherine A. M., 'Literary Production Before and After the Conquest', in *The History of British Women's Writing, 700–1500*, ed. Liz Herbert McAvoy and Diane Watt, (Basingstoke: Palgrave Macmillan, 2012), 40–50.

Clarke, Catherine A. M., *Writing Power in Anglo-Saxon England: Texts, Hierarchies, Economies* (Cambridge: D.S. Brewer, 2012).

Clay, John-Henry Wilson, 'Gift-Giving and Books in the Letters of St. Boniface and Lul', *Journal of Medieval History* 35 (2009): 313–25.

Clayton, Mary, *The Cult of the Virgin Mary in Anglo-Saxon England* (Cambridge: Cambridge University Press, 1990).

Colker, Marvin L., 'A Gotha Codex Dealing with the Saints of Barking Abbey', *Studia Monastica* 10 (1968): 321–24.

Colker, Marvin L., *Trinity College Dublin: Descriptive Catalogue of the Mediaeval and Renaissance Latin Manuscripts*, intro. William O'Sullivan (Aldershot: Scolar Press, 1991), vol. 1.

Collins, Kirsten, 'Pictures and the Devotional Imagination in the St Albans Psalter', in Kirsten Collins, Peter Kidd and Nancy K. Turner, *The St Albans Psalter: Painting and Prayer in Medieval England* (Los Angeles: The J. Paul Getty Museum, 2013), 9–63.

Conti, Aidan, 'The Literate Memory of Hugeburc of Heidenheim', in *Feminist Approaches to Anglo-Saxon Studies*, ed. Robin Norris, Rebecca Stephenson and Renée Trilling (Tempe, AZ: Arizona Center for Medieval Studies, forthcoming).

Cotter-Lynch, Margaret, 'Rereading Leoba, or Hagiography as Compromise', *Medieval Feminist Forum* 46.1 (2010): 14–37.

Cross, J. E., 'A Lost Life of Hilda of Whitby: the Evidence of the *Old English Martyrology*', *The Early Middle Ages*, *Acta* 6 (1979): 21–43.

Cubitt, Catherine, 'St Wilfrid: A Man for his Times', in *Wilfrid Abbot Bishop Saint: Papers from the 1300th Anniversary Conferences*, ed. N. J. Higham (Donington: Shaun Tyas, 2013), 311–30.

Cubitt, Catherine, 'Virginity and Misogyny in Tenth- and Eleventh-Century England', *Gender & History* 12, no. 1 (2000): 1–32.

Dailey, Erin Thomas A., 'The *Vita Gregorii* and Ethnogenesis in Anglo-Saxon Britain', *Northern History* 47 (2010), 195–207.

Damico, Helen, and Alexandra Hennessey Olsen, eds., *New Readings on Women in Old English Literature* (Bloomington, IN: Indiana University Press, 1990).

Damon, John Edward, *Soldier Saints and Holy Warriors: Warfare and Sanctity in the Literature of Early England* (Aldershot: Ashgate, 2003).

Danielli, Sonja, '"Wulf, min Wulf": An Eclectic Analysis of the Wolf-man', *Neophilologus* 91 (2007): 505–24.

Davies, Joshua, 'The Landscapes of Thanet and the Legend of St Mildrith: Human and Nonhuman Voices, Agencies and Histories', *English Studies* 96 (2015): 487–506.

DeGregorio, Scott, 'Affective Spirituality: Theory and Practice in Bede and Alfred the Great', *Essays in Medieval Studies* 22 (2005): 129–39.

Desmond, Marilynn, 'The Voice of Exile: Feminist Literary History and the Anonymous Anglo-Saxon Elegy', *Critical Inquiry* 16 (1990): 572–90.

Dinshaw, Carolyn, *Getting Medieval: Sexualities and Communities, Pre- and Postmodern* (Durham, NC: Duke University Press, 1999).

Dinshaw, Carolyn, *How Soon is Now? Medieval Texts, Amateur Readers, and the Queerness of Time.* (Durham, NC: Duke University Press, 2012).

Dinshaw, Carolyn, and David Wallace, eds., *The Cambridge Companion to Medieval Women's Writing* (Cambridge: Cambridge University Press, 2003).

Dockray-Miller, Mary, 'Goscelin and Queer Edith: Lexomics Project Update', available online: https://blogs.surrey.ac.uk/medievalwomen/2016/06/01/goscelin-and-queen-edith-lexomics-project-update/ (accessed 18 August 2017).

Dockray-Miller, Mary, 'Judith of Flanders and Her Books: Patronage, Piety, and Politics in mid-eleventh century Europe', in *Telling Tales and Crafting Books, Essays in Honor of Thomas H. Ohlgren*, eds. Dorsey A. Armstrong, Shaun F. D. Hughes, and Alexander L. Kaufman (Kalamazoo, MI: Medieval Institute Publications, 2016), 267–322.

Dockray-Miller, Mary, *Motherhood and Mothering in Anglo-Saxon England* (London: Macmillan, 2000).

Dockray-Miller, Mary, 'Old English Literature and Feminist Theory: A State of the Field', *Literature Compass* 5, no. 6 (2008): 1049–59.

Dockray-Miller, Mary, *Saints Edith and Æthelthryth: Princesses, Miracle Workers, and their Late Medieval Audience* (Turnhout: Brepols, 2009).

Downey, Sarah, Michael D.C. Drout, Veronica E. Kerekes and Douglas C. Raffle, 'Lexomic Analysis of Medieval Latin Texts', *The Journal of Medieval Latin* 24 (2014): 225–74.

Dronke, Peter, *Women Writers of the Middle Ages: A Critical Study of Texts from Perpetua (†203) to Marguerite Porete (†1310)* (Cambridge: Cambridge University Press, 1984).

Dumitrescu, Irina, *The Experience of Education in Anglo-Saxon Literature* (Cambridge: Cambridge University Press, 2018).

Dunn, Marilyn, *The Vision of St. Fursey and the Development of Purgatory* (Norwich: Fursey Pilgrims, 2007).

Elliott, Dyan, 'Alternative Intimacies: Men, Women and Spiritual Direction in the Twelfth Century', in *Christina of Markyate: A Twelfth-Century Holy Woman*, ed. Samuel Fanous and Henrietta Leyser (London: Routledge, 2005), 160–83.

Elliott, Dyan, *Spiritual Marriage: Sexual Abstinence in Medieval Wedlock* (Princeton, NJ: Princeton University Press, 1993).

Estes, Heide, 'Feasting with Holofernes: Digesting Judith in Anglo-Saxon England', *Exemplaria* 15 (2003): 325–50.

Ezell, Margaret J. M., *Writing Women's Literary History* (Baltimore: Johns Hopkins University Press, 1993).

Fell, Christine E., 'Hild, Abbess of Streonæshalch', in *Hagiography and Medieval Literature: A Symposium*, ed. Hans Bekker-Nielsen, Peter Foote, Jørgen Højgaard Jørgensen, and Tore Nyberg (Odense: Odense University Press, 1981), 76–99.

Fell, Christine E., 'Some Implications of the Boniface Correspondence', in *New Readings on Women in Old English Literature*, ed. Helen Damico and Alexandra Hennessey Olsen (Bloomington, IN: Indiana University Press, 1990), 29–43.

Ferrante, Joan M., *To The Glory of Her Sex: Women's Roles in the Composition of Medieval Texts* (Bloomington, IN: Indiana University Press, 1997).

Finke, Laurie A., *Women's Writing in English: Medieval England* (London: Longman, 1999).

Foot, Sarah, 'Anglo-Saxon Minsters: A Review of Terminology', in *Pastoral Care Before the Parish*, ed. John Blair and Richard Sharpe (Leicester: Leicester University Press, 1992), 212–25.

Foot, Sarah, '*Flores ecclesiae*: Women in Early Anglo-Saxon Monasticism', in *Female* vita religiosa *between Late Antiquity and the High Middle Ages: Structures, Developments and Spatial Contexts*, ed. Gert Melville and Anne Müller (Berlin: LIT Verlag, 2011), 173–85.

Foot, Sarah, *Veiled Women 1: the Disappearance of Nuns from Anglo-Saxon England* (Aldershot: Ashgate, 2000).

Foot, Sarah, *Veiled Women II: Female Religious Communities in England, 871–1066* (Aldershot: Ashgate, 2000).

Frantzen, Allen J., 'Bede and Bawdy Bale: Gregory the Great, Angels, and the "Angli"', in *Anglo-Saxonism and the Construction of Social Identity*, ed. Allen J. Frantzen and John D. Niles (Gainesville, FL: University Press of Florida, 1997), 17–39.

Frantzen, Allen J., 'The Fragmentation of Cultural Studies and the Fragments of Anglo-Saxon England', *Anglia* 114 (1996): 310–339.

Frantzen, Allen J., 'Spirituality and Devotion in the Anglo-Saxon Penitentials', *Essays in Medieval Studies* 22 (2005): 117–128.

Frese, Dorothy Warwick, '"Wulf and Eadwacer": The Adulterous Woman Reconsidered', *Notre Dame English Journal* 15 (1983): 1–22.

Gallistl, Bernhard, 'Codex and Room: The St Albans Psalter', *European Research Centre for Book and Paper Conservation Restoration Newsletter* 2 (2015): 4–17.

Garver, Valerie, *Women and Aristocratic Culture in the Carolingian World* (Ithaca, NY: Cornell University Press, 2009).

Gathen, Joachim von zur, *CryptoSchool* (Berlin: Springer Verlag, 2015).

Geddes, Jane, *The St Albans Psalter: A Book for Christina of Markyate* (London: British Library, 2005).

Geddes, Jane, 'The St Albans Psalter: the Abbot and the Anchoress', in *Christina of Markyate: a Twelfth-Century Holy Woman*, ed. Samuel Fanous and Henrietta Leyser (London: Routledge, 2005), 197–216.

Geddes, Jane, 'The St Albans Psalter: Sex, Desire and the Middle-Aged Woman', in *Middle-Aged Women in the Middle Ages*, ed. Sue Niebrzydowski (Cambridge: D.S. Brewer, 2011), 69–82.

Gerry, Kathryn, 'The Alexis quire and the Cult of Saints at St Albans', *Historical Research* 82 (2008): 593–612.

Gerry, Kathryn, 'Cult and Codex: Alexis, Christina and the Saint Albans Psalter', in *Der Albani-Psalter: Stand und Perspektiven der Forschung/The St Albans Psalter: Current Research and Perspectives*, ed. Jochen Bepler and Christian Heitzmann (Hildesheim: Georg Olms Verlag, 2013), 69–95.

Gilbert, Sandra M., and Susan Gubar, *The Madwoman in the Attic: The Woman Writer and the Nineteenth-Century Literary Imagination* (New Haven, CT: Yale University Press, 1979).

Gilbert, Sandra M., and Susan Gubar, eds., *The Norton Anthology of Literature by Women: the Traditions in English* (New York: W.W. Norton, 1st edn, 1985).

Gilbert, Sandra M., and Susan Gubar, eds., *The Norton Anthology of Literature by Women: the Traditions in English*, 2 vols (New York: W.W. Norton, 3rd edn, 2007).

Gilchrist, Roberta, *Gender and Material Culture: The Archaeology of Religious Women* (London: Routledge, 1994).

Goffart, Walter, *The Narrators of Barbarian History (AD 550–800): Jordanes, Gregory of Tours, Bede, and Paul the Deacon* (Princeton, NJ: Princeton University Press, 1988).

Gottschaller, Eva, *Hugeburc von Heidenheim. Philologische Untersuchungen zu den Heiligenbiographien einer Nonne des achten Jahrhunderts* (Munich: Arbeo-Gesellschaft, 1973).

Grau, Marion, *Rethinking Mission in the Postcolony: Salvation, Society and Subversion* (New York: T&T Clarke International, 2011).

Gray, Douglas 'Christina of Markyate: The Literary Background', in *Christina of Markyate: A Twelfth-Century Holy Woman*, ed. Samuel Fanous and Henrietta Leyser (London: Routledge, 2005), 12–24.

Gretsch, Mechthild, *Ælfric and the Cult of Saints in Late-Anglo-Saxon England* (Cambridge: Cambridge University Press, 2005).

Gretsch, Mechthild, 'Æthelwold's Translation of the *Regula Sancti Benedicti* and Its Latin Exemplar', *Anglo-Saxon England* 3 (1974): 125–51.

Grosjean, Paul, 'De Codice Hagiogaphica Gothano', *Analecta Bollandiana* 58 (1940): 90–103.

Gunn, Cate, and Liz Herbert McAvoy, eds, *Medieval Anchorites in their Communities* (Cambridge: D.S. Brewer, 2017).

Hall, Stuart, 'Cultural Identity and Diaspora', in *Theorizing Diaspora: A Reader*, ed. Jana Evans Braziel and Anita Mannur (Oxford: Blackwell, 2003), 233–46.

Hayward, Paul Antony, 'Translation-Narratives in Post-Conquest Hagiography and English Resistance to the Norman Conquest', *Anglo-Norman Studies* 21 (1998): 67–93.

Hayward, Rebecca, and Stephanie Hollis, 'The Anchorite's Progress: Structure and Motif in the *Liber confortatorius*', in *Writing the Wilton Women: Goscelin's Legend of Edith and* Liber confortatorius, ed. Stephanie Hollis, with W. R. Barnes, Rebecca Hayward, Kathleen Loncar and Michael Wright (Turnhout: Brepols, 2004), 369–83.

Hayward, Rebecca, and Stephanie Hollis, 'The Female Reader in the *Liber confortatorius*', in *Writing the Wilton Women: Goscelin's Legend of Edith and* Liber confortatorius, ed. Stephanie Hollis, with W. R. Barnes, Rebecca Hayward, Kathleen Loncar and Michael Wright (Turnhout: Brepols, 2004), 385–99.

Head, Pauline, '"Integras" in Rudolf of Fulda's *Vita Leobae Abbatissae*', *Parergon* 13 (1995): 33–51.

Head, Pauline, 'Who is the Nun from Heidenheim? A Study of Hugeburc's *Vita Willibaldi*', *Medium Ævum* 71 (2002): 29–46.

Hen, Yitzhak, *Culture and Religion in Merovingian Gaul: AD 481–751* (Leiden: Brill, 1995).

Hill, Joyce, 'The *Regularis Concordia* Glossed and Translated', in *Rethinking and Recontextualizing Glosses: New Perspectives on the Study of Late Anglo-Saxon Glossography*, ed. Patrizia Lendinara, Loredana Lazzari and Claudia Di Sciacca (Porto: Fédération Internationale des Instituts d'Études Médiévales, 2011), 249–67.

Hill, Joyce, 'Rending the Garment and Reading By the Rood: *Regularis Concordia* Rituals for Men and Women', in *The Liturgy of the Late Anglo-Saxon Church*, ed. Helen Gittos and M. Bradford Bedingfield (London: Henry Bradshaw Society, 2005), 53–64.

Hill, Joyce, '"Þaet Waes Geomuru Ides!" A Female Stereotype Examined', in *New Readings on Women in Old English Literature*, ed. Helen Damico and Alexandra Hennessey Olsen (Bloomington: Indiana University Press, 1990), 235–47.

Hollis, Stephanie, *Anglo-Saxon Women and the Church: Sharing a Common Fate* (Woodbridge: Boydell Press, 1992).

Hollis, Stephanie, 'Barking's Monastic School, Late Seventh to Twelfth Century: History, Saint-Making and Literary Culture', in *Barking Abbey and Medieval Literary Culture: Authorship and Authority in a Female Community* (York: York Medieval Press, 2012), ed. Jennifer R. Brown and Donna Alfano Bussell, 33–55.

Hollis, Stephanie, 'Edith as Contemplative and Bride of Christ', in *Writing the Wilton Women: Goscelin's Legend of Edith and* Liber confortatorius, ed. Stephanie Hollis, with W. R. Barnes, Rebecca Hayward, Kathleen Loncar and Michael Wright (Turnhout: Brepols, 2004), 281–306.

Hollis, Stephanie, 'Goscelin's Writings and the Wilton Women', in *Writing the Wilton Women: Goscelin's Legend of Edith and* Liber confortatorius, ed. Stephanie Hollis, with W. R. Barnes, Rebecca Hayward, Kathleen Loncar and Michael Wright (Turnhout: Brepols, 2004), 217–44.

Hollis, Stephanie, 'The Minster-in-Thanet Foundation Story', *Anglo-Saxon England* 27 (1998): 41–64.

Hollis, Stephanie, 'The Old English "Ritual of the Admission of Mildrith" (London, Lambeth Palace 427, fol. 210)', *Journal of English and Germanic Philology* 97 (1998): 311–21.

Hollis, Stephanie, 'St Edith and the Wilton Community', in *Writing the Wilton Women: Goscelin's Legend of Edith and* Liber confortatorius, ed. Stephanie Hollis, with W. R. Barnes, Rebecca Hayward, Kathleen Loncar and Michael Wright (Turnhout: Brepols, 2004), 245–80.

Hollis, Stephanie, 'Strategies of Emplacement and Displacement: St. Edith and the Wilton Community in Goscelin's Legend of Edith and *Liber confortatorius*', in *A Place to Believe in: Locating Medieval Landscapes*, ed. Clare A. Lees and Gillian R. Overing (University Park, PA: Pennsylvania State University Press, 2006), 150–69.

Hollis, Stephanie, 'Wilton as a Centre of Learning', in *Writing the Wilton Women: Goscelin's Legend of Edith and* Liber confortatorius, ed. Stephanie Hollis, with W. R. Barnes, Rebecca Hayward, Kathleen Loncar and Michael Wright (Turnhout: Brepols, 2004), 307–38.

Hollis, Stephanie, with W. R. Barnes, Rebecca Hayward, Kathleen Loncar and Michael Wright, eds., *Writing the Wilton Women: Goscelin's* Legend of Edith *and* Liber confortatorius (Turnhout: Brepols, 2004).

Hollis, Stephanie, and Jocelyn Wogan-Browne, 'St Albans and Women's Monasticism: Lives and their Foundations in Christina's World', in *Christina of Markyate: A Twelfth-Century Holy Woman*, ed. Samuel Fanous and Henrietta Leyser (London: Routledge, 2005), 25–52.

Hopf, Cornelia, ed., *Die abendländischen Handschriften der Forschungs- und Landesbibliothek Gotha. 1. Die großformatigen Pergamenthandschriften Memb. I* (Erfurt: Universitäts- u. Forschungsbibliothek Erfurt, 1997).

Horner, Shari, *The Discourse of Enclosure: Representing Women in Old English Literature* (Albany, NY: SUNY Press, 2001).

Houts, Elisabeth van, *Memory and Gender in Medieval Europe 900–1200* (Basingstoke: Macmillan, 1999).

Houts, Elisabeth van, 'Women and the Writing of History in the Early Middle Ages: The Case of Abbess Matilda of Essen and Aethelweard', *Early Medieval Europe* 1 (1992): 53–68.

Howe, Nicholas. *Migration and Mythmaking in Anglo-Saxon England* (New Haven, CT: Yale University Press, 1989).

Hughes-Edward, Mari, 'The Role of the Anchoritic Guidance Writer: Goscelin of St Bertin', in *Anchoritism in the Middle Ages: Text and Traditions*, ed. Catherine Innes-Parker and Naoë Kukita Yoshikawa (Cardiff: University of Wales Press, 2013), 31–45.

Huneycutt, Lois L., 'The Idea of the Perfect Princess: the *Life of St Margaret* in the Reign of Matilda II (1100–1118)', *Anglo-Norman Studies* 12 (1989): 81–97.

Huneycutt, Lois L., *Matilda of Scotland: A Study in Medieval Queenship* (Woodbridge: Boydell Press, 2003).

Ingham, Patricia Clare. 'From Kinship to Kingship: Mourning, Gender, and Anglo-Saxon Community', in *Grief and Gender: 700–1700*, ed. Jennifer C. Vaught with Lynne Dickson Bruckner (Basingstoke: Palgrave Macmillan, 2003), 17–31.

Karkov, Catherine E., 'Pictured in the Heart: the Ediths at Wilton', in *Intertexts: Studies in Anglo-Saxon Culture Presented to Paul E. Szarmach*, ed. Virginia Blanton and Helene Scheck (Turnhout: Brepols, 2008), 273–85.

Karkov, Catherine E., *The Ruler Portraits of Anglo-Saxon England* (Woodbridge: Boydell Press, 2004).

Karkov, Catherine E., 'Whitby, Jarrow and the Commemoration of Death in Northumbria', in *Northumbria's Golden Age*, ed. Jane Hawkes and Susan Mills (Stroud: Sutton, 1999), 126–35.

Ker, N. R., *Medieval Manuscripts in British Libraries II, Abbotsford-Keele* (Oxford: Clarendon Press, 1977).

Klein, Stacy S., 'Gender and the Nature of Exile in Old English Elegies', in *A Place to Believe in: Locating Medieval Landscapes*, ed. Clare A. Lees and Gillian R. Overing (University Park, PA: Pennsylvania State University Press, 2006), 113–31.

Klink, Anne L., 'Anglo-Saxon Women and the Law', *Journal of Medieval History* 8 (1982): 107–21.

Klinck, Anne L., *The Old English Elegies: A Critical Edition and Genre Study* (Montreal: McGill-Queen's University Press, 1992).

Koopmans, Rachel M., 'The Conclusion of Christina of Markyate's *Vita*', *Journal of Ecclesiastical History* 51 (2000): 663–98.

Lapidge, Michael, 'The Career of Aldhelm', *Anglo-Saxon England* 36 (2007): 15–69.

Lapidge, Michael, John Blair, Simon Keynes and Donald Scragg, eds, *The Wiley Blackwell Encyclopedia of Anglo-Saxon England* (Chichester: Wiley Blackwell, 2nd edn, 2014).

Lavezzo, Kathy, *Angels on the Edge of the World: Geography, Literature, and English Community, 1000–1534* (Ithaca, NY: Cornell University Press, 2006).

Lavezzo, Kathy, 'Gregory's Boys: The Homoerotic Production of English Whiteness', in *Sex and Sexuality in Anglo-Saxon England: Essays in Memory of Daniel Gillmore Calder*, ed. Carol Braun Pasternack and Lisa M. C. Weston (Tempe, AZ: Arizona Center for Medieval and Renaissance Studies, 2004), 63–90.

Lees, Clare A., ed., *The Cambridge History of Early Medieval English Literature* (Cambridge: Cambridge University Press, 2012).

Lees, Clare A., 'In Ælfric's Words: Conversion, Vigilance and the Nation', in Ælfric's *Life of Gregory the Great* in *A Companion to Ælfric*, ed. Hugh Magennis and Mary Swan (Leiden and Boston: Brill, 2009), 271–96.

Lees, Clare A., and Gillian R. Overing, 'Birthing Bishops and Fathering Poets: Bede, Hild, and the Relations of Cultural Production', *Exemplaria* 6 (1994): 35–65.

Lees, Clare A., and Gillian R. Overing, *Double Agents: Women and Clerical Culture in Anglo-Saxon England*, (2001, reprinted with a new preface, Cardiff: University of Wales Press, 2009).

Lees, Clare A., and Gillian R. Overing, 'Women and the Origins of English Literature', in *The The History of British Women's Writing, 700–1500*, ed. Liz Herbert McAvoy and Diane Watt, (Basingstoke: Palgrave Macmillan, 2012), 31–40.

Levison, Wilhelm, *England and the Continent in the Eighth Century* (Oxford: Clarendon Press, 1946).

Licence, Tom, *Hermits and Recluses in English Society, 950–1200* (Oxford: Oxford University Press, 2011).

Lifshitz, Felice, *Women in Early Carolingian Francia: A Study of Manuscript Transmission and Monastic Culture* (New York: Fordham University Press, 2014).

Limor, Ora, 'Pilgrims and Authors: Adomnán's *De locis sanctis* and Hugeburc's *Hodoeporicon Sancti Willibaldi*', *Revue Bénédictine* 114 (2004): 253–75.

Liuzza, R. M., ed. *Old English Literature: Critical Essays* (New Haven, CT: Yale University Press, 2012).

Love, Rosalind, '"Torture Me, Rend Me, Burn Me, Kill Me!" Goscelin of Saint-Bertin and the Depiction of Female Sanctity', in *Writing Women Saints in Anglo-Saxon England*, ed. Paul E. Szarmach (Toronto: University of Toronto Press, 2013), 274–306.

Matthew, Donald, 'The Incongruities of the St Albans Psalter', *Journal of Medieval History* 34 (2008): 396–416.

McAvoy, Liz Herbert, *Medieval Anchoriticisms: Gender, Space and the Solitary Life* (Woodbridge: D.S. Brewer, 2011).

McAvoy, Liz Herbert, and Diane Watt, eds., *The History of British Women's Writing, 700–1500* (Basingstoke: Palgrave Macmillan, 2012).

McCormick, Michael, 'New Light on the "Dark Ages": How the Slave Trade Fuelled the Carolingian Economy', *Past & Present* 177 (2002): 17–54.

McDaniel, Rhonda L., *The Third Gender and Ælfric's Lives of Saints* (Kalamazoo, MI: Medieval Institute Publications, 2018).

McKitterick, Rosamond, *Anglo-Saxon Missionaries in Germany: Personal Connections and Local Influences*, The Eighth Annual Brixworth Lecture, Vaughan Paper 36 (Leicester: Leicester University Press, 1991).

McKitterick, Rosamond, 'Nuns' Scriptoria in England and Francia in the Eighth Century', *Francia* 19 (1992): 1–35.

McNamer, Sarah, *Affective Meditation and the Invention of Medieval Compassion* (Philadelphia, PA: University of Pennsylvania Press, 2010).

Maude, Kathryn, '"Look at my Hands": Physical Presence and the Saintly Intercessor at Wilton', in *Dealing With The Dead: Mortality and Community in Medieval and Early Modern Europe*, ed. Thea Tomaini (Leiden, the Netherlands: Brill, 2018), 129–47.

Maude, Kathryn, '"She Fled from the Uproar of the World": Eve of Wilton and the Rhetorics of Solitude', *Magistra* 21.1 (2015): 36–50.

Meale, Carole M., ed., *Women and Literature in Britain, 1150–1500* (Cambridge: Cambridge University Press, 2nd edn, 1996).

Mehan, Uppinder, and David Townsend, '"Nation" and the Gaze of the Other in Eighth-Century Northumbria', *Comparative Literature* 53 (2001): 1–26.

Millett, Bella, 'Women in No Man's Land: English Recluses and the Development of Vernacular Literature in the Twelfth and Thirteenth Centuries', in *Women and Literature in Britain, 1150–1500*, ed. Carole M. Meale (Cambridge: Cambridge University Press, 1993), 86–103.

Millett, Kate, *Sexual Politics* (Garden City, NY: Doubleday, 1970).

Minnis, A.J., *Medieval Theory of Authorship: Scholastic Literary Attitudes in the Later Middle Ages* (Aldershot: Scholar Press, 2nd edition, 1988).

Moers, Ellen, *Literary Women: The Great Writers* (Garden City, NY: Doubleday, 1976).

Munns, John, *Cross and Culture in Anglo-Norman England: Theology, Imagery, Devotion* (Woodbridge: Boydell Press, 2016).

Moreira, Isabel, *Dreams, Visions, and Spiritual Authority in Merovingian Gaul* (Ithaca, NY: Cornell University Press, 2000).

Newman, Barbara, *From Virile Woman to WomanChrist: Studies in Medieval Religion and Literature* (Philadelphia, PA: University of Pennsylvania Press, 1995).

Newman, Barbara, 'Liminalities: Literate Women in the Long Twelfth Century', in *European Transformations: The Long Twelfth Century*, ed. Thomas F. X. Noble and John van Engen (Notre Dame, IN: University of Notre Dame Press, 2012), 354–402.

Nolte, Cordula, *Conversio und Christianitas: Frauen in der Christianisierung von 5. bis 8. Jahrhundert* (Stuttgart: Hiersemann, 1995).

O'Brien O'Keeffe, Katherine, 'Edith's Choice', in *Latin Learning and English Lore: Studies in Anglo-Saxon Literature for Michael Lapidge*, ed. Katherine O'Brien O'Keeffe and Andy Orchard, 2 vols (Toronto: University of Toronto Press, 2005), vol. 2, 253–74.

O'Brien O'Keeffe, Katherine, *Stealing Obedience: Narratives of Agency and Identity in Later Anglo-Saxon England* (Toronto: University of Toronto Press, 2012).

Olson, Linda, 'Did Medieval English Women Read Augustine's *Confessiones*? Constructing Female Interiority and Literacy in the Eleventh and Twelfth Centuries', in *Learning and Literacy in Medieval England and Abroad*, ed. Sarah Rees Jones (Turnhout: Brepols, 2003), 69–96.

Orchard, Andy, 'Old Sources, New Resources: Finding the Right Formula for Boniface', *Anglo-Saxon England* 30 (2001): 15–38.

Orchard, Andy, *The Poetic Art of Aldhelm* (Cambridge: Cambridge University Press, 1994).

Osborn, Marijane, 'The Text and Context of Wulf and Eadwacer', in *The Old English Elegies: New Essays in Criticism and Research*, ed. by Martin Green (Toronto and London: Fairleigh Dickinson University Press, 1983), 174–89.

Pächt, Otto, C. R. Dodwell and Francis Wormald, *The St Albans Psalter (Albani Psalter)* (London: Warburg Institute, 1960).

Palmer, James, *Anglo-Saxons in a Frankish World, 690–900* (Turnhout: Brepols, 2009).

Palmer, James, 'Saxon or European? Interpreting and Reinterpreting St Boniface', *History Compass*, 4 (2006): 852–69.

Pasternack, Carol Braun, 'The Sexual Practices of Virginity and Chastity in Aldhelm's *De Virginitate*', in *Sex and Sexuality in Anglo-Saxon England: Essays in Memory of Daniel Gillmore Calder*, ed. Carol Braun Pasternack and Lisa M. C. Weston (Tempe, AZ: Arizona Center for Medieval and Renaissance Studies, 2004), 93–120.

Pasternack, Carol Braun, and Lisa M. C. Weston, eds., *Sex and Sexuality in Anglo-Saxon England: Essays in Memory of Daniel Gillmore Calder* (Tempe, AZ: Arizona Center for Medieval and Renaissance Studies, 2004).

Paxton, Frederick S., *Anchoress and Abbess in Ninth-Century Saxony: The Lives of Liutbirga of Wendhausen and Hathumoda of Gandersheim* (Washington, DC: The Catholic University of America Press, 2009).

Petroff, Elizabeth Alvilda, *Medieval Women's Visionary Literature* (Oxford: Oxford University Press, 1986).

Powell, Morgan, 'Making the Psalter of Christina of Markyate (The St Albans Psalter)', *Viator* 36 (2005): 293–335.

Powell, Morgan, 'The Visual, the Visionary, and Her Viewer: Media and Presence in the Psalter of Christina of Markyate (The St Albans Psalter)', *Word and Image* 22 (2006): 340–62.

Raaijmakers, Janneke, *The Making of the Monastic Community of Fulda, c. 744–c. 900* (Cambridge: Cambridge University Press, 2012).

Rauer, Christine, 'Female Hagiography in the *Old English Martyrology*', in *Writing Women Saints in Anglo-Saxon England*, ed. Paul E. Szarmach (Toronto: University of Toronto Press, 2013), 13–29.

Ridyard, Susan J., '*Condigna veneratio*: Post-Conquest Attitudes to the Saints of the Anglo-Saxons', *Anglo-Norman Studies* 9 (1986): 179–206.

Ridyard, Susan J., *The Royal Saints of Anglo-Saxon England: a Study of West Saxon and East Anglian Cults* (Cambridge: Cambridge University Press, 1988).

Robinson, P. R., 'A Twelfth-Century Scriptrix from Nunnaminster', in *Of the Making of Books: Medieval Manuscripts, Their Scribes and Readers: Essays Presented to M.B. Parkes*, ed. P. R. Robinson and Rivkah Zim (Aldershot: Ashgate, 1997), 77–93.

Rollason, D. W., 'Goscelin of Canterbury's Account of the Translation and Miracles of St Mildrith (BHL 5961/4). An Edition with Notes', *Mediaeval Studies* 48 (1986): 139–210.

Rollason, D. W., *The Mildrith Legend: A Study in Early Medieval Hagiography in England* (Leicester: Leicester University Press, 1982).

Rollason, David [D. W.], *Saints and Relics in Anglo-Saxon England* (Oxford: Basil Blackwell, 1989).

Sanock, Catherine, *Her Life Historical: Exemplarity and Female Saints' Lives in Late Medieval England* (Philadelphia, PA: University of Pennsylvania Press, 2007).

Scheck, Helene, *Reform and Resistance: Formations of Female Subjectivity in Early Medieval Ecclesiastical Culture* (Albany, NY: SUNY Press, 2008).

Scheck, Helene and Virginia Blanton, 'Leoba's Legacy: the Carolingian Transformation of an Iconography of Literacy', in *Nuns' Literacies in Medieval Europe: the Antwerp Dialogue*, ed. Virginia Blanton, Veronica O'Mara and Patricia Stoop (Turnhout: Brepols, 2017), 3–126.

Scheck, Helene, and Virginia Blanton, 'Women', in *A Handbook of Anglo-Saxon Studies*, ed. Jacqueline Stodnick and Renée R. Trilling (Chichester: Blackwell, 2012), 265–79.

Schulenburg, Jane Tibbetts, *Forgetful of Their Sex: Female Sanctity and Society, ca. 500–1100* (Chicago: University of Chicago Press, 1998).

Showalter, Elaine, *A Literature of their Own: From Charlotte Brontë to Doris Lessing* (Princeton, NJ: Princeton University Press, 1977).

Simpson, James, *Reform and Cultural Revolution: 1350–1547*, The Oxford English Literary History, vol. 2 (Oxford: Oxford University Press, 2002).

Sims-Williams, Patrick, 'Cuthswith, Seventh-Century Abbess of Inkberrow, near Worcester, and the Würzburg Manuscript of Jerome on Ecclesiastes', *Anglo-Saxon England* 5 (1976) : 1–21.

Sims-Williams, Patrick, 'A Recension of Boniface's Letter to Eadburg about the Monk of Much Wenlock's Vision', in *Latin Learning and English Lore: Studies in Anglo-Saxon Literature for Michael Lapidge*, ed. Katherine O'Brien O'Keeffe and Andy Orchard, 2 vols (Toronto: University of Toronto Press, 2005), vol. 1, 194–214.

Sims-Williams, Patrick, *Religion and Literature in Western England 600–800* (Cambridge: Cambridge University Press, 1990).

Sobecki, Sebastian, '"The writyng of this tretys": Margery Kempe's Son and the Authorship of Her Book', *Studies in the Age of Chaucer* 37 (2015): 257–83.

Stafford, Pauline, *Queen Emma and Queen Edith: Queenship and Women's Power in Eleventh-Century England* (Oxford: Blackwell, 1997).

Stanley, Eric, 'Wulf, My Wolf!', in *Old English and New: Studies in Language and Linguistics in Honor of Frederic G. Cassidy*, ed. Joan H. Hall, Nick Doane and Dick Ringler (New York: Garland, 1992), 46–62.

Stevenson, Jane, 'Anglo-Latin Women Poets', in *Latin Learning and English Lore: Studies in Anglo-Saxon Literature for Michael Lapidge*, ed. Katherine O'Brien O'Keeffe and Andy Orchard, 2 vols (Toronto: University of Toronto Press, 2005), vol. 2, 86–107.

Stevenson, Jane, 'Brothers and Sisters: Women and Monastic Life in Eighth-Century England and Frankia', *Nederlandsch archief voor kerkgeschiedenis* 82 (2002): 1–34.

Stevenson, Jane, *Women Latin Poets: Language, Gender, and Authority from Antiquity to the Eighteenth Century* (Oxford: Oxford University Press, 2005).

Straus, Barrie Ruth, 'Women's Words as Weapons: Speech as Action in "The Wife's Lament"', *Texas Studies in Literature and Language* 23 (1981): 268–85.

Summit, Jennifer, *Lost Property: The Woman Writer and English Literary History, 1380–1589* (Chicago: University of Chicago Press, 2000).

Summit, Jennifer, 'Women and Authorship', in *The Cambridge Companion to Medieval Women's Writing*, ed. Carolyn Dinshaw and David Wallace (Cambridge: Cambridge University Press, 2003), 91–108.

Swan, Mary, and Elaine M. Treharne, eds., *Rewriting Old English in the Twelfth Century* (Cambridge: Cambridge University Press, 2000).

Swanton, M. J., 'A Fragmentary Life of St. Mildred and other Kentish Royal Saints', *Archæologia Cantiana* 91 (1975): 15–27.

Tasioulas, J. A., 'The Mother's Lament: Wulf and Eadwacer Reconsidered', *Medium Ævum* 65 (1996): 1–18.

Tatlock, J. S. P., 'Muriel: The Earliest English Poetess', *PMLA* 48 (1933): 317–21.

Thomas, Gabor and Alexandra Knox, eds, *Early Medieval Monasticism in the North Sea Zone* (Oxford: Oxbow, 2017).

Thomson, Rodney M. *Manuscripts from St Albans Abbey*, vol. 1 (Woodbridge: D.S. Brewer, 1982).

Thompson, Robert, 'The St Albans Psalter: Abbot Geoffrey's Book?', *Der Albani-Psalter: Stand und Perspektiven der Forschung/The St Albans Psalter: Current Research and Perspectives*, ed. Jochen Bepler and Christian Heitzmann (Hildesheim: Georg Olms Verlag, 2013), 57–68.

Thornbury, Emily V., *Becoming a Poet in Anglo-Saxon England* (Cambridge: Cambridge University Press, 2014).

Todd, Janet, *Feminist Literary History: A Defence* (Cambridge: Polity, 1988).

Treharne, Elaine, *Living Through Conquest: The Politics of Early English, 1020–1220* (Oxford: Oxford University Press, 2012).

Treharne, Elaine, and Greg Walker with William Green, eds, *The Oxford Handbook of Medieval Literature in English* (Oxford: Oxford University Press, 2010).

Turner, D. H., 'Illuminated Manuscripts', in *The Golden Age of Anglo-Saxon Art and Culture, 966–1066*, ed. Janet Backhouse, D. H. Turner and Leslie Webster (Bloomington, IN: Indiana University Presss, 1984), 46–87.

Tyler, Elizabeth M., *England in Europe: Royal Women and Literary Patronage c.1000–c. 1150* (Toronto: Toronto University Press, 2017).

Tyler, Elizabeth M., 'Fictions of Family: the *Encomium Emmae Reginae* and Virgil's *Aeneid*', Viator 36 (2005): 149–79.

Tyler, Elizabeth M., 'From Old English to Old French', in *Language and Culture in Medieval Britain: The French of England, c. 1100–c. 1500*, ed. Jocelyn Wogan-Browne with Carolyn Collette, Maryanne Kowaleski, Linne Mooney, Ad Putter and David Trotter (Woodbridge: York Medieval Press, 2009), 164–78.

Wallace, D. Patricia, 'Feminine Rhetoric and the Epistolary Tradition: The Boniface Correspondence', *Women's Studies* 24 (1995): 229–46.

Wallace, David, ed., *The Cambridge History of Medieval English Literature* (Cambridge: Cambridge University Press, 1999).

Wallace, David, *Strong Women: Life, Text, and Territory 1347–1645* (Oxford: Oxford University Press, 2011).

Ward, Benedicta, '"To My Dearest Sister": Bede and the Educated Woman', in *Women, the Book and the Godly: Selected Proceedings of the St. Hilda's Conference, 1993, vol. 1* ed. Lesley Smith and Jane H. M. Taylor (Cambridge: D.S. Brewer, 1995), 105–11.

Watt, Diane, 'Authorizing Female Piety', in *The Oxford Handbook of Medieval Literature in English*, ed. Elaine Treharneand, Greg Walker with William Green (Oxford: Oxford University Press, 2010), 240–55.

Watt, Diane, 'Literature in Pieces: Female Sanctity and the Relics of Early Women's Writing', in *The Cambridge History of Early Medieval English Literature*, ed. Clare A. Lees (Cambridge: Cambridge University Press, 2012), 357–80.

Watt, Diane, 'The Manly Middle Ages', *English* 49 (2000): 177–81.

Watt, Diane, 'Mary the Physician: Women, Religion and Medicine in the Middle Ages', in *Medicine, Religion and Gender in Medieval Culture*, ed. Naoë Kukita Yoshikawa (Cambridge: D.S. Brewer, 2015), 27–44.

Watt, Diane, *Medieval Women's Writing: Works by and for Women in England, 1100–1500* (Cambridge: Polity, 2007).

Watt, Diane, *Secretaries of God: Women Prophets in Late Medieval and Early Modern England* (Cambridge: D.S. Brewer, 1997).

Watt, Diane, 'Small Consolation?: Goscelin of St. Bertin's *Liber confortatorius* and the Middle English *Pearl*', *Chaucer Review* 51 (2016): 31–48.

Watt, Diane, and Clare A. Lees, 'Age and Desire in the Old English Mary of Egypt: A Queerer Time and Place?', in *Middle-Aged Women in the Middle Ages,* ed. Sue Niebrzydowski (Cambridge: D.S. Brewer, 2011), 53–67.

Weston, Lisa M. C., 'Conceiving the Word(s): Habits of Literacy Among Earlier Anglo-Saxon Monastic Women', in *Nuns' Literacies in Medieval Europe: The Hull Dialogue*, ed. Virginia Blanton, Veronica O'Mara and Patricia Stoop (Turnhout: Brepols, 2013), 149–67.

Weston, Lisa M. C., 'Reading the Textual Shadows of Anglo-Saxon Monastic Women's Friendships', *Magistra* 14 (2008): 68–78.

Weston, Lisa M. C., 'The Saint-Maker and the Saint: Hildelith Creates Ethelburg', in *Barking Abbey and Medieval Literary Culture: Authorship and Authority in a Female Community* (York: York Medieval Press, 2012), ed. Jennifer R. Brown and Donna Alfano Bussell, 56–72.

Weston, Lisa M. C., 'Saintly Lives: Friendship, Kinship, Gender and Sexuality', in *The Cambridge History of Early Medieval English Literature,* ed. Clare A. Lees (Cambridge: Cambridge University Press, 2013), 381–405.

Weston, Lisa M. C., '*Sanctimoniales Cum Sanctimoniale*: Particular Friendships and Female Community in Anglo-Saxon England', in *Sex and Sexuality in Anglo-Saxon England: Essays in Memory of Daniel Gillmore Calder*, ed. Carol Braun Pasternack and Lisa M. C. Weston (Tempe, AZ: Arizona Center for Medieval and Renaissance Studies, 2004), 35–62.

Weston, Lisa M. C., 'Where Textual Bodies Meet: Anglo-Saxon Women's Epistolary Friendship', in *Friendship in the Middle Ages and Early Modern Age*, ed. Albrecht Classen and Marilyn Sandidge (Berlin: De Gruyter, 2010), 231–46.

Whalen, Georges, 'Patronage Engendered: How Goscelin Allayed the Concerns of Nuns' Discriminatory Publics', in *Women, the Book and the Godly: Selected Proceedings of the St Hilda's Conference, 1993*, vol. 1, ed. Lesley Smith and Jane H. M. Taylor (Cambridge: D.S. Brewer, 1995), 123–35.

Whitelock, Dorothy, 'The Interpretation of *The Seafarer*', in *The Early Cultures of North-West Europe* (*H.M. Chadwick Memorial Studies*), ed. Sir Cyril Fox and Bruce Dickens (Cambridge: Cambridge University Press, 1950), 261–72.

Wogan-Browne, Jocelyn, '"Clerc u lai, muĭne u dame": Women and Anglo-Norman Hagiography in the Twelfth and Thirteenth Centuries', in *Women and Literature in Britain: 1150–1500* (Cambridge: Cambridge University Press, 2nd edn, 1996), ed. Carole M. Meale, 61–85.

Wogan-Browne, Jocelyn, 'Dead to the World? Death and the Maiden Revisited in Medieval Women's Convent Culture', in *Guidance for Women in Twelfth-Century Convents*, trans. Vera Morton with an Interpretative Essay by Jocelyn Wogan-Browne (Cambridge: D.S. Brewer, 2003), 157–80.

Wogan-Browne, Jocelyn, *Saints' Lives and Women's Literary Culture c. 1150–1300: Virginity and its Authorizations* (Oxford: Oxford University Press, 2001).

Wood, Ian N., 'The Continental Connections of Anglo-Saxon Courts from Æthelberht to Offa', in *Le relazioni internazionali nell'alto medioevo: Spoleto, 8–12 aprile 2010*, (Spoleto: Fondazione Centro italiano di studi sull'alto medioevo, 2011), 443–78.

Wood, Ian N., 'Differing Emotions in Luxeuil, Bobbio, and Faremoutiers', in *Emotions, Communities, and Difference in Medieval Europe: Essays in Honor of Barbara H. Rosenwein*, ed. Maureen C. Miller and Edward Wheatley (Abingdon: Routledge, 2017), 31–45.

Wood, Ian, 'Merovingian Monasticism and England', in *Early Medieval Monasticism in the North Sea Zone*, ed. Gabor Thomas and Alexandra Knox (Oxford: Oxbow, 2017), 17–24.

Wood, Ian, 'Missionary Hagiography in the Eighth and Ninth Centuries', in *Ethnogenese und Überlieferung: Angewandte Methoden der Frühmittelalterforschung*, ed. Karl Brunner and Brigitte Merta (Vienna: R. Oldenbourg, 1994), 189–99.

Wood, Ian, *The Missionary Life: Saints and the Evangelisation of Europe 400–1050* (Harlow: Longman, 2001).

Wood, Ian, 'Monastères et Ports dans l'Angleterre du VIIᵉ–VIIIᵉ Siècles', in *Échanges, Communications et Réseaux dans le Haut Moyen Âge: Études et Textes offerts à Stéphane Lebecq*, ed. Alban Gautier and Céline Martin (Turnhout: Brepols, 2011), 89–100.

Wood, Ian, 'Quentovic et le Sud-Est britannique (VIe–IXe siècle)', in *Quentovic: Environnement, Archéologie, Histoire*, ed. Stéphane Lebecq, Bruno Béthouart and Laurent Verslype (Lille: Conseil Scientifique de l'Université Charles-de-Gaulle, 2010), 165–75.

Wood, Ian N., 'Ripon, Francia and the Franks Casket in the Early Middle Ages', *Northern History* 26 (1990): 1–19.

Wood, Ian, 'The *Vita Columbani* and Merovingian Hagiography', *Peritia* 1 (1982): 63–80.

Woolf, Virginia, *A Room of One's Own* (1929, reprinted Harmondsworth: Penguin, 1945).

Yorke, Barbara, 'The Bonifacian Mission and Female Religious in Wessex', *Early Medieval Europe* 7 (1998): 145–72.

Yorke, Barbara, '"Carriers of Truth": Writing the Biographies of Anglo-Saxon Female Saints', in *Writing Medieval Biography, 750–1250: Essays in Honour of Frank Barlow*, ed. David Bates, Julia Crick and Sarah Hamilton (Woodbridge: Boydell Press, 2006), 49–60.

Yorke, Barbara, 'Queen Balthild's "Monastic Policy" and the Origins of Female Religious Houses in Southern England', in *Early Medieval Monasticism in the North Sea Zone*, ed. Gabor Thomas and Alexandra Knox (Oxford: Oxbow, 2017), 7–16.

Yorke, Barbara, 'Rudolf of Fulda's *VITA S. LEOBÆ*: Hagiography and Historical Reality', in *Anglo-Saxon England and the Continent*, ed. Hans Sauer and Joanna Story with Gaby Waxenberger (Tempe, AZ: ACMRS, 2011), 199–216.

Index

CPSIA information can be obtained
at www.ICGtesting.com
Printed in the USA
LVHW010415260221
679957LV00007B/75